SUSTAINABILITY

Sustainability

Approaches to Environmental Justice and Social Power

Edited by
Julie Sze

NEW YORK UNIVERSITY PRESS
New York

NEW YORK UNIVERSITY PRESS
New York
www.nyupress.org

References to Internet websites (URLs) were accurate at the time of writing. Neither the author nor New York University Press is responsible for URLs that may have expired or changed since the manuscript was prepared.

ISBN: 978-1-4798-9456-7 (hardback)
ISBN: 978-1-4798-7034-9 (paperback)

For Library of Congress Cataloging-in-Publication data, please contact the Library of Congress.

New York University Press books are printed on acid-free paper, and their binding materials are chosen for strength and durability. We strive to use environmentally responsible suppliers and materials to the greatest extent possible in publishing our books.

Manufactured in the United States of America

10 9 8 7 6 5 4 3 2 1

Also available as an ebook

CONTENTS

Introduction

JULIE SZE, WITH ANNE RADEMACHER, TOM BEAMISH,
LIZA GRANDIA, JONATHAN LONDON, LOUIS WARREN,
BETH ROSE MIDDLETON, AND MIKE ZISER

In 2008, the residents of Kivalina in northwest Alaska filed a ground-breaking lawsuit. This Iñupiaq village of four hundred people is in danger of being destroyed as sea ice melts and rates of coastal erosion increase. In *Kivalina v. ExxonMobil Corporation, et al.*, the residents of Kivalina, represented by the Center for Race, Poverty and the Environment and the Native American Rights Fund, among other major law firms, charged twenty-four of the largest oil and electric companies in the United States with contributing to global warming and claimed that the companies are liable for the damage suffered by the village. The lawsuit also alleged that the defendants have engaged in a conspiracy to mislead the public about the causes and effects of climate change.[1] The suit, based on the common-law theory of nuisance, claimed up to $400 million in monetary damages to pay for the relocation of the village. The U.S. District Court dismissed the case on the grounds that regulating greenhouse gas emissions was a political, rather than a legal, issue. Although the residents were not successful legally, their case raised important issues of responsibility and sustainability. Kivalina garnered global attention for climate change, their situation, and the relocation process they had initiated. How could a small Native village which had very little to do with the causes of environmental damage—in this case, climate change—survive?

The pressing issues of sustainability and social justice that the lawsuit raised remain largely unaddressed, and in many ways, the challenges of achieving both sustainability and social justice have only magnified.[2] Yet, paradoxically, there is potential today for a broader base of concern, activism, and solidarity than ever before. Important social movements for environmental and climate justice are mobilizing large numbers of people, with broad impact outside of their local political contexts. Kivalina is just one example. Others include oil pipeline protests on the Standing Rock Sioux Reservation; global coverage of mass lead poisonings in Flint, Michigan; the urgent entreaties of small Pacific islands and Arctic Indigenous villages in response to rising sea levels caused by climate change; and the struggles of the working classes, immigrants, and people of color on waterfronts in San Francisco and New York against high-end ecologically themed "sustainable" developments in gentrifying cities. All of these instances have combined elements of environmentalism, sustainability, and concerns about social injustice/inequality.

Spurred by climate change and taken together with questions of increasing water scarcity and the negative impacts of dirty energy systems, promoting sustainability may be one of the key global issues of our era. In its absence, the very demise of humanity seems plausible. As ecological change exacts urgent, and often unprecedented, tolls on human and nonhuman life, this sense of urgency sometimes obscures the extent to which sustainability and its underlying pillars are carefully analyzed and understood as products of social and ecological dynamics. These dynamics form mosaics of moral logic, aspiration, and struggles over power. Yet studies examining how sustainability issues and issues of social justice are linked remain underdeveloped.[3] This book contends that environmental crises and social inequality are in fact twins, born of coexisting cultural, political, and economic processes. Thus social justice and sustainability are intimately connected.

Sustainability and social justice remain elusive, even as it has become increasingly clear that each is unattainable without the other. Unsustainable practices diminish social justice: The effects of animal extinctions, toxic waste, and air pollution alike have fallen disproportionately on the poor. Meanwhile, efforts at achieving sustainability in the industrialized West and Global South have often aggravated social inequities—for example, when Indigenous people have been displaced to create wildlife or natural reserves or when governments have mandated expensive new environmental management technologies that exacerbate the burden of the poor. One result is that sustainability is sometimes perceived as an elite, technologically driven project in an increasingly diverse world, and opposition to environmental reform finds a solid footing among the expanding ranks of the world's working and impoverished peoples.

Moreover, "sustainability" seems so vague a concept that it invites skepticism. The environmental scientist Lucas Seghezzo argues that it is the ambiguity of the term "sustainability" that has contributed to its large-scale acceptance as a framework for environmental and social action.[4] In this volume, we argue that to aspire to something called "sustainability" is to reject this ambiguity. Our task is to *contextualize* and *situate* sustainability. This volume does so through engaging with three central questions:

1. What does sustainability mean? How does sustainability function in multiple dimensions, including material, pragmatic, ideological, and discursive dimensions?
2. What are the key contexts for how sustainability is conceptualized, enacted, and contested?
3. What is sustainable, for whom, why, and how? Where and how do social justice and sustainability connect? How is that connection achieved?

The short answer we propose to the first question in this book is this: Sustainability depends on context. Our case studies range widely. Sustainability, as one chapter shows, can mean a range of more or less water quality in a particular urban watershed in Baltimore, Maryland. Another chapter shows that, in the Menominee Nation, sustainability is squarely focused on Indigenous planning principles and projects centered on land sovereignty. And another chapter describes Dinner 2040, a planning exercise website and actual event that imagined what a sustainable dinner would be like in Maricopa County, Arizona, in the future. For all the chapters in this book, social justice and/or interdisciplinarity are central factors. The questions of whether and how social justice is achieved in a sustainability project, and what it looks like, must also take many different disciplinary perspectives into account. This diversity of approaches and perspectives is a necessary precondition to achieving sustainability.

The sociologists Julian Agyeman, Robert Bullard, and Bob Evans argue in their ground-breaking 2003 book *Just Sustainabilities* that a "sustainable society is a just society."[5] This volume updates their contention in a different political moment. We also believe that sustainability and justice are indeed, as those scholars articulated, "joined up."[6] They wrote of the problems that connect sustainability and justice: the linked relationship between poverty and environmental problems, the disproportionality of pollution exposures among disenfranchised populations (i.e., low-income and/or racial minorities), and the need to move toward sustainable development. They defined "just sustainability" as "the need to ensure a better quality of life for all, now and into the future, in a just and equitable manner, whilst living within the limits of supporting ecosystems."[7]

The task they outlined has not yet been achieved, although their framework remains powerful. To develop just sustainability now, our focus is on two distinct and overlapping groups: those concerned with social justice and those interested in sustainability. We assume these domains to be linked—but we also acknowledge that many trained and conversant in one camp do not necessarily seek common cause in the other. This divide is not accidental, as a generation of environmental justice scholars and environmental historians has documented. Rather, the perception that environmentalism is both overwhelmingly elite and white in the United States is part and parcel of the history of mainstream environmentalism. The elitism and whiteness of mainstream environmentalism has deep roots, and the perception of environmental protection as distinct from issues of social justice derives from a complex history. Two important examples are John Muir's denigration of the Yosemite Indians as a "blight" on the land and the expansion of the national park system as tied to Indian removal.[8] These histories of which bodies have been perceived to belong in which natural landscapes matter, as do counterhistories that show the deep connection between race, justice, and the environment.[9]

At the same time, recent developments in climate justice and in certain mainstream environmental organizations reveal that structural change is indeed possible. In the 1990s, the Sierra Club took an anti-immigrant, pro–population control position on the grounds that expanding immigration was bad for the environment. This position was widely understood by poor people, immigrants, and people of color to show how mainstream environmentalism eschewed their perspectives.[10] Yet despite the anti-immigrant position the organization took, perceived by many to be a form of racism and classism (and gender violence), in 2016 the Sierra

Club endorsed the platform for Black Lives Matter. The Sierra Club's position was that police violence was an environmental issue. This stance was an indication of their leadership taking a racial justice stand, one unimaginable in the 1990s. Only by understanding that proponents of social justice and sustainability have not necessarily made common cause in the past can we create and strengthen new alliances.

These alliances are essential, given the scope of the problems we now face. The literary scholar Rob Nixon (drawing from earlier environmental humanist and environmental justice work) argues that how people *talk about* and *visually represent* environmental crises is important. Part of the strength of the environmental justice movement in the 1980s was to broaden "environment" to mean race, urban spaces, labor, and pollution. This widened conception of "environmentalism" was a rebuke of a conception of nature-as-wilderness. Current stories and *narratives* about climate change, Nixon argues, have generally "sidestepped the question of unequal human agency, unequal human impacts, and unequal human vulnerabilities." He contends that "stories matter. . . . In a world drowning in data, stories can play a vital role . . . in the making of environmental publics and in the shaping of environmental policy."[11] Following this impetus, this book attempts to "reshape" the contours, parameters, and stories of sustainability so that social justice is understood as a central factor for everyone involved in sustainability research and concerned with inequality (environmental and otherwise).

Sustainability is implicitly connected to the term "nature." The idea of nature is tied to the sense that the world has natural systems able to support the continuation of human society. This conception was formalized by economists, philosophers, scientists, and social reformers in the eighteenth century. Of course, Indigenous societies practice sustainability to ensure their survival. The limits of these natural systems have been the focal point of much environmental science research in the twentieth century. As the socialist culture critic Raymond Williams famously argued, ideas about nature "contain an extraordinary amount of human history,"[12] and this complexity lies at the contested heart of sustainability. From Williams onward, many scholars have attempted to outline human history in nature, beginning with the intellectual history of the connection between political economy and nature and the exchange of ideas between European and American intellectuals.

In the latter half of the twentieth century, the biological, physical, and ecological sciences and economics dominated much contemporary sustainability research and action at the relative expense of the humanities and humanistic social sciences. Despite the rapid expansion of sustainability research since the turn of the twenty-first century, fundamental questions about core concepts and values of sustainability as it relates to social justice have remained largely unexplored.

Drawing from the urban ecologists Mary Cadenasso and S. T. A. Pickett's contribution in this volume, we contend that sustainability must be *situated*. In chapter 1 they write that "sustainability, like all ecologically relevant concepts, is multidimensional, and these dimensions can be identified as metaphor, meaning, and model. . . . These three dimensions can be exploited to situate sustainability." This book seeks to *situate* sustainability within interdisciplinary frameworks and from the standpoint of social justice. Cadenasso and Pickett ask, "Why is a shared vision of sustainability so elusive, especially given that it is so widely invoked?" The contributions in this book provide key insights as to how interdisciplinary synergy can happen and why these forays matter. We take these gestures toward interdisciplinarity that they signal to be fundamental starting points for a more robust understanding about, and overcoming of, the barriers to achieving sustainability.

Sustainability Meanings: Sustainability/Sustainable Development

Sustainability is a flexible concept, open to a great deal of projection and lack of clarity. There is no standard definition that is generally agreed upon. What is probably better understood is the *lack* of sustainability. As we saw earlier, sustainability seems so ubiquitous and undefined that it provokes "skepticism."[13] Rather than provide a single definitive explanation of "sustainability," it is useful to consider how time, place, scale, and politics help to enact debates about it. The German journalist Ulrich Grober's *Sustainability: A Cultural History* traces the recent history of sustainability to a 1972 report called *The Limits to Growth*.[14] The report—written for the Club of Rome, a global think tank that distributed over thirty million copies—suggested that sustainability was seen as an "antonym" for collapse. It was the first to suggest that there are indeed limits to growth and to a world system capable of supporting human life, and it suggested action.[15] However, sustainability's roots go far back, beyond 1972.

Earth and its resources have been understood as finite and subject to collapse since at least the eighteenth century. This understanding draws from forestry, but extends far beyond it. The first generation of forestry research set the stage for later concepts of sustainability knowledge and language. These later accounts suggested that, as Grober recounts, "another world was possible," one in which the "material needs of each person on earth are satisfied and each person has an equal opportunity to realize his or her individual human potential."[16] In many ways, sustainability and its closely linked cousin, sustainable development, are both simultaneously radical and reformist. They are potentially radical because they posit that there may be environmental limits to economic growth but reformist in that they presuppose the existing capitalist system.

Lucas Seghezzo, in contending that it is the ambiguity of the term "sustainability" that has contributed to its large-scale acceptance, focuses on the *limitations* of the sustainability framework put forth by the World Commission on Environment and Development (WCED) for sustainable development. The WCED's 1987 report *Our Common Future* and the development of the UN Conferences on Environment and Development (beginning in 1992) were signal achievements in the field.[17] According to Grober, "sustainable development" is in the 1987 report as development that meets the needs of the present without compromising the ability of future generations to meet their own needs.[18] Seghezzo identifies key limits of the WCED paradigm of sustainable development. It is anthropocentric, the role of the economy is overstated, it is incompatible with intergenerational justice, it neglects space and time, and it ignores personal aspects of development. To address these weaknesses, he proposes a new framework for use in academic analysis and policy making that includes considerations of *place*, *permanence*, and *persons*.[19] To Seghezzo's list, we would add *praxis* and *positionality*.

How Do We Achieve Sustainability? Praxis and Positionality

Sustainability emerges out of a sense—and empirical documentation—of environmental crises. The International Geosphere–Biosphere Programme publishes what it calls the "Great Acceleration" indicators, which have shown an uptick in human activity since 1950. Its data shows that "human activity, predominantly the global economic system, is now the prime driver of change in the Earth System (the sum of our planet's interacting physical, chemical, biological and human processes), according to a set of 24 global indicators," including carbon emissions, ocean acidification, and tropical land loss, to name just a few categories.[20] The rapid growth of environmental problems maps onto socioeconomic trends (e.g., rising populations, energy use, and fertilizer consumption). Environmental crises have been linked to economic growth over the last fifty years, and rising social inequalities in the last decade have exacerbated already dangerous conditions of life, land, and labor.

Sustainability Science and Reflexivity

Despite the growth and influence of environmental history, sociology, and the humanities, these approaches to sustainability exist far too often on parallel, not intersecting, tracks with environmental science research. Some of this lack of confluence arises from epistemological and disciplinary differences. Generally, sustainability programs rely heavily on mathematical models and economic methods, whereas humanities and social science agendas tend to draw from the study of culture, history, and the philosophy of values.

For example, modeling of future climates dominates climate change analysis. But the profound inequalities associated with rapid changes in climate—including massive population displacement, catastrophic disruptions in food systems, and political instability—require scholarship that can uncover the human costs and possible human responses to climate change. In fact, societies have, in different parts of the worlds and at different times, long experienced climate change, albeit not at this pace and scale. The humanities and humanistic social sciences are critical to any effort to understand the experience of climate-change mitigation and adaptation, and they are one of our best, and underutilized, resources for envisioning alternative and just futures. Encouraging interdisciplinary and justice-oriented sustainability collaborations to partly overcome their differences in approach with dominant sustainability and environmental science-oriented research has the potential to bring scholarship into meaningful and productive dialogue with the broader public around our era's most pressing questions.

This separation between the environmental sciences and the humanities and humanistic social sciences is a persistent problem. The geographer John Robinson clarifies the role of science in sustainability research, writing that "good science is necessary, but . . . in the end, sustainability is an issue of human behavior and negotiation over preferred futures, under conditions of deep contingency and uncertainty. It is an inherently normative concept, rooted in real world problems and very different sets of values and moral judgments."[21] In other words, "Science can inform but not resolve, scientific analysis embeds values, other forms of knowledge."[22] Further, "if sustainability is to mean anything, it must act as an integrating concept. . . . Social dimensions of sustainability must be integrated with the biophysical dimensions . . . and integrating across fields [and] sectors. . . . There will not develop a single coherent conceptual approach to sustainability."[23] Social justice and interdisciplinarity are central precepts to this essential task of integration.

Because environmental crises and social inequality are born of coexisting political and economic processes, we need diverse tools to address both. Dynamic conversations around sustainability and social justice have rarely been the subject of the inclusive inquiry that takes interdisciplinarity and questions of social justice as its center. This book draws inspiration from *Uncommon Ground: Rethinking the Human Place in Nature*, edited by the environmental historian William Cronon and published in 1996. This book was groundbreaking in its central argument about the human place in nature, not only vis-à-vis wilderness but also in relation to work, consumption, and a host of other human activities.[24] It demonstrated the importance of interdisciplinarity among environmental historians, ecologists, feminist science/technology scholars, and environmental justice scholars.

Reflexive interdisciplinary research is difficult to embark upon, as the chapters in this volume illustrate. Segregating academic knowledge from lived/community knowledge—especially the knowledge of politically and culturally marginalized people—is a form of epistemic exclusion, as the community development scholar Jonathan London, Mary Cadenasso, and I have argued elsewhere.[25] Indeed, the move for collaboration across disciplines needs to be accelerated, according to the sustainability scientist Thaddeus Miller and his colleagues. They suggest that sustainability science and knowledge as currently generated by academic institutions is inadequate for actually transitioning to a sustainable society.[26] Part of the sustainability knowledge we are advancing here is a more inclusive and radical notion of sustainability. We are not advocating against sustainability science. Rather, we contend that sustainability science offers one set of approaches. We also need sustainability humanities, sustainability histories, praxis-oriented sustainability, community-oriented sustainability, and radical sustainability. Taken together, these approaches begin to answer the question of "how" we begin to move toward sustainability.

Sustainability Stories: Environmental Humanities

Miller's call for sustainability scientists to take seriously cultural values and other works of knowledge—including different disciplinary approaches—is echoed in the work of environmental humanists, linguists, and historians. Some environmental humanists trace environmental knowledge back to narratives, stories, and images documenting the first Indigenous uprisings and slave revolts in the colonial world.[27] The work of this group touched off a new interdisciplinary movement in the humanities to pursue a wide range of conversations on environmental issues in this time of growing awareness of the challenges facing all life on Earth.

If, as Robinson argues, "sustainability is an issue of human behavior and negotiation over preferred futures," then the question of futures is tied implicitly to storytelling and imagination. Science fiction writers have been plumbing the real world to imagine dystopian and utopian futures along the lines of those described by science fiction writers like Octavia Butler.[28] Understanding culture through storytelling, art, and history is an effort to develop other ways of developing knowledge about environmental issues. We can understand the future, in part, by understanding the past. Different ways of environmental knowing, living, and thinking in interdisciplinary ways makes sustainability stronger. Making sustainability more socially just benefits those who are the most environmentally harmed.

Sustainability Histories

Sustainability research also needs to take history, especially from postcolonial and decolonial perspectives, seriously. These perspectives have tended to be overlooked, yet they are crucial in emergent discussions on the Anthropocene, the era during which human impacts have begun to shape geologic time.[29] Intense scientific debate has taken place about whether the Anthropocene exists (i.e., is the Anthropocene "real"?) and when the era began. Some argue that a new geologic epoch started in the early seventeenth century (specifically 1610, as recorded by a dip in carbon dioxide levels in ice core records connected to the "Little Ice Age") as a result of atmospheric change that followed mass deaths, slavery, and war after 1492.[30] In August 2016, a working group of the International Geological Congress recommended that the starting point of the Anthropocene be set after the 1940s because that was when radioactive elements were dispersed across the planet by nuclear tests.[31] Although the recommendation has not yet been adopted by the Geological Congress, scientific acceptance of the Anthropocene has accelerated rapidly since 2000.

Despite the considerable scientific discussion in the last two decades about the Anthropocene, there has been far less research on how history, justice, and inequality are related to climate change. (Notable exceptions include Amitav Ghosh's *The Great Derangement: Climate Change and the Unthinkable*, the journalist-activist Naomi Klein's *This Changes Everything: Capitalism vs. the Climate*, and cultural explorations of climate change in literature and film.)[32] This relative omission of the humanities and social sciences is ultimately counterproductive, specifically in addressing the scientific problems of global environmental change.[33]

The particular contribution of social science and humanities-based historical research is to better center politics, power, and global flows. Research that centers the "anthro/human" without taking colonialism—and the communities and ecosystems most affected by colonialism—into account is arguably limited in scope and impact. Anthropocene research must be decolonized from the standpoint of Indigenous studies, but as the Indigenous scholar Eve Tuck and the radical educator K. Wayne Yang note (on a different set of topics), "decolonization is not a metaphor."[34]

This decolonization of knowledge is what the Indigenous scholar Makere Stewart-Harawira calls the "challenge to knowledge capitalism."[35] Although she does not address the Anthropocene/climate change or environmentalism/sustainability specifically, there are many important points in her work to be reckoned with, specifically regarding the centrality of indigenous knowledge. The historian Dipesh Chakrabarty examines the limits of dominant paradigms of the Anthropocene from the standpoint of colonial history in his seminal work, "Climate and Capital: On Conjoined Histories."[36] In his overview of the collisions of "histories" of "the earth system, history of life, history of industrial civilization (mostly, capitalism)," he identifies issues of spatial and temporal justice.[37] Like Agyeman, Bullard, and Evans, he uses the word "conjoining" to describe the need for unification. He explains that "the history of populations belongs to two histories simultaneously—the short term history of the industrial way of life, and the evolutionary deep history of our species."[38] To avoid (or at least address) anthropocentrism, he quotes Gayatri Spivak, known primarily as a postcolonial theorist: "The planet is in the specific alterity, belonging to another system, and yet we inhabit it."[39] In other words, "The realization that humans—all humans, rich or poor—come late in the planet's life and dwell more in the position of passing guests than possessive hosts, has to be an integral part of the perspective from which we pursue our all-too-human but legitimate quest for justice on issues to do with the iniquitous impact of anthropogenic climate change."[40]

Postcolonial and decolonial Indigenous scholarship, by necessity, position, and perspective, asks a different set of questions from dominant versions of sustainability research. Some of this positionality necessarily invites a different history and perspective on sustainability, as this volume contends. Take, for example, the history of Native nations and their impact on modern conservation. Although it is not generally discussed in the history of North American environmental stewardship, the birth of sustainable forestry can be traced back to when the first federal laws mandating sustainable forest harvesting in the United States were enacted on the Menominee Indian Reservation.[41]

What's the Point of Situated/Situating Sustainabilities?: Positionality, Power, Perspective

The question to which we now turn is this: How does sustainability, however interdisciplinary, avoid the trap of reinforcing dominant ideologies that produce social injustice and environmental harm?

The answer draws from, and extends beyond the work of, environmental justice scholars, in what we call "situated sustainabilities."

"Situated" sustainability is based on four factors. First, it draws from sustainability and sustainable development. Second, it emerges out of just sustainability and environmental justice research. Third, it is indebted to the environmental humanities/radical interdisciplinarity and to developing cross-sector knowledge coproduction with communities and knowledge makers. Last, it differs from earlier works in all these fields in how it balances among the first three, and it centralizes issues of gender, race, and indigeneity and, to some degree (although not all writers in this volume would agree), gestures toward anti-capitalism. It emerges from, and transforms, the environmental justice agenda. It embraces core values that link environmental justice scholarship—a focus on praxis and social/racial justice and a fundamentally respectful appreciation of history and other modes of knowing and engaging in the world—including arts and the humanities.

Situated sustainabilities imply an awareness of the multiple ways in which sustainability is marshaled and deployed in social and political life. Some of this integrative and interdisciplinary work is already under way in a number of different fields.[42] Sustainability science and environmental justice research provide one important crossroads. Case studies show how Baltimore's sustainability plan explicitly called for social equity in recreation and transportation.[43] At the same time, even a more expansive sustainability science and environmental justice research does not necessarily address the *fundamental* political conditions that set the parameters for why and how vulnerability (environmental or otherwise) is disproportionately distributed, one of the key questions in environmental justice research. Recent work from environmental justice scholars David Pellow and Laura Pulido take aim squarely at this question of politics. Both critique the state-centered approach of reformist environmental justice analysis—Pellow through "critical environmental justice studies" and Pulido by offering a critique of normative policy.[44] To this end, Pulido argues that environmental justice must by analyzed from a framework of "racial capitalism." She borrows this term from Cedric Robinson, who argued in 1983 that racism was a structuring logic of capitalism.[45] Pulido argues that environmental racism is "state-sanctioned violence."

These radical critiques from major environmental justice scholars join many others in insisting that ideologies inherent in sustainability be named as such. The literary scholar Leerom Medovoi asks: "What is it about sustainability that enables the particular word . . . to express the ecological hopes and fears of so diverse and antagonistic an array of social actors?"[46] Drawing on the political scientist Wendy Brown's critique of tolerance as a political discourse, he argues that sustainability "serves to sustain economic liberalism and ultimately, capitalism itself." Thus, sustainability "stand(s) as a compensatory substitute for . . . more profound ethical critique in lieu of the impulse to a deeper political transformation."[47] In outlining the convergence between ecological Marxist critiques and corporate sustainability/business management, Medovoi suggests that the "discourse of sustainability is a new intensification in the exercise of biopower . . . of what is the value of what we kill when we extract value from what remains living."[48]

In other words, many who inhabit a "sustainability" space exist in a discursive and political fantasyland of "solutions" (primarily, but not only, technological). To better achieve sustainability, we need to take the frame of analysis out of the literal "business as usual," albeit with a "green" frame. This means addressing politics, history, displacement, theft, violence, and the not-so-feel-good roots of how we got to the socially unjust and environmentally precarious planet we currently inhabit.

The idea that disciplinary perspectives or differently positioned social groups "know" and assign meaning to ecology and sustainability in ways that are shaped by different geographies (e.g., rural/urban, Global South) and social and cultural factors—including race, class, gender, ethnicity, age, ability, and other modes of marking or experiencing social difference—is not new. This effort to situate sustainability is, of course, indebted to the classic essay by the feminist science studies scholar Donna Haraway, "Situated Knowledges: The Science Question in Feminism and the Privilege of Partial Perspective." She argues for "politics and epistemologies of location, positioning, and situating," and her oft-cited text remains relevant.[49] She suggests that "rational knowledge is a process of ongoing critical interpretation among 'fields' of interpreters and decoders."[50] Specifically, Haraway argues that "situated knowledges are about communities, not about the isolated individual. The only way to find a larger vision is to be somewhere in particular."[51]

But where? Outside the academy, surely. More recently, the geographers Paul Routledge and Kate Derickson called for "situated solidarities" in their recent article, "Situated Solidarities and the Practice of Scholar-Activism."[52] For them, "situated solidarities require that we ask how knowledge produced through research might be of use to multiple others without reinscribing the interests of the privileged; and how such knowledge might be actively tied to a material politics of social change that works in the interests of the disadvantaged." They describe situated solidarities as "a goal of and a strategy for doing scholar-activism. . . . The form of knowledge that can be of value is context specific and changes over time." Specifically, they call for a *convergence space*, which they define as "the convergence of interests, dreams, and goals that are generated through the process of cooperation through the process of cooperation between scholar-activists and their collaborators."[53]

Conjoining, Converging, Confounding: A Framework for the Study of Situated/Situating Sustainabilities

This book is about convergence: between academic fields, between research and practice, between campus and community. This call for convergence and conjoining echoes the earlier calls for new vocabularies and approaches.

The environmental justice movement famously defined the "environment" as where we "live, work and play." The movement did so to complicate the view of environment-as-nature and to put a more complicated set of spaces into environmentalism (e.g., urban, housing, workplace, Native lands). This discursive expansion also expanded the bodies in environmental spaces—the lead poisoned, the occupationally injured, the food insecure. But environmental injustice is also more than human. As Pellow writes in his account of critical environmental justice, environmental justice was never anthropocentric, but includes animals, the watershed, and the air basin.[54]

To this expansion, we further argue in this book that the "environment" that needs to be expanded and decolonized includes the curriculum in sustainability studies. The lack of knowledge about, and hence lack of imagination for, different worlds and futures when students of sustainability read only scientific studies—and not literature or Native origin tales—is a form of epistemic violence.

We don't need just more research as usual but entirely different conversations and lines of sustainability research. Without throwing the baby out with the proverbial bathwater (or inadvertently endorsing an anti-scientific approach), we bridge the praxis-oriented and positionality approach as a central contribution of this volume, thereby suggesting what *situated sustainabilities* might look like. We are calling for a *process*, rather than an object-oriented sustainability. Thus, in addition to situated sustainabilities, we call for the politics of knowledge coproduction, environmental science, and democracy in action. The chapters in this volume engage with the questions of why and how to situate sustainability through interdisciplinarity, place, and praxis, and through social justice, and power.

Interdisciplinarity, Place, and Praxis

Part I of this book offers case studies that are situated in relation to interdisciplinary engagements that span the ecosystem and health sciences, community-university praxis, and the arts and humanities. Grounding their analyses in particular cases and questions, the contributors in this section foreground those projects that intentionally cross boundaries among sustainability sciences, the arts and humanities, and social practice, highlighting research that has wrestled with how to balance different disciplinary approaches. What is gained and what is lost by doing or not doing so? Although this section—as with the volume as a whole—advocates interdisciplinary approaches, praxis-oriented work offers useful insights, as both interdisciplinary and praxis-oriented approaches call for a similar skill set. Chief among these are humility and the bravery to step out of one's own domains—whether in terms of an intellectual "field" or one's campus/community engagement.

The ecologists M. L. Cadenasso and S. T. A. Pickett open Part I with a case analysis from the pathbreaking Baltimore Ecosystem Study, one of a group of important long-term urban ecosystem studies. The studies show that, when properly specified, the concept of sustainability offers a critical opportunity to forge conceptual and methodological links that are otherwise impossible. But Cadenasso and Pickett argue that the key is specification. They demonstrate the utility of sustainability in Baltimore, using it to lay down completely new pathways for understanding the intersection of urban landscape design, ecosystem processes, and community dynamics.

Joni Adamson, in chapter 2, describes one of the most ambitious international projects in the fast-rising field of the environmental humanities, Humanities for the Environment (HfE). The Humanities for the Environment initiative was designed to explore the roots and consequences of human-caused change in the Anthropocene. Adamson explains how humanities disciplines are transforming themselves to allow for greater collaboration with social scientists and scientists and for greater international networking.

In chapter 3, the renowned environmental justice scholar Giovanna Di Chiro and organizer Laura Rigell discuss a campus-community partnership between community leaders in North Philadelphia and a group of faculty and students. Their project, Sustainable Serenity, represents a productive model for interdisciplinary, intersectional, and broad-based sustainability efforts. Their collaboration embraces the vision of engaged scholarship and learning that makes a difference in the world with a focus on real-life, community-based, and collaborative projects that address the interconnected social, economic, and environmental issues underlying economic disparity, environmental racism, and climate change.

The sociologist Tracy Perkins and filmmaker Aaron Soto-Karlin integrate their approaches in a global look at climate change in chapter 4. They present the global policy debate over forest carbon offsets as it plays out on the ground, specifically the first subnational (i.e., California) international memorandum of understanding on forest carbon offsets. As California is emerging as a de facto environmental leader in the face of U.S. national retrenchment from global environmental policy, this prescient analysis suggests some pitfalls amid opportunities to cross geographic and political scales.

Lawrence Baker, an applied biogeochemist with expertise in "translational research," further demonstrates what collaboration across fields looks like in chapter 5, which uses drought resistance and resilience to examine urban sustainability. Recognizing the profound importance of water supply, scarcity, and distribution for urban biophysical function and social harmony, Baker proposes an analytical approach for evaluating a city's capacity to adapt to dramatic changes in its water regime.

Positionality, Power, and Situated Sustainabilities

Part II considers sustainability and social justice explicitly through an exploration of identities and social power. The chapters in this section examine how practices of sustainability are shaped by specific temporal and spatial scales. In short, this section is focused on how notions of sustainability travel.

The contention in this section is that it is only in *situating sustainabilities* as dynamic, traveling bundles of concepts and practices that we may assess their meaning. Here, the frame of the analysis matters profoundly. These ways of knowing often compete with one another for prominence, and through those competitions we come to understand how specific forms of environmental change carry distinctly social consequences.

Each factor—indigeneity, race, class, gender, and ethnicity, among others—in marking or experiencing social difference potentially forges its own ecological discourse, or articulation of how environmental change occurs, and what kinds of environmental improvement *should* occur. Attendant efforts to ensure, promote, or imagine specific kinds of environmental change extend from these multiple ecologies and compel us to notice that sustainability is inherently plural and contested. The questions of who, how, and why sustainability serves has been key to scholars in the fields of environmental justice and just sustainability. This section draws upon these fields to grapple with how social power frames sustainability practice. Highlighting the influence of these factors of social power, including gender, race, global indigeneity, militarization, and violence is the goal of this section.

In chapter 6, Kyle Whyte, Chris Caldwell, and Marie Schaefer address how Indigenous people's cultures are widely recognized as holding insights into, or principles about, how humans and human societies can live sustainably or resiliently. Yet people rarely acknowledge that, for Indigenous peoples living in settler states such as the United States or New Zealand, their own efforts to sustain their communities' and nations' social, cultural, and ecological integrity rest heavily on their capacity to negotiate settler colonial oppression. For Indigenous peoples, then, sustainability requires an active concept of "Indigenous planning," which refers to the ways in which many Indigenous people reflect critically on sustainability in relation to what actions are needed to negotiate settler colonialism. The chapter develops these ideas by drawing on the work of the Sustainable Development Institute of the College of Menominee Nation.

Miriam Greenberg, a sociologist and leading figure in the field of critical urban sustainabilities, writes about global urban, spatial, and environmental inequality in chapter 7. Drawing on the example of the contentious displacement of a 1970s-era recycling center by a corporate-sponsored community garden in the rapidly gentrifying Haight Ashbury neighborhood of San Francisco, she argues that we must contextualize these projects—both those that succeed and those that fail—within contemporary urban social relations. When we do so, we find how rooted leading sustainability projects are in modes of market-oriented urban development tethered to luxury development, exacerbating unaffordability and inequality and leading to new forms of "uneven sustainable development." The impact of the dominance of this version of sustainability at the expense of other forms of sustainability is having the effect of redefining urban sustainability itself in a more instrumentalist, market-oriented direction.

Traci Brynne Voyles explores in chapter 8 how the fields of environmental history, feminist environmentalism, and environmental justice studies each provide us with important tools to destabilize entrenched environmental narratives and, in particular, the dominant declensionist narrative that all human interactions with nature end in destruction. In doing so, these fields offer opportunities to think more critically about "man," "nature," and "destruction" alike. Voyles explores key themes and contributions that offer new insights into how we can understand the complex milieu of our human relationships to the non-human world—thinking and acting beyond the binary of "destroying" and "saving" nature. Sustainability, like feminist epistemology, must be situated in contingent and intersectional environmental knowledges and experiences.

In chapter 9, Michael Lujan Bevacqua and Isa Ua Ceallaigh Bowman write about global militarized uses of sustainability rhetoric. In 2009, the United States announced its intention to dramatically increase its military presence on the island of Guam, moving troops from the nearby more publicly controversial base on Okinawa. Although this military buildup would cause severe damage to the environment, society, and economy, discourse from island leaders and media reports focused primarily on this increase as being the key to a "sustainability" future for the island. Such "sustainability" is tied to Guam's history since the Second World War, with the U.S. military in the role of liberator from the Japanese and socioeconomic savior. Indigenous Chamorro activists from groups such as Nasion Chamoru and We Are Guahan used the public comment period for the U.S. military's plans to disrupt the fantasy of the buildup's sustainability and help the community to develop a more critical position in relation to its potential impacts.

Finally, in chapter 10 Lindsey Dillon and Julie Sze explore the ways in which anti-racist social movements offer an alternate concept of sustainability. Anti-racist movements, such as Black Lives Matter, offer a different version of "sustainability" in that they work toward life-sustaining social and environmental conditions. The experiences of people of color on U.S. cities' streets are often structured by race and racism, producing the kinds of urban ecologies and health inequalities that inspired the Black Panthers to offer free medical clinics and breakfast programs in the 1960s and that inspire environmental justice activism today. Through two case studies the authors rethink sustainability from the lived experience of environmental inequality: (1) the intersection of racism, toxic ecologies, and a market-driven sustainable development project in San Francisco; and (2) the metaphor and materiality of Eric Garner's final words, "I can't breathe." They focus on the interrelatedness of police killings, gentrification, and pollution as different modalities of racism on U.S. streets today.

Conclusion

The contributors to this book situate sustainability and social justice through boundary crossings—among fields, community/university, and praxis. By assembling chapters from a range of arenas that are central to simultaneously diagnosing and solving environmental problems, this book explores how our own perspectives foreground specific aspects of sustainability while backgrounding others.

In presenting, in one volume, analyses of sustainability in interdisciplinary and social justice contexts, we make the case that the social and political *meanings* attributed to sustainability must be centralized. *Any efforts at sustainability that do not take interdisciplinary and social justice approaches at their core are unsustainable.* In this book we aim, in short, to move beyond the mere *observation* that sustainability has multiple meanings and to focus on empirical demonstrations of how and why this is the case. Ultimately, the contributions here are meant to inspire the next generation of sustainability researchers and practitioners to take on the biggest questions facing the world today.

Our hope is that through empirical case studies we can illustrate how environmental renewal can happen without creating social inequity. By understanding history, diverse cultural traditions, and complexity in relation to race, class, and gender, we can help shape better and more robust solutions to the world's most pressing problems. Through these innovative case studies and analytics, we demonstrate the analytical and methodological skills from the humanities and humanistic social sciences that are needed to prepare the next generation of global citizens. Scholars broadly interested in sustainability from across the disciplinary divides must continue to collaborate in a critical and constructive way, and with broader environmental publics.

As David Pellow notes in his afterword, we need to move forward from analyses of just/unjust sustainability to just resilience. To better move toward robust and just sustainability, we need a better vocabulary and analytic not only to diagnose problems but also to understand how their efforts replicate existing epistemological and political problems. To better dislodge inequality, sustainability advocates require better tools, rather than reusing poor ones or tinkering around the edges of systems on the verge of collapse. Pellow writes that existing "systems and structures are often forced to display resilience, as they frequently deflect, displace, absorb, incorporate, and assimilate myriad challenges from various corners of society, whether it be the entry of new ethnic groups, the emergence of revolutionary social movements, or the growth of political ideologies that might challenge their hegemony."

States, corporations, markets, and their constituent institutions seek to maintain their dominance through a number of methods—including particular forms of sustainability. To move toward a more just sustainability, we must situate sustainability in both interdisciplinary and political terms. Without situating sustainability in these ways, we risk exacerbating the existing reality: lots of sustainability research, but less sustainability *and* justice on all fronts.

NOTES

1   Center on Race, Poverty and the Environment, "Climate Justice in Kivalina," n.d., www.crpe-ej.org.

2   To address the issues of sustainability and disciplinarity, Anne Rademacher began a project called "Situating Sustainability" in 2009, working with diverse practitioners (such as green architects) and theorists in the United States and globally. These have included conferences and events in Abu Dhabi and the United States.

3   At the University of California, Davis, for example, more students from the environmental sciences are taking aim at what they don't learn in their environmental science and policy classes. It is entirely possible to learn, for example, about the twenty-year struggle by a low-income, primarily Latino population against the siting, and then expansion, of a hazardous waste facility in Kettleman City, California, and never talk about social justice. Some of us find this to be problematic. The Environmental Justice Project, with Julie Sze as founding director and Beth Rose Middleton as second director, began within the institutional context of the John Muir Institute of the Environment at UC Davis. The Center for Regional Change, also at UC Davis and directed by Jonathan London, is committed as well to addressing environmental injustice through research, policy, and action. Although there are a number of renowned environmental historians, literary scholars, sociologists, and geographers and a strong history of interdisciplinary approaches to environmental issues that have been associated with the University of California, Davis (e.g., a now defunct "Nature and Culture" program), the university has had a particularly contested history in relation to industrial agriculture and economic development in California. In this institutional and historical context, where much agricultural research is focused on developing commodity chains, there historically has not been a strong focus on environmental and social justice issues or on environmental inquiry from the humanities and humanistic social sciences.

4   Lucas Seghezzo, "The Five Dimensions of Sustainability," *Environmental Politics* 18, no. 4 (2009): 539–556.

5   Julian Agyeman, Robert Doyle Bullard, and Bob Evans, "Introduction: Joined-Up Thinking: Bringing Together Sustainability, Environmental Justice and Equity," in *Just Sustainabilities: Development in an Unequal World*, ed. Julian Agyeman, Robert Doyle Bullard, and Bob Evans (Cambridge, MA: MIT Press, 2003), 3.

6 Ibid., 1.

7 Ibid., 5.

8 Mark David Spence, *Dispossessing the Wilderness: Indian Removal and the Making of the National Parks* (New York: Oxford University Press, 1999).

9 Carolyn Finney, *Black Faces, White Spaces: Reimagining the Relationship of African Americans to the Great Outdoors* (Durham: University of North Carolina Press, 2014).

10 Ronald Sandler and Phaedra Pezzullo, eds., *Environmental Justice and Environmentalism: The Social Justice Challenge to the Environmental Movement* (Cambridge, MA: MIT Press, 2007).

11 Rob Nixon, "The Great Acceleration and the Great Divergence: Vulnerability in the Anthropocene," *Profession*, Presidential Forum, March 19, 2014, Modern Language Association, www.mla.org.

12 Raymond Williams, *Problems in Materialism and Culture: Selected Essays* (London: Verso, 1980), 67.

13 John Robinson, "Squaring the Circle? Some Thoughts on the Idea of Sustainable Development," *Ecological Economics* 48, no. 4 (2004): 369–384, quote at 373.

14 Donella H. Meadows, Dennis L. Meadows, Jørgen Randers, and William W. Behrens III, *The Limits to Growth: A Report for the Club of Rome's Project on the Predicatment of Mankind* (New York: Universe Books, 1972); and Ulrich Grober, *Sustainability: A Cultural History*, trans. R. Cunningham (Devon: Green Books, 2012).

15 Grober, *Sustainability*, 155, 158.

16 Ibid., 159.

17 World Commission on Environment and Development, *Our Common Future* (Oxford: Oxford University Press, 1987), www.un.org.

18 Grober, *Sustainability*, 182.

19 Seghezzo, "The Five Dimensions of Sustainability."

20 International Geosphere–Biosphere Programme, "Planetary Dashboard Shows 'Great Acceleration' in Human Activity since 1950," *Global Change*, January 15, 2015, www.igbp.net.

21 John Robinson, "Squaring the Circle? Some Thoughts on the Idea of Sustainable Development," *Ecological Economics* 48, no. 4 (2004): 369–384, quote at 379.

22 Ibid., 380.

23 Ibid., 378.

24 William Cronon, ed., *Uncommon Ground: Toward Reinventing Nature* (New York: Norton, 1996).

25 Jonathan K. London, Julie Sze, and Mary L. Cadenasso, "Facilitating Transdisciplinary Conversations in Environmental Justice Studies," in *The Routledge Handbook of Environmental Justice*, ed. Ryan Holifield, Jayajit Chakraborty, and Gordon Walker (New York: Routledge, 2018), 252–263.

26 Thaddeus R. Miller, Tischa Munoz-Erickson, and Charles L. Redman, "Transforming Knowledge for Sustainability: Towards Adaptive Academic

Institutions," *International Journal of Sustainability in Higher Education* 12, no. 2 (2011): 177–192.

27 Joni Adamson, "Introduction: Integrating Knowledge, Forging New Constellations of Practice," in *Humanities for the Environment: Integrating Knowledge, Forging New Constellations of Practice*, ed. Joni Adamson and Michael Davis (New York: Routledge, 2017), 3–19; Elizabeth DeLoughrey and George Handley, eds., *Postcolonial Ecologies: Literatures of the Environment* (Oxford: Oxford University Press, 2011); and Deborah Bird Rose, Thom van Dooren, Matthew Chrulew, Stuart Cooke, Matthew Kearnes, and Emily O'Gorman, "Thinking through the Environment, Unsettling the Humanities," *Environmental Humanities* 1 (2012): 1–5.

28 See Donna Haraway, *Staying with the Trouble: Making Kin in the Chthulucene* (Durham, NC: Duke University Press, 2016), and in novels and fiction. Shelley Streeby describes Butler's world-making in her Parable novels in *Imagining the Future of Climate Change: World-Making through Science Fiction and Activism* (Berkeley: University of California Press, 2017).

29 The term "Anthropocene" was introduced in the year 2000 by Paul J. Crutzen and Eugene F. Stoermer, "The 'Anthropocene,'" *Global Change Newsletter*, no. 41, May 2000, 17–18.

30 David Biello, "Mass Deaths in Americas Start New CO2 Epoch," *Scientific American*, March 11, 2015, www.scientificamerican.com.

31 David Carrington, "The Anthropocene Epoch: Scientists Declare Dawn of Human-Influenced Age," *Guardian*, August 29, 2016, www.theguardian.com.

32 Amitav Ghosh, *The Great Derangement: Climate Change and the Unthinkable* (Chicago: University of Chicago Press, 2016); and Naomi Klein, *This Changes Everything: Capitalism vs. the Climate* (London: Penguin Books, 2014). Some of these cultural examples are stories and worlds within art/science activism and cultural production (weaving, indigenous video game making in the circumpolar North) as discussed by Haraway in *Staying with the Trouble* and in novels and fiction (see Streeby, *Imagining the Future of Climate Change*).

33 Noel Castree, "The Anthropocene and the Environmental Humanities: Extending the Conversation," *Environmental Humanities* 5 (2014): 233–260.

34 Eve Tuck and K. Wayne Yang, "Decolonization Is Not a Metaphor," *Decolonization: Indigeneity, Education and Society* 1, no. 1 (2012): 1–40.

35 Makere Stewart-Harawira, "Challenging Knowledge Capitalism: Indigenous Research in the 21st Century," *Socialist Studies / Études Socialistes* 9, no. 1 (Spring 2013), www.socialiststudies.com.

36 Dipesh Chakrabarty, "Climate and Capital: On Conjoined Histories," *Critical Inquiry* 41, no. 1 (Autumn 2014): 1–23.

37 Ibid., 1.

38 Ibid., 14.

39 Gayatri Spivak, as quoted in ibid., 21.

40 Ibid., 23.

41 David Beck, *The Struggle for Self-Determination: History of the Menominee Indians since 1854* (Lincoln: University of Nebraska Press, 2005); Michael J. Dockry, "Indigenous Forestry in the Americas: Comparative Environmental Histories in Bolivia and Wisconsin" (PhD diss., University of Wisconsin–Madison, 2012).

42 Anne Rademacher and K. Sivamakrishnan, eds., *Places of Nature in Ecologies of Urbanism* (Hong Kong: Hong Kong University Press, 2017).

43 Michail Fragkias and Christopher G. Boone, "Connecting Environmental Justice, Sustainability, and Vulnerability," *Urbanization and Sustainability* 3 (2013): 49–59.

44 David N. Pellow, "Toward a Critical Environmental Justice Studies: Black Lives Matter as an Environmental Justice Challenge," *Du Bois Review* 13, no. 2 (October 2016): 221–236; and Laura Pulido, "Geographies of Race and Ethnicity II: Environmental Racism, Racial Capitalism, and State-Sanctioned Violence," *Progress in Human Geography* 41, no. 4 (2017): 524–533.

45 Cedric J. Robinson, *Black Marxism: The Making of the Black Radical Tradition* (Chapel Hill: University of North Carolina Press, 1983).

46 Leerom Medovoi, "A Contribution to the Critique of Political Ecology: Sustainability as Disavowal," *New Formations* 69 (July 2010): 129–143, quote on 129–130.

47 Ibid., 132. Specifically, Medovoi draws from Wendy Brown, *Regulating Aversion: Tolerance in the Age of Identity and Empire* (Princeton, NJ: Princeton University Press, 2008), 10.

48 Medovoi, "A Contribution to the Critique of Political Ecology," 142.

49 Donna Haraway, "Situated Knowledges: The Science Question in Feminism and the Privilege of Partial Perspective," *Feminist Studies* 14, no. 3 (Autumn 1988): 575–599, quote on 589.

50 Ibid., 590.

51 Ibid.

52 Paul Routledge and Kate Driscoll Derickson, "Situated Solidarities and the Practice of Scholar-Activism," *Environment and Planning D: Society and Space* 33, no. 3 (2015): 391–407.

53 Ibid., 393.

54 David N. Pellow, "Toward a Critical Environmental Justice Studies: Black Lives Matter as an Environmental Justice Challenge," *Du Bois Review* 13, no. 2 (2016): 6.

PART I

Interdisciplinarity, Place, and Praxis

1

Situating Sustainability from an Ecological Science Perspective

Ecosystem Services, Resilience, and Environmental Justice

M. L. CADENASSO AND S. T. A. PICKETT

Bernie Fowler, a ninety-one-year-old former Maryland state senator, remembers the clear waters of the Chesapeake Bay when he was a child. Concerned with the deteriorating water quality of the Bay that merited its listing in the Clean Water Act of 1972 as "impaired waters," he has worked to raise awareness about its condition and to promote efforts to improve its ecology. Senator Fowler remembers wading up to his shoulders into the Patuxent River, one of the estuarine tributaries of the Bay, and seeing fish, crabs, and abundant bottom-dwelling plants. So in 1988, he began an annual ritual; for the last twenty-nine years, he has waded into the Patuxent on the second Sunday in June. He—joined more recently by a crowd of family, friends, and politicos—wades into the water until he can no longer see his white sneakers. The depth is indexed by how far up the water has wetted his denim overalls.

Although Senator Fowler was not conducting the sneaker test in the 1950s, calibrating his personal index with less subjective measurements from the era suggests that a sneaker test would have scored a very deep 57 inches back then. By 1988 water clarity had diminished dramatically, and Bernie Fowler's overalls measured a mere 10 inches of visibility. Since that time, water clarity has improved, but there is much variability year to year owing to inputs of nutrients, pollutants, and sediments into the Bay (fig. 1.1).

Bernie Fowler wades in the water because he is concerned with the sustainability of the Chesapeake Bay and its crabs, oysters, fish, and waterfowl. He is motivated by the images he remembers from his

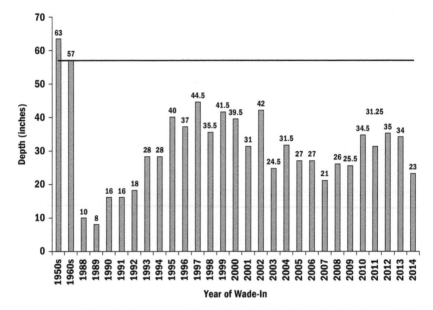

Figure 1.1. Depth at which Bernie Fowler could see his feet during his "sneaker test" for water clarity in the Patuxent River, a tributary of the Chesapeake Bay. The black line indicates the benchmark used as a goal for restoration efforts. Source: Maryland Department of Planning, www.mdp.state.md.us.

childhood and by the abundance that has become a cultural symbol for the Bay. This symbolism encompasses the culinary history of the city of Baltimore, the work ethic of coastal towns of the Eastern Shore of Maryland, the meticulous labor of the African American workers in the shellfish packing plants, and the back-breaking work of watermen, both black and white, as they raked for oysters in the shallows.

This rich array of social, cultural, economic, environmental, and place-based images points to different facets of sustainability. The Chesapeake has provided livelihoods, food, leisure, environmental benefits, cultural symbolism, and a sense of place for generations. How do the images of Bernie Fowler's obscured white sneakers and the efforts to regulate the 11,601-square-kilometer Chesapeake Bay watershed and its urban, suburban, rural, and wild lands coalesce into a rigorous understanding and application of the concept and practice of sustainability?

The Concept of Sustainability

Many scholars and policy makers have experienced the frustration of attempting to define sustainability at the beginning of a meeting or workshop. Participants bring different assumptions and motivations to their view of sustainability, and it seems as though these different views are often in conflict with one another. Water clarity, development, equity, and conservation concerns bump and clash. Why is a shared vision of sustainability so elusive, especially given that it is so widely invoked? Like all concepts, sustainability is an abstraction; it is an aggregated concept that must be unpacked and the components specified in order for it to be applied to a particular situation. In the process of specification, assumptions of spatial and temporal scales and about sustainability goals and motivations are revealed. Participants frequently bring these assumptions to the table without calling them out specifically, which leads to seemingly incompatible visions of sustainability. The good news is that the sustainability "tent" is large and inclusive, but, at the same time, the abstract concept of sustainability must be situated in time, place, and motivation in order to establish measureable goals for sustainability to be used in discussion or practice. It is for this reason that situating sustainability is crucial. It is only when the motivations and corresponding goals are articulated, and the spatial and temporal scales determined, that sustainability is situated and, with a shared vision of sustainability, action can be taken.

Sustainability as a concept may engender frustration because it is both complex and broad. It is complex because it has multiple layers of meaning and use that can result in confusion that diminishes the concept's utility. Sustainability, like all ecologically relevant concepts, is multidimensional, and these dimensions can be identified as metaphor, meaning, and model (Pickett and Cadenasso 2002). These three dimensions can be exploited to effectively situate sustainability. Metaphors can spur creativity and foster communication within a discipline or across disciplinary traditions. Metaphors are images that can be useful when concepts are first being developed. Metaphors, such as the image of Bernie Fowler's disappearing sneakers, can also be the stimuli for public understanding and civic action, as well as a call for increased scientific rigor. They are also valuable as a communication tool when understanding within a discipline has advanced to the stage of sharing that understanding with non-specialists.

To advance understanding of the concept beyond evocative images, however, a technical definition must be developed. This definition should be inclusive, apply to a wide array of situations, and indicate what needs to be specified before it can be applied or tested. Once the meaning of the concept has been articulated, then specific models can be generated to guide the testing, application, and refinement of the meaning and, therefore, the concept. A model must specify the components of the concept that are relevant for a particular time and place. There can be many models generated to accomplish this specification, and the models can translate the concept to numerous real or hypothetical situations. Through testing and application, the models can be refined because new relationships among components may be found or the relative strength of different relationships may be discovered (fig. 1.2).

Sustainability consists of three pillars popularly referred to as the 3 E's: economy, environment, and equity. Leach, Scoones, and Stirling (2010) have suggested that these three pillars be more broadly conceived of as human well-being, ecological integrity, and equity. We adopt Leach et al.'s three normative spheres but translate them into the corresponding theoretical realms of ecosystem services, resilience, and environmental justice, respectively. Ecosystem services are benefits that ecosystems provide to humans that enhance human well-being (Millennium Ecosystem Assessment 2005); resilience is the ability of a system to adapt and adjust to changing internal or external processes while at the same time remaining ecologically functional (Childers et al. 2014); and, finally, equity in terms of environmental justice suggests that environmental benefits and burdens should not be disproportionately experienced by those who lack power or access to the decision-making process, including those living outside the area of particular focus or future generations (Boone 2008; Sze and London 2008). All three of these theoretical realms contribute to understanding sustainability.

Once the three pillars of sustainability are translated into the three spheres of models, there is still an additional step toward practicality. To operationalize sustainability, two things must occur in this step. First, it must be situated in time, place, and motivation. Second, indices or benchmarks must be established so that progress toward a specified goal

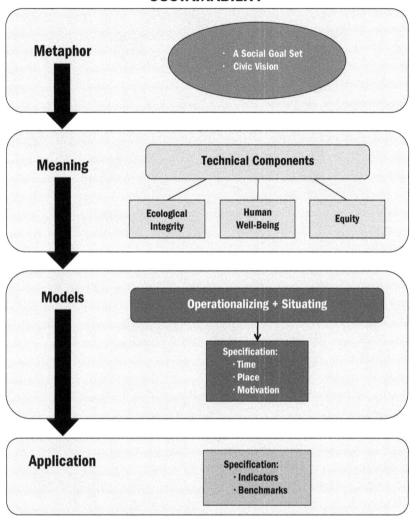

Figure 1.2. Tools for situating sustainability—metaphor, meaning, and models. Metaphors are images useful for generating ideas. But assumptions that underlie metaphors must be removed as the technical definition or meaning of the concept is determined. This meaning should be broad and inclusive and draw on established theoretical realms. The role of models is to specify or translate the meaning for a particular situation—hypothetical or real. Models represent the system and include the physical components, indicate how those components are related to each other, and describe how components interact—all within the context of time, place, and motivation. Finally, applying models and determining how well they represent the system informs changes needed to future models and, potentially, the core meaning of the concept.

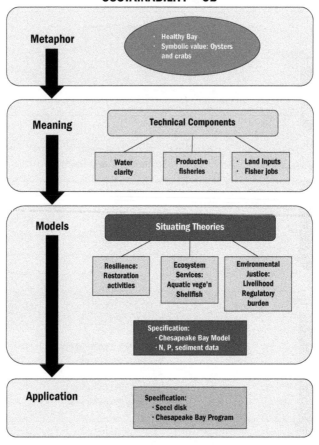

Figure 1.3. One approach to specifying the tools needed to situate sustainability for the Chesapeake Bay. Bernie Fowler's "sneaker test" is an imagistic metaphor for the role of water clarity as an indicator of Bay health and the impacts of water clarity on important economic and cultural icons such as the blue crab and oysters. The technical components that need to be understood to move toward a more sustainable Chesapeake Bay include water clarity as a measure of ecological integrity, the re-creation of productive fisheries as an indication of human well-being, equitable distribution of pollution (e.g., fertilizer runoff) and sediment inputs from the land, and jobs. Models need to be developed to articulate the links among the technical components and to aid in hypothesis generation and testing. These models can be informed by the theoretical realms of resilience, ecosystem services, and environmental justice, all of which will need to be specified within the context of time, place, and motivation. Finally, changes in water clarity can be determined using a Secci disk, a common tool in aquatic sciences, and lessons learned can feed back to affect the priorities and activities of the Chesapeake Bay Program. CB = Chesapeake Bay; vege'n = vegetation; N = nitrogen and P = phosphorus (both indicators of fertilizer runoff).

can be measured. Seeking measurables isn't meant to imply that an end point is achievable; rather, it's to emphasize that evaluation of whether progress toward sustainability is being made must be measureable. Some of these measurables can be truly quantitative, such as a specific decrease in a pollutant of concern, for example. But others are measureable in the sense of relative changes—whether something has gotten better or has gotten worse after a particular time or point of action. The depth at which Bernie Fowler's sneakers disappear is an admittedly informal attempt at measurement.

This chapter is organized to follow closely the steps introduced above to expose and work with the assumptions attending sustainability (fig. 1.2). We first discuss the three dimensions of concepts—metaphor, meaning, and model—as they apply to sustainability in particular. We then discuss the three core theoretical realms—ecosystem services, resilience, and environmental justice—as components of sustainability. Finally, we operationalize these realms within the context of enhancing the water quality of the Chesapeake Bay to sustain aquatic life and important fisheries as a case study (fig. 1.3).

Sustainability: Metaphor—Meaning—Model

Metaphor

Metaphors are valuable tools for creating new ideas and syntheses within a discipline because the new idea can be likened to some other, already familiar, phenomenon. Metaphors provide a jumping-off point for beginning to define and shape the understanding of new ideas by clarifying where the new idea parallels or deviates from the concepts already familiar to the discipline. In this sense, the metaphor is generative (Pickett 1999). Generative metaphors are also useful tools for multidisciplinary interactions because metaphors draw on the imagination and encourage informal and non-technical discussions focused on creating what may be possible instead of being constrained or limited to what already is.

Sustainability is a powerful metaphor (Larson 2011). It conjures up of images of healthy environments, socially cohesive communities, and economies that persist into the future. Sustainability encourages wise and equitable uses of resources such that those resources will continue to be available for future generations. Sustainability recognizes the connections among humans and the natural world (Chapin et al. 2011). As a metaphor, sustainability has motivated individuals, institutions, municipalities and even corporations to modify behaviors in such a way that they work toward protecting the environment, promoting social equity, and enhancing economic vitality (Pierce et al. 2014).

Meaning

Sustainability, however, must move beyond metaphor and toward clear definition in order to set goals and ultimately assess whether those goals have been met. The second dimension of sustainability is therefore its meaning, or technical definition. The definition should be (1) abstract or generalizable, (2) free of unnecessary limiting assumptions, and (3) scale neutral. These three features ensure that the basic definition is inclusive of the broadest array of situations. The definition should not be constrained by assumptions of system stability or persistence through time and space, equilibrium at a determined set point, or even the identity of components and the kinds of interactions among components. A scale-neutral definition allows the concept to be applied across all spatial and temporal scales. This is not the same as scale independence because the scale of application will affect the development, method of application, and interpretation of whether goals have been met. The dimension of meaning answers the question, "What is sustainability?"

Sustainability, at its root, means to maintain, support, and endure through time. Sustainability is founded on ecological principles of mass balance in systems, of conservation of limiting resources in ecosystems, and of allocation of assimilated resources in closed systems. It is about improving the quality of human life within the limits, of resources and otherwise, imposed by the supporting system. Cities, like most ecological systems, are not closed to inputs and influences from the surrounding system; rather, they are fundamentally reliant on resources and processes from beyond their boundaries. Because cities must draw upon resources from beyond their boundaries, sustainability cannot mean a state of autotrophy or completely closed material cycles (Odum 1971). If cities are not closed systems, then sustainability must be expressed in comparative terms. A city can become more, or less, sustainable. In addition, sustainability comprises three principles: human well-being, ecological integrity, and equity. But the decisions about how exactly to relate the three principles of sustainability are not scientific decisions. They emerge from social, political, and power relationships as well as from the understanding of the workings of material systems (Pincetl 2012). There are several directives inherent in this definition: (1) maintain balance among the three principles or pillars, (2) set quantifiable limits, (3) articulate desired goals decided upon by a social community, (4) minimize negative impacts, and (5) include concern not only with current but also with future inhabitants and conditions. Sustainability is not an end point or a state of a system but rather a process or trajectory relative to established goals (Childers et al. 2014).

This basic definition and set of characteristics is intentionally broad and inclusive. The power of the sustainability concept can only be captured and used effectively if there is a way to organize the huge array of situations and approaches. This is the goal of the third dimension of concepts—models. Models specify how the abstract definition is being used—"situated"—in a particular case or range of cases (Jax 1998).

Models

The role of models is to specify or translate the abstract definition for a particular situation—hypothetical or real (Pickett, Kolasa, and Jones 2007). A model is a representation of a system, and it specifies the system's physical components, indicates how those components are related to each other, and describes how components interact. A model also sets the spatial and temporal boundaries of the system. Once a model's contents—components, interactions, and spatial and temporal boundaries—are established, the kind and range of dynamics the interactions can exhibit can also be specified, and the underlying assumptions revealed. Model components vary with particular research questions, the scope and intent of application, and the characteristics of particular sites or situations a model is meant to represent. Therefore, many different models can be generated from the same abstract definition. Although a model is intended to represent a specific situation, it is important to recognize the spatial, temporal, and social context within which the model fits (fig. 1.2). The important role of the model is to establish the domain of the topic under consideration within a specified set of circumstances or a demarcated spatial area or, in other words, to determine "what is in and what is out."

Sustainability plans can be viewed as a type of general model. The overarching goal of a sustainability plan is to provide a series of measures to document the health of a suite of characteristics that the social community cares about. These plans indicate the specific targets that can be quantified and the time and space boundaries in which they will be evaluated. Because sustainability consists of human well-being, ecological integrity, and equity, the details of how these three realms, or pillars, can be modeled as subsets of sustainability is explored in the next section.

Theoretical Realms of Sustainability: Ecosystem Services, Resilience, and Environmental Justice

Each of the three pillars of human well-being, ecological integrity, and equity draws on a recognized body of scholarship—ecosystem services, resilience, and environmental justice, respectively. These three theoretical realms will each be evaluated in terms of their contribution to sustainability. Because sustainability must also be situated in time, place, and motivation in order to advance discussions on setting goals and evaluating progress toward those goals, each of these three realms must also be situated in order to move beyond abstraction. Ecosystem services refer to the goods and functions provided by ecosystems that benefit humans and enhance human well-being. The concept of resilience is a key tool or mechanism by which sustainability is generated. The characteristic of a resilient ecological system is one that can absorb changes to processes, either internal or external to the system, and retain its ecological integrity. Finally, because sustainability goals are the result of community decisions, equity is necessarily a concern. The theoretical realm of environmental justice can be brought to bear on the evaluation of ecosystem services and whether systems are moving toward enhanced sustainability (Escobedo, Kroeger, and Wagner 2011). Each of these theoretical realms is more fully examined below.

Ecosystem Services

Ecosystem services are defined as the benefits that people can derive from the structures and functions of ecosystems. There are four categories of services (Millennium Ecosystem Assessment 2005). Supporting services are those that are necessary for all other services to exist and include such processes as soil formation, nutrient cycling, and seed dispersal. Provisioning services are those that provide products that are consumed, such as food, fiber, and energy. Ecosystems also perform regulating services—the many functions that modulate water, soil, and air quality, and climate and pollination processes. Finally, ecosystems can provide cultural services, which are non-material benefits and which include things such as spiritual fulfillment, recreation, and intellectual inspiration.

The services provided by ecosystem structures and functions depend on several factors. First, by definition, whether something is a service depends on the values and perceptions of the people that might "receive" the service. Therefore, the social community must recognize the service as a good. Second, the same ecosystem structure can provide multiple services. For example, a tree in an urban setting can provide the services of climate regulation and aesthetic enjoyment, among others. Third, what may be perceived as a service by one individual or social group may be perceived as a disservice by another individual or social group. For example, the same tree that provided climate regulation and aesthetic enjoyment may also generate allergens, leaf litter to rake, or damage to infrastructure. The burdens this tree causes for some people may outweigh its benefits, and hence the tree may be a disservice for those people (Battaglia et al. 2014). Finally, in order to evaluate whether a service or disservice is being created by ecosystem structures and functions, those phenomena must be situated in time and place. A young tree may not provide the same type or amount of services as a full-grown tree, and an older, deteriorating tree may also provide different services and disservices than a younger tree. Alternatively, what is perceived by the social community as a benefit at one moment may not be so at a different time. In addition, a tree located in the neighborhood park will provide different services and disservices for a resident than one located on the resident's property. Alternatively, the capacity of an ecosystem to provide a service may shift over space owing to differing biogeophysical constraints. This scalar complexity in both time and space suggests that an ecosystem service may exist at a scale different from the scale at which sustainability goals are being developed.

While it is generally understood that services are provided by ecosystems, the quantification of those services is frequently lacking (Pataki et al. 2011). Instead, it is assumed that, if the system structures and functions are present, the service is being provided. Much more research is needed to determine at what magnitude and rate services are being provided and what factors, both internal and external to the ecosystem, influence the capacity of the system to provide services. Trade-offs and synergies among services also need to be better understood (Rodriguez et al. 2006; Bennett, Peterson, and Gordon 2009). For ecosystem services to contribute to sustainability, the provided services have to be noticeable, and they have to matter to the social community determining sustainability goals. Therefore, sustainability provides the filter to determine whether those services matter in a particular situation.

Resilience

Ecological resilience is a conceptual model for examining the processes underlying sustainability. Resilience is defined as the ability of a system to absorb disturbances, respond to and reorganize from the disturbance, and retain essentially the same basic structure and ways of functioning (Walker et al. 2004). Disturbances can originate from within a system or be external to it. This definition explicitly recognizes that systems are dynamic and that non-equilibrium is the norm. Remaining ecologically functional is the ultimate criterion, and recovery and flexibility are emphasized. This definition is in contrast to what is frequently referred to as "engineering resilience," which emphasizes returning to a stable equilibrium point after a disruption (Holling 1973; Wu and Wu 2013). Engineering resilience comes out of an equilibrium paradigm and is better thought of as a special case (Pickett and Ostfeld 1995). Here we are referring only to ecological resilience that is derived from the non-equilibrium paradigm and that emphasizes dynamics and multiple pathways of change in systems, within limits, that allow the system to ultimately retain its characteristic structures and functions.

Resilience has two key assumptions. One assumption is that systems can exist in multiple stable states under the same environmental conditions. A system is resilient if it can absorb a disturbance and remain within the same state, governed by similar processes. There are several factors that determine whether a system will stay within the same state (Walker et al. 2004). First is the resistance of the system to change states, or how much change has to occur for the system to change state. Second, the larger the range of variability the system can exhibit and still retain the same state will determine how much latitude the system has. Finally, where the system is within its current state at the time of the disturbance will affect how precarious the system is to tipping into another state. Although a system may be resilient, this doesn't mean that the system will initially look and behave exactly the same as the pre-disturbance system; rather, the system will have the capacity to undergo reorganization and growth such that it will retain the same identity in terms of key processes and structures. If the system is not resilient, then it will shift from one state to another in response to a disturbance or as a result of some fundamental change to the underlying parameters determining the capacity of the system to retain the multiple states (Beisner, Haydon, and Cuddington 2003).

The second key assumption of resilience is that, in the face of a disruption, the system does not respond linearly but, rather, in the form of a threshold. The system absorbs the disruption with no noticeable shift until a threshold is reached, and then the system rapidly changes into another state. This characteristic makes it very difficult to predict changes to systems and complicates the ability to manage the system in an effort to reverse the change (Scheffer, Carpenter, et al. 2001). A classic example of this is the impact of nutrient enrichment on the water clarity of a lake (Scheffer, Hosper, et al. 1993). The lake can exist in two distinct states, one with clear water and the other with cloudy water. In the clear-water state, the lake maintains submerged aquatic plants that are rooted in the sediment and help keep the water clear. The aquatic plants need clear water so they can acquire enough light to photosynthesize and survive. The plants also provide hiding places for zooplankton that graze on the algae but are also themselves eaten by fish in the lake. This complex series of interactions maintains water clarity. However, as nutrient additions to the lake occur, the system can maintain water clarity only until a threshold is exceeded; then nutrient enrichment is too much for the system. This disrupts the interactions among system components. Excess nutrients lead to a bloom of algae that block the light reaching the aquatic plants, and the aquatic plants decline. Water clarity is lost as sediments are no longer held in place by the plants and as the algae continue to multiply. The zooplankton are not as effective in keeping algal populations down because they have lost their hiding place from predatory fish. Consequently, the lake transitions into a cloudy state. The transition to a cloudy state can be sudden, which makes managing the lake to maintain it in the clear-water state difficult. The clear state can tolerate or absorb nutrient inputs without any noticeable changes in water clarity until a tipping point, or threshold, is reached and the water suddenly becomes cloudy. In addition, taking management steps to reverse the transition is also difficult because the system has moved to an alternative stable state—cloudy water. Simply reducing nutrient input will not send the system back into the previous clear state because other interactions among system components have been altered (Scheffer, Hosper, et al. 1993). There is a concern that the Chesapeake Bay may have passed such a threshold in sediment load, pollution concentration, and food web structure.

Environmental Justice

The third pillar of sustainability is equity. This is expressed in the definition of sustainability as the ability to support the quality of life of the current generation without impairing the ability of future generations to meet their needs for well-being. Not only should hazards and vulnerabilities not be externalized to future generations, but they should also not be externalized to those elsewhere who lack power or access to environmentally significant decisions. Hence sustainability is founded on concepts of equity across time and space. While definitions may vary, social scientists generally agree that environmental justice exists when environmental "goods" (e.g., parks, playgrounds, and street trees) and "bads" (e.g., landfills, power plants, and polluting industries) are distributed equitably among members of a community, regardless of race, ethnicity, income, or other demographic characteristics (Boone and Fragkias 2012). Conversely, an environmental injustice exists when "goods" and "bads" are distributed inequitably across space, enhancing the environmental opportunities of some residents while exposing others to greater risks (Boone 2008; Sze and London 2008). This aspect of environmental justice is labeled *distributive justice* (Shrader-Frechette and McCoy 1993).

Environmental injustice also exists when residents are excluded from the decision-making process that determines their access to amenities and exposure to disamenities. This dimension is referred to as *participative justice* (Shrader-Frechette and McCoy 1993) or *participatory justice* (Schlosberg 2004). Meaningful incorporation into the decision-making process requires more than simply a place at the table. It also means that residents can gain and contribute information in ways that are accessible to them. Scientific information, and interpretation of that information, should be available in a style free of jargon and in languages spoken by residents. Residents should also be encouraged to contribute information and feedback in forms that are best for them to communicate—verbal, written, or otherwise. In addition, multiple "ways of knowing" should be recognized (Schlosberg 2004). For example, scientific data is one way of knowing, but experiential, historical, and indigenous knowledge are additional ways of knowing, and all should be recognized in a process seeking equity.

Sustainability, as a socially constructed set of goals, lays out the compromises and values of peoples and institutions for addressing human well-being, ecological integrity, and equity in particular places. The best use of sustainability does not export negative effects to the future or to distant or disenfranchised peoples and places in any of the three realms. Sustainability is not a fixed state but a trajectory that can be continually improved upon and balanced (Childers et al. 2014). Resilience is a scientific tool for understanding the changes in complex systems that can either promote or inhibit the societally determined goals of sustainability. The greatest value of resilience is in promoting sustainability and as a model structure for understanding how systems adjust to radical and surprising change. Applying sustainability and its three pillars can be exemplified by the case of the Chesapeake Bay.

Situating Sustainability: The Case of Water Quality in the Chesapeake Bay and Aquatic Resources

Bernie Fowler's annual "sneaker test," which provides a simple, aggregated view of the condition of the Chesapeake Bay, is highly metaphorical (fig. 1.3). It is important and powerful. Yet it also points toward a more rigorous evaluation of Bay water quality. To move past the concept of sustainability as a metaphor and toward developing a series of actions to promote sustainability, two things must be achieved. First, sustainability must be situated. We have explored the three theoretical realms that constitute sustainability—ecosystems services, resilience, and environmental justice. Each of these realms can be understood only when placed in context: context in terms of time, biogeophysical setting, and social milieu. Second, indices or measures to track progress toward sustainability must be developed. Keeping in mind that sustainability is a process rather than a fixed state that is achieved, we must measure sustainability in relative terms. As noted above, some of these measurables can be quantitative, such as a specific decrease in a pollutant of concern. But others are measureable in the sense of relative changes—whether something has gotten better or, has gotten worse over time or following a particular change in the system, such as a disturbance or regulatory action. The sneaker test is an ideal example of this second approach. Specifying temporal, spatial, and social context and developing measures to track progress are both elements of any model of sustainability. We provide here an example of situating sustainability using the case of improving water quality in the Chesapeake Bay to sustain aquatic life and important fisheries.

The Chesapeake Bay is the largest estuary in the United States, with a watershed that drains portions of six states and the District of Columbia. The Bay is uniquely productive for aquatic life because of its size, nutrient inputs from a large watershed, convoluted shoreline, and its shallowness. Consequently, the Bay has been an important commercial fisheries hub for generations, particularly for crab, oysters, and fish. This productivity and the lifestyles, livelihood, and cultural symbols it has supported are some of the metaphorical connotations of the Chesapeake Bay. Over time, as both agricultural and urban development increased within the Chesapeake Bay's watershed, inputs of nutrients, pollutants, and sediment to the Bay also increased (Curtin, Fisher, and Brush 2001). These inputs damaged water quality, and the populations of aquatic organisms greatly decreased. The U.S. Environmental Protection Agency declared the waters of the Bay impaired and mandated that nutrient inputs, specifically nitrate, into the Bay be decreased by 40 percent. Such a specific policy goal is motivated by the cultural and economic images of the Bay, but it implies a model of how the Bay functions. That model suggests some of the levers that can be manipulated to improve Bay environment and productivity.

Nitrate is a common water pollutant worldwide. Nitrogen makes up more than 75 percent of our atmosphere as a non-reactive gas. It enters the terrestrial system through fixation by microorganisms and lightening. Since the industrial revolution however, humans have doubled the amount of nitrogen in the terrestrial system through fossil fuel combustion and atmospheric deposition and through fertilizer application (Vitousek et al. 1997). Nitrogen has several forms, but nitrate is the inorganic form of nitrogen that is highly mobile because it is soluble in water and quickly travels through the soil into groundwater or off land surfaces into infrastructure. Once in the water, nitrate causes algal blooms because nitrogen is often a limiting resource for plants. As algae die and heterotrophic bacteria decompose algal tissue, oxygen in the water column is reduced, causing die-offs of aquatic life. These processes create areas termed "dead zones," and since 1985 the size of the dead zone in the Chesapeake Bay from June to August has varied between 15 and 30 percent of the total volume of the Bay (Maryland Department of Natural Resources 2012). Although invisible to Fowler's sneaker test, nitrogen is a key aspect of the model for understanding and thus improving the Bay ecosystem.

From this background, it is easy to imagine that a sustainability goal for the Chesapeake Bay and its watershed would be to reduce the nitrate loadings into the Bay in order to improve water quality and bring back sustainable levels of aquatic life. The statement of this goal informs the spatial and temporal extent of concern and the measures that would be used to evaluate whether progress toward the goal has been made. For example, the changes in the concentrations of nitrogen in the Bay can be tracked through time. An assumption of Fowler's sneaker test is that invisible pollutants like nitrate can also be indexed by water clarity as a linked feature in the complex model of Chesapeake Bay ecological functioning. The detailed scientific model would take into account not only the traditionally recognized point sources of water pollution—sanitary sewer effluent, for example—but also non-point pollution from urban and rural sources. Taking water samples around the Bay can help to determine which stream or infrastructural outfall is contributing nitrogen to the Bay. This determination can then be used to prioritize activities upstream in the watershed to limit the amount of nitrogen entering the Bay by reducing it at its source. The ultimate measure or benchmark for success, however, may be the change in populations of aquatic organisms. This aspect of the Bay ecosystem echoes Bernie Fowler's ability to see an active bottom-dwelling community of organisms through the clear waters of his youth. Establishing measures to determine whether progress toward a sustainability goal has been made may be the relatively easy part, however. More challenging will be determining what actions need to be taken in the watershed to decrease nitrate concentrations in the Bay in an effort to enhance the sustainability of Bay fisheries. Fowler's sneaker index seems to acknowledge that water clarity is important, permitting aquatic plants the light they need for photosynthesis. These plants are, in turn, important fish nursery sites. But the sneaker test also acknowledges that filter-feeding oysters can be damaged by sediment loading directly. Thus the sneaker test connects with important components of scientific models of Bay food webs and limiting environmental factors.

The Chesapeake Bay watershed contains metropolitan regions and agricultural activities. Both of these land uses are sources of nitrate and sediments that work their way into the waters of the Bay. Agricultural fertilizer addition is an obvious source of nutrients. In urban regions nitrogen is added through lawn fertilizer, sewage, and fossil fuel combustion, including manufacturing, home heating, and vehicle use. Sediment can be added to the Bay through construction practices that grade or erode land as well as through changes to stream flow that may lead to bank erosion. Sources that are from one discernible location are called point-source pollution, and they are relatively easy to control. More difficult to control are the non-point sources of pollution that are distributed around the landscape. In order to reduce nitrate loading into the Bay, the sources of nitrogen input have to be reduced, or strategies have to be employed to keep the nitrogen that is added to the watershed from entering waterways and ultimately the Bay. These two approaches are much more difficult because they involve changing human behaviors affecting fertilizer and vehicle use, for example.

Those engaged in developing a management plan must be motivated by similar goals. For this example, the goals include improved water quality as measured by nitrate concentration and the growth of the populations of targeted organisms of concern. Potential strategies to reduce nitrate loading into the Bay in an effort to enhance the sustainability of Bay aquatic life must be situated not only in motivation but also in time and in place. Strategies to reduce nitrate loading into the Bay may be more effective in particular places in the watershed than others. For example, because nitrate is soluble and enters waterways as runoff, capturing that runoff and treating it to remove the nitrate before it is released into the waterways may be effective. This activity may require restoring riparian areas to enhance their function in terms of nitrogen retention. Another option may be to reduce the amount of runoff or the amount of nitrogen in the runoff by installing broadly distributed storm-water management infrastructure, such as bioswales and rain gardens, that could remove nitrogen and sediments from the water before releasing it into streams draining into the Chesapeake, or by removing impervious surfaces and by planting areas that are currently bare in an effort to retain both water and nitrogen throughout the watershed (Cadenasso et al. 2008). Alternatively, strategies could be employed to reduce the inputs of nitrogen to the system by regulating fertilization of home lawns or agricultural fields, upgrading sewage systems to minimize leaking, decreasing vehicle emissions, or otherwise lessening deposition from fossil fuel combustion.

Not only will each of these suggested strategies have greater or lesser success depending on where in the landscape they are implemented, but each of these potential strategies may also result in differential benefits and burdens to residents. Some residents may have to change behaviors or incur other costs, such as time, money, or risk. The storm-water utility fee established in 2012 by the city of Baltimore aims at reducing the amount, and improving the quality of, storm water flowing from the city. In addition, activities at one spatial and temporal scale to achieve a goal may result in benefits or burdens to individuals at a different scale. By situating each of the three realms of sustainability, trade-offs and synergies among actions undertaken to promote sustainability can be evaluated.

The Chesapeake Bay is a complex system that is driven by water salinity, sediment concentration, nitrogen and phosphorus amounts, and dissolved oxygen in the water. These biophysical attributes are affected by human decisions, the built infrastructure, policies, and the incidental effects of construction, transportation, agriculture, and daily life. Understanding and improving the water quality of the Chesapeake exercises imagistic metaphors—as when Bernie Fowler wades into the Patuxent branch of the Bay—along with the specification of Bay structure and function in detailed scientific models. The models operationalize the definition—that is, the meaning—of the Chesapeake as a complex, social-ecological system whose components, connections, feedbacks, dynamics, and boundaries must be specified in technical terms. If those models can be articulated in metaphors, then activists and policy makers like Bernie Fowler can engage the complexities of the Chesapeake as meaning and model in the imagistic and value-driven public realm.

Conclusion

As we have seen, the concept of sustainability has three dimensions—metaphor, meaning, and model. Metaphors are helpful for generating initial understanding and beginning conversations across disciplinary divides. They can also engage the public and non-specialists in productively understanding systems that they care about. To move forward, however, the assumptions underlying the metaphorical dimension must be stripped from the core definition. The core definition is broad and inclusive and is translated to specific situations by models. Models, therefore, have the job of identifying the temporal and spatial scale, content, bounds, and dynamics of a particular situation.

Sustainability is not solely a scientific concept. It draws on ecological concepts and processes but incorporates social perceptions and values. The three pillars of sustainability—human well-being, ecological integrity, and equity—resonate with the specific theoretical realms of ecosystem services, resilience, and environmental justice, respectively. Resilience is the ability of a system to adapt and adjust to changing internal and external shocks and structurally disruptive events. Resilience is a scientific tool for understanding the changes in complex systems that can either promote or inhibit the societally determined goals of sustainability. The goals of sustainability are generally motivated by a desire to improve human well-being without compromising the well-being of future generations or of distant or disenfranchised communities.

This definition of sustainability is in reality highly metaphorical. It is translated through the technical dimensions of such concepts as ecosystem services or environmental justice. Ecosystem services are benefits that ecosystems provide to humans. Therefore, human well-being is inherently influenced by the state of ecological systems. Whether those systems provide benefits or burdens to humans is ultimately determined by the perceptions and values of affected social communities. The last pillar, equity, can be informed by scientific measurements and understanding in terms of the distribution of benefits and burdens through time and across space. However, whether equity among peoples has been achieved is a social decision. Hence, it will likely have significant metaphorical or imagistic content.

In an attempt to balance these three pillars, sustainability encompasses a series of socially derived goals that embody the values, priorities, and compromises of a social community. Although sustainability is usually articulated in terms of a series of goals, sustainability is not a fixed state or something achievable per se. Sustainability is more usefully thought of as a trajectory along which the balancing of trade-offs and synergies among goals results in making systems relatively more sustainable (Childers et al. 2014). Finally, sustainability and its component concepts—ecosystem services, resilience, and equity—are all abstract. All of these concepts depend on specification to a particular situation, including being situated in time, place, and motivation, in order to translate the abstract meaning into specific models for testing and evaluation (fig. 1.2). Situating sustainability requires recognizing its metaphorical content, its meaning, and the models that translate it into rigorous measures.

Acknowledgments

We are grateful for the opportunity to contribute to this volume and express thanks to Anne Rademacher and Julie Sze, who were instrumental to sparking this conversation and carrying it through to publication.

We have learned much from our many colleagues in Baltimore and the numerous stimulating interdisciplinary conversations had over the years, and we thank them for their intellectual generosity. We acknowledge support by the U.S. National Science Foundation's Long-Term Ecological Research program (DEB-1027188) and the Urban Sustainability Research Coordination Network (DEB-1140077).

WORKS CITED

Battaglia, M., G. L. Buckley, M. Galvin, and J. M. Grove. 2014. "It's Not Easy Going Green: Obstacles to Tree-Planting Programs in East Baltimore." *Cities and the Environment* 7, no. 2, article 6.

Beisner, B. E., D. T. Haydon, and K. Cuddington. 2003. "Alternative Stable States in Ecology." *Frontiers in Ecology and the Environment* 1, no. 7:376–382.

Bennett, E. M., G. D. Peterson, and L. Gordon. 2009. "Understanding Relationships among Multiple Ecosystem Services." *Ecology Letters* 12:1–11.

Boone, C. G. 2008. "Environmental Justice as Process and New Avenues for Research." *Environmental Justice* 1:149–153.

Boone, C. G., and M. Fragkias. 2012. *Urbanization and Sustainability: Linking Urban Ecology, Environmental Justice and Global Environmental Change.* New York: Springer.

Cadenasso, M. L., S. T. A. Pickett, P. M. Groffman, G. S. Brush, M. F. Galvin, J. M. Grove, G. Hagar, V. Marshall, B. P. McGrath, J. P. M. O'Neil-Dunne, W. P. Stack, and A. R. Troy. 2008. "Exchanges across Land-Water-Scape Boundaries in Urban Systems: Strategies for Reducing Nitrate Pollution." *Annals of the New York Academy of Sciences* 1134:213–232.

Chapin, F. S., III, M. E. Power, S. T. A. Pickett, A. Freitag, J. A. Reynolds, R. B. Jackson, D. M. Lodge, C. Duke, S. L. Collins, A. G. Power, and A. Bartuska. 2011. "Earth Stewardship: Science for Action to Sustain the Human-Earth System." *Ecosphere* 2, no. 8:1–20, article 89.

Childers, D. L., S. T. A. Pickett, J. M. Grove, L. Ogden, and A. Whitmer. 2014. "Advancing Urban Sustainability Theory and Action: Challenges and Opportunities." *Landscape and Urban Planning* 125:320–328. DOI: www.dx.doi.org/10.1016/j.landurbplan.2014.01.022.

Curtin, P., G. W. Fisher, and G. S. Brush, eds. 2001. *Discovering the Chesapeake: The History of an Ecosystem.* Baltimore: Johns Hopkins University Press.

Escobedo, F. J., T. Kroeger, and J. E. Wagner. 2011. "Urban Forests and Pollution Mitigation: Analyzing Ecosystem Services and Disservices." *Environmental Pollution* 159:2078–2087.

Holling, C. S. 1973. "Resilience and Stability of Ecological Systems." *Annual Review of Ecology and Systematics* 4:1–23.

Jax, K. 1998. "Holocoen and Ecosystem: On the Origin and Historical Consequences of Two Concepts." *Journal of the History of Biology* 31:113–142.

Larson, B. 2011. *Metaphors for Environmental Sustainability: Redefining Our Relationship with Nature*. New Haven, CT: Yale University Press.

Leach, M., I. Scoones, and A. Stirling, eds. 2010. *Dynamic Sustainabilities: Technology, Environment, Social Justice*. New York: Earthscan.

Maryland Department of Natural Resources. 2012. "The 2012 Chesapeake Bay Summer Dead Zone." *Eyes on the Bay*. http://dnr.maryland.gov.

Millennium Ecosystem Assessment. 2005. *Ecosystems and Human Well-Being: Synthesis*. Washington, DC: Island Press.

Odum, H. T. 1971. *Environment, Power, and Society*. New York: John Wiley.

Pataki, D. E., M. M. Carreiro, J. Cherrier, N. E. Grulke, V. Jennings, S. Pincetl, R. V. Pouyat, T. H. Whitlow, and W. C. Zipperer. 2011. "Coupling Biogeochemical Cycles in Urban Environments: Ecosystem Services, Green Solutions, and Misconceptions." *Frontiers in Ecology and the Environment* 9:27–36.

Pickett, S. T. A. 1999. "The Culture of Synthesis: Habits of Mind in Novel Ecological Integration." *Oikos* 87:479–487.

Pickett, S. T. A., and M. L. Cadenasso. 2002. "The Ecosystem as a Multidimensional Concept: Meaning, Model and Metaphor." *Ecosystems* 5: 1–10.

Pickett, S. T. A., J. Kolasa, and C. Jones. 2007. *Ecological Understanding: The Nature of Theory and the Theory of Nature*. 2nd ed. Boston: Academic Press.

Pickett, S. T. A., and R. S. Ostfeld. 1995. "The Shifting Paradigm in Ecology." In *A New Century for Natural Resources Management*, edited by R. L. Knight and S. F. Bates, 261–278. Washington, DC: Island Press.

Pierce, J., N. Lovrich, B. Johnson, T. Reames, and W. Budd. 2014. "Social Capital and Longitudinal Change in Sustainability Plans and Policies: US Cities from 2000 to 2010." *Sustainability* 6:136–157.

Pincetl, S. 2012. "Nature, Urban Development and Sustainability—What New Elements Are Needed for a More Comprehensive Understanding?" In "Current Research on Cities," edited by Andrew Kirby. Special issue, *Cities* 29, suppl. no. 2:S32–S37.

Rodriguez, J. P., T. D. Beard, E. M. Bennett, G. S. Cumming, S. J. Cork, J. Agard, A. P. Dobson, and G. D. Peterson. 2006. "Trade-Offs across Space, Time, and Ecosystem Services." *Ecology and Society* 11, no. 1, article 28. www.ecologyandsociety.org.

Scheffer, M. S., S. Carpenter, J. A. Foley, C. Folke, and B. Walker. 2001. "Catastrophic Shifts in Ecosystems." *Nature* 413:591–596.

Scheffer, M., S. H. Hosper, M. L. Meijer, and B. Moss. 1993. "Alternative Equilibria in Shallow Lakes." *Trends in Ecology and Evolution* 8:275–279.

Schlosberg, D. 2004. "Reconceiving Environmental Justice: Global Movements and Political Theories." *Environmental Politics* 13:517–540.

Shrader-Frechette, K. S., and E. D. McCoy. 1993. *Method in Ecology: Strategies for Conservation*. Cambridge: Cambridge University Press.

Sze, J., and J. K. London. 2008. "Environmental Justice at the Crossroads." *Sociology Compass* 2, no. 4 (2008): 1331–1354.

Vitousek, P. M., H. A. Mooney, J. Lubchenco, and J. M. Melillo. 1997. "Human Domination of Earth's Ecosystems." *Science* 277:494–499.

Walker, B., C. S. Holling, S. R. Carpenter, and A. Kinzig. 2004. "Resilience, Adaptability and Transformability in Social-Ecological Systems." *Ecology and Society* 9, no. 2, article 5. www.ecologyandsociety.org.

Wu, J., and T. Wu. 2013. "Ecological Resilience as a Foundation for Urban Design and Sustainability." In *Resilience in Ecology and Urban Design: Linking Theory and Practice for Sustainable Cities*, edited by S. T. A. Pickett, M. L. Cadenasso, and B. P. McGrath, 211–229. New York: Springer.

2

Situating New Constellations of Practice in the Humanities

Toward a Just and Sustainable Future

JONI ADAMSON

In advance of the 2015 Paris climate talks, Pope Francis of the Roman Catholic Church published an encyclical, "On Care for Our Common Home: Laudato Si'" (Francis 2015), widely said to have influenced the outcomes of the meetings. Anticipated by the press as a statement on climate change, the pope, in fact, addresses climate change only briefly in the lengthy document. Instead, like the framers of "The Future We Want," the outcome document of the 2012 Rio+20 UN Conference on Sustainable Development (United Nations 2012), the pope takes on economic development and consumerism directly, arguing that accelerating environmental change is a symptom of human attitudes and practices in an unconstrained era of global capitalism. He emphasizes, more than any of his papal predecessors, "the extent to which humankind must be understood as a part of nature, not as something alien to or outside of it" (Zimmerman 2017, 150). As a religious leader, he calls upon the religions of all the world to recognize the moral standing of all living beings, not just the human.

Both "The Future We Want" and "On Care for Our Common Home" reframe sustainable development as an issue involving more than economics. Introduced into global consciousness in 1987 by the publication of *Our Common Future* (also known as the Brundtland Report), early notions of sustainable development often failed to address the issues of justice and equity or to emphasize the role that human values, attitudes, and imagination play in sustaining—or interrupting—cultural and biological diversity (World Commission on Environment and Development 1987). Twenty-five years later, "The Future We Want," signed by all UN member states, confirms broad general agreement that global society should strive for a high quality of life that is equitably shared and sustainable for all species, not just the human. The document recognizes that global efforts to monitor, measure, and reverse the biogeophysical drivers of climate change will require science, but it calls for change in the ways in which research is done in international research programs, such as the UN Intergovernmental Panel on Climate Change (IPCC; www.ipcc.ch) and Future Earth (www.futureearth.org).[1]

The IPCC, which was formed to study accelerating environmental change, has over a thousand scientists, very few social scientists, and less than a handful of humanists contributing to its research and reports. Future Earth has also been dominated by scientists. Change is needed in these programs—as groups of interdisciplinary humanists, social scientists, and scientists have observed—because, while Big Science provides facts and data about earth systems, it has offered little understanding of "humans as diverse, interpretive creatures who frequently disagree about values, means, and ends" (Castree et al., 2014, 765). Neither has science, until more recently, acknowledged that, as the pope argues in the encyclical, "humankind is a creature dependent on the other creatures constituting the biosphere" (Zimmerman 2017, 151).

In responding to these calls for change from both the international and religious communities, both the IPCC and Future Earth have been working to "reconstitute themselves for the future" by integrating the insights and practices of the humanities, which have long focused on the study of human values, attitudes, and diversity, into their projects and programming (Castree 2014, 248). Scholars working in the humanities who also study the physical and sustainability sciences, as articulated in "Humanities for the Environment—a Manifesto for Research and Action," are affirming the expertise of their fields for transforming human preferences, practices, and actions in a time when there is a need for greater sustainability and justice in the ways that humans live on the planet. The turn to the humanities, these researchers argue, is important since what humans believe and value, how they organize themselves, and what they are willing to invest to achieve their goals are factors that lie largely outside scientific calculation (Holm et al. 2015, 978). Moreover, the 2015 papal encyclical and, arguably, the 2016 election of Donald Trump both offer evidence that religion, long one of the most important fields in the humanities and long a shaper of human values, is not going to be relegated to the "dustbin of history" any time soon (Zimmerman 2017, 149). Religion, like literature, history, philosophy, and the arts, continues to shape global affairs and, as a part of human cultures, is also a significant influence on how notions of sustainability, equity, and justice are conceived and debated.

As noted in the introduction to this volume, this is the reason many scholars are calling for more interdisciplinarity in sustainability discourse and praxis. But what forms will integrated or interdisciplinary sustainability research take? Sze et. al observe in the introduction that there is a need for "a toolkit" to help us innovate integrated sustainability research. This chapter contributes to such a toolkit by exploring ongoing projects that have been innovated by one of the most ambitious humanities efforts to emerge from calls at international levels for more equity- and justice-focused definitions of sustainability (Hartman 2015; Holm et al. 2015; Birgersson, Hartman, and Norrman 2016). Seed-funded from 2013 to 2015 by the Andrew W. Mellon Foundation, the Humanities for the Environment project, or HfE (https://hfe-observatories.org), is modeling new constellations of interdisciplinary practice that respond to calls for better integration of the humanities into sustainability research. The Mellon Foundation persistently defends the value of the humanities while consistently encouraging "scholars and institutions to experiment and adapt" and to engage in more collaborative projects with digital components (Howard 2014, 4). The Mellon Foundation awarded a grant to the Consortium of Humanities Centers and Institutes (CHCI), which, in turn, dispersed funds to three international "Observatories" located at Arizona State University (North America), Trinity College Dublin (Europe) and the University of Sydney (Australia-Pacific).[2] The term "Observatory" was chosen as the formal mechanism that HfE researchers would use to organize within their own institutions and to network and map the environmental humanities initiatives in their own regions. Each Observatory—in North America, Europe, and Australia-Pacific—was also tasked with working to enhance global networking among universities, nongovernmental organizations, businesses, and communities and to represent this work on a common international website.[3]

Although the Observatories would innovate themes, projects, programming, and activities tailored to their own regional interests and issues, they would also be guided by some common agreements and principles. They agreed that "sustainability" would be defined as "just sustainability," or a sustainability that works to "ensure a better quality of life for all, now and into the future" while "living within the limits of supporting ecosystems" (Agyeman, Bullard, and Evans 2003, 5). Humanities for the Environment principle investigators also wrote a set of guiding concepts, or "Common Threads," that would connect and articulate the shared ideas informing the outlooks and research outcomes of the Observatories. The first of these threads states that

> we recognize the role that humans have played in transforming the chemical, physical and biological processes of the Earth's atmosphere, land surfaces and oceans at an ever-increasing pace, leading a wide range of scientists to propose that we are now living in the Anthropocene, a term that is catching the public's imagination, as it suggests that human activities have ramped up to become a geological force as significant as volcanic outbursts or meteorite impacts, and requiring us to take responsibility and action for the future of the planet and its inhabitants.[4]

This chapter provides a brief field genealogy of the environmental humanities and situates the humanities within sustainability discourses, explaining why discussion of the Anthropocene has sparked interest among humanities scholars for deepening critical engagement with the concepts of "sustainability" and "sustainable development." It then describes three ongoing HfE projects at the North America Observatory that illustrate a growing interdisciplinary toolkit of approaches to sustainability praxis that takes the humanities and humanities methodologies seriously: The Archive of Hope and Cautionary Tales, Life Overlooked, and Dinner 2040.

The Environmental Humanities and the Anthropocene

Generally defined, the environmental humanities include historical, philosophical, aesthetic, religious, literary, filmic, and media studies informed by the most recent research in the sciences of nature and sustainability. Academic institutionalization of the environmental humanities began in the early 1970s, with the organization of the American Society of Environmental History (ASEH). Later in the 1990s, the

International Society for Environmental Ethics, the Association for the Study of Literature and Environment (ASLE) and its sister organizations around the world, and the International Association for Environmental Philosophy were organized. Soon after, the Environment and Culture Caucus (ECC) of the American Studies Association was founded. By 2000, all of these organizations were networking internationally in very robust ways.

Before the 1970s, most humanists "regarded as absurd the idea that trees or even biomes could have moral standing" (Zimmerman 2017, 146). Most still sharply distinguished between mind and body, freedom and necessity, and they had little interest in nature as studied by the natural sciences. As the philosopher Michael Zimmerman has observed, the "humanities were devoted to studying and assessing human products, such as texts and works of art, and human events, including those deemed significant in human history" (Zimmerman 2017, 146). However, with the growth of the professional organizations described above, by the turn of the twenty-first century, the environmental humanities were growing rapidly, and infrastructural support and funding for curricular innovation and programming were expanding.[5]

The roots of the environmental humanities are arguably much older and more rhizomatic, however, than even the early 1990s dates usually given to the emergence of environmental literary criticism, history, and philosophy. Some humanists working in ethnic studies, Indigenous studies, environmental justice and postcolonial studies, political ecology, and religion and ecology trace the roots of their disciplines back to the earliest cosmological narratives, stories and symbols from among the world's oldest cultures. Many cosmologies, recorded in the modern day, tell not only of cultural origins but also include references to postcolonial uprisings, resistance, and revolts, and some suggest critiques of imperialism and forced conversions to Western religions (DeLoughrey and Handley 2011, 20; Adamson 2016, 136; 2017b, 5). Interestingly, Pope Francis takes a stance in his encyclical that alludes to these older cosmologies through the figure of Saint Francis and his care for animals and plants. Without embracing pre-Christian pantheism, of course, the pope refers to the Earth as our "sister" and gives equal moral standing to our Earth/sister and the peoples and animals made most vulnerable and at risk by colonial activities and, now, modern economic development and climate change. Today's daunting social and environmental problems, he remarks, "have caused sister earth, along with all the abandoned of our world, to cry out, pleading that we take another course. Never have we so hurt and mistreated our common home as we have in the last two hundred years" (Francis 2015, 53; Zimmerman 2017, 154).

In 2001 in Australia, Libby Robin, Deborah Bird Rose, and Val Plumwood co-founded a group to study the "ecological humanities," which was the first use of the term. They fully embraced not only the integrated study of science and the humanities but the study of Indigenous/ Aboriginal cosmologies and the impacts of colonization and climate change on vulnerable peoples, animals, and ecosystems (Robin 2013; Adamson 2017b, 5). The work of this group touched off a new interdisciplinary movement in the humanities to pursue "a wide range of conversations on environmental issues in this time of growing awareness of the . . . challenges facing all life on Earth" (Rose et al. 2012, 1). Indeed, as the Citizen Potawatami tribal member and philosopher Kyle Whyte asserts, stories about climate change suggest something like "déjà vu" for the world's Indigenous peoples, since recent anthropogenic environmental change continues patterns "that have been part of settler colonialism for quite some time" (Whyte 2017, 49). Today, three decades after the first visible emergence of what would become the "environmental humanities," it is safe to say that there are thousands of humanists around the world taking environmental justice and social equity approaches to their work with particular attention to the knowledges of the world's Indigenous and Aboriginal peoples.[6]

As a field and as a methodological approach, the environmental humanities explore and address the anthropogenic factors contributing to increasingly extreme weather events and linked social disparities and risk, including drought, fire, hurricanes, melting glaciers, and warming and rising oceans (Adamson 2016, 135). Many environmental literary critics, historians, ecofeminists, and philosophers have commented on a "coterminous turn" toward discussion of the "Anthropocene" at the turn of the twenty-first century and the rise of the environmental humanities (Nixon 2014; Deloughrey 2015, 352). This development is linked to publication of a short essay by Paul Crutzen and Eugene Stoermer titled "The 'Anthropocene.'" Crutzen and Stoermer proposed this term to describe a new, post-Holocene epoch in which, they argued, humans had become like "Nature" itself, a geomorphic force so powerful that they were changing every biogeochemical system on the planet (Crutzen and Stoermer 2000).

The cultural critic Rob Nixon has observed that soon after the appearance of this essay, humanists "in their interdisciplinary masses" began pouring into symposiums and conferences to discuss and debate this "epochal idea" (Nixon 2014). Crutzen and Stoermer likely did not anticipate that their essay would lead researchers in once rigidly separated disciplines to begin building infrastructure and fora in which scholars from across disciplines would willingly cross divides that had existed at least since 1959, when C. P. Snow famously wrote about a "rift" between the humanities and sciences, an idea that helped build disciplinary walls and separations resting on increasingly unquestioned assumption "of active human cultures working upon the passive raw material of . . . nature" (Snow [1959] 2001; see also Rocheleau and Padini 2016, 51).

There are several reasons why the keyword "Anthropocene" is deemed problematic by many humanists. It is often deployed as if there is an "aggregate Anthropos" or homogenous species—"the human"—that is equally responsible and equally aware of the processes of environmental change taking place on a planetary scale (Di Chiro 2015, 369). Indeed, aggregate narratives about "the human," as Nixon has observed, almost always fail to describe "unequal human agency, unequal human impacts, and unequal human vulnerabilities" (2015). This also points to the reasons "sustainable development" has not been a term that has caught the imagination in the environmental humanities. As Zimmerman observes, recent humanities scholarship has been highly critical of the idea that human history reveals waves of cultural evolution or cultural development. Today, the idea of cultural development is often the object of suspicion, given that supposedly more "developed" Europeans and Americans assumed that they were justified in invading and colonizing "backward" peoples. In the contemporary multicultural, postcolonial context in which the environmental humanities is taking shape, "terms like 'development' call to mind exploitative hierarchies that must be resisted"; however, Zimmerman observes that they should not be dismissed completely because "developmental models can be useful in making sense of complex cultural arrangement" (Zimmerman 2017, 146). For this reason, as a metaconcept, the Anthropocene is catalyzing productive discussion and debate about both anthropogenic activities and sustainable development.

Also, Nixon notes, the Anthropocene has sparked the imagination of scholars in the humanities because it is becoming a term that is increasingly associated with the early twenty-first century expansion of neoliberal capitalism, in a time in which most societies around the world have experienced a deep and "widening chasm between the super rich and the ultra poor" (Nixon 2014, n.p.; see also Zalasiewicz, Williams, and Waters 2016). Three decades after the publication of *Our Common Future*, awareness of this widening chasm is expanding and enriching definitions of "sustainability." In "Welcome to the Anthropocene," the short three-minute film that debuted at Rio+20, "sustainability," as a term, has been infused with concerns for justice and equity in its presentation of economics and development.[7] Screen-sized images of the globe are superimposed with an uninterrupted succession of hockey stick-shaped graphs illustrating the "great acceleration" of human activities in the last two hundred fifty years leading to steadily rising CO_2 emissions, tropical forest loss, and population growth (Di Chiro 2015, 364). The film ends with the assurance that "our creativity, energy, and industry offer hope" to shape our future. This focus on hope and creativity, increasingly seen to be missing in Big Science and in many discussions of sustainable development, has energized scholars in the humanities, who tend to focus on anthropogenic activities and human motivations, behaviors, and desires, rather than on strictly economic—or "ecosystem services"—perspectives. What environmental humanists are seeking to produce are shifts in human imagination and societal values and norms. They hope to catalyze integrated interventions lead by "artists, writers, scientists, educators, community leaders and activists" (Birgersson, Hartman, and Norrman 2016; see also Hartman 2015). Without the integration of all the disciplines, writes Noel Castree and a venerable group of humanists and social scientists, multiple potential responses in potential decision making processes about sustainability or sustainable development "relevant to different constituencies" might be missing (Castree et al. 2014, 765–766). By integrating imagination and creativity and attention to race, class, gender, ethnicity, and social inequities—topics that tend to be the focus of the humanities—into interdisciplinary projects, there is increased potential to enrich and expand insights and outcomes.

Humanities for the Environment

Can the humanities (which typically are characterized as weakly tooled to address social and environmental crises) catalyze the imagination of new ideas, narratives, frameworks, alternatives, demands, and projects that will enable people to envision plausibly different futures, even "livable futures"? (Adamson 2016, 139). This is exactly the question that humanists working together in the North American Observatory in the summer of 2013 came together to answer.

As one of the North American Observatory principle investigators and lead developer for the HfE international website, I was tasked with organizing a steering committee from various universities with ongoing environmental humanities initiatives or programs to collaborate on the innovation of three experimental projects. Nine researchers from twelve U.S. and Canadian universities and nine researchers from Arizona State University gathered to begin planning projects that would aim to tackle the complex challenges of the Anthropocene. Several members of this committee had long been involved as scholars and public intellectuals in grassroots environmental justice and conservation movements and in pioneering the environmental humanities.[8] Most had been networking for over a decade through the Association for the Study of Literature and Environment, the American Society of Environmental History, and the Environment and Culture Caucus of the American Studies Association. Some had networked previously through other Mellon Foundation grants, including the Initiative on Environments and Societies at the University of California, Davis.[9] Through these associations and others, steering committee members brought a wealth of public humanities and collaborative experience in environmental justice and sustainability community outreach to their work at the North American Observatory.

Each of the projects they designed is archived on the HfE website, which is itself one of the outcomes of this Mellon-funded project. To use a phrase that I find useful to describe this work, each of the projects and the website on which they are archived seek to innovate "new constellations of narrative, visual, digital, and curatorial practice" for the purpose of addressing social and environmental justice challenges and modeling sustainable solutions and guidelines for community praxis. The word "constellation" was chosen not only because of my own longtime scholarly interest in ancient observatories and oral cosmologies focused on the stars and constellations that continue even today to be used to think about both the immensity of the universe and the ecological limits of the only planet that humans can call home (Adamson 2016, 136–138). "Constellations of practice" also suggests that what the HfE project aspires to contribute to sustainability discourses is not only a collaborative approach to working across the disciplines but also a deep knowledge of practices that have worked sustainably in the past and that work today and that may be as crucial to survival of "our common home" as the futuristic technologies being innovated to transition to a time beyond fossil fuel dependence.

None of the methodologies or practices being innovated by HfE researchers are, in themselves, new. What is "new" is the ways in which they are being "constellated" and imagined by collaborative teams working across the disciplines and with locally, regionally, and internationally networked partners. In terms of imagining new methods and projects, the term "Observatory" was chosen to quicken the imagination of humanists being called upon to think outside the limitations of traditional humanities research protocols, such as the single-authored monograph, and to engage in more collaborative, interdisciplinary, or web-based projects and research focused on global sustainability challenges. "Observatory" would also align HfE projects well with other international research platforms and scientific initiatives, such as Future Earth, by evoking a sense of a humanities "laboratory" or "research space" offering humanities points of view.

At Arizona State University, the first HfE workshop aimed to innovate how a humanities "Observatory" space might work. Giovanna Di Chiro, a noted cultural geographer and a consultant to the HfE project, was invited to offer a concise overview of the histories of the environmental justice and sustainability movements and consult with the steering committee about "best practices" for working in stakeholder communities. Di Chiro, who has worked both inside and outside academia on sustainability initiatives with community groups, explained that "environmental justice" is now a term used "to describe a global network of social movements fiercely critical of the disparities and depredations caused by the unchecked expansion and neocolonial logic of fossil fuel-driven modern industrial development" (Di Chiro 2016, 105).[10] She summarized the historical milestone sustainability and environmental justice documents, summits, and conferences, from the Brundtland Report to "The Future We Want," and delved into the inspired leadership of a growing movement mapping "the issues vital to building environmentally sound and socially equitable societies" and increasingly taking up the complex challenges of climate change (Di Chiro 2016, 105). She also referenced the work of David Suzuki, who is considered an elder statesman in the global environmental justice movement. Suzuki believes that active hope is required to imagine and make manifest notions of intergenerational justice or caring for the future. Di Chiro introduced the group to Suzuki's argument that an "imaginary of hope" must be driven by a primary commitment "to care, think, and act" (Suzuki 2013). From here, she extrapolated that an "Anthropocene humanities" might work to forge an "active hope" that would motivate academics and community members alike. With this inspiring beginning, HfE North American Observatory (NAO) researchers began designing three experimental projects.

The Archive of Hope and Cautionary Tales

With notions of "active hope" and the goal to move beyond declensionist narratives and to reimagine the meanings of survivability, thriveability, and the longue durée, HfE researchers began by first designing a project to archive stories they hoped would, at the very least, forestall or shift the litanies of trauma, disaster, and extirpation that we face everyday in the news toward thinking about plausible and livable futures on a constantly changing planet. The Archive of Hope and Cautionary Tales,[11] still in its pilot phase, is a digital collection of stories about frontline communities organizing to advocate for the right to meaningful, democratic participation in environmental decision making. As Rob Nixon has cautioned, the narratives shaping the "Anthropocene story" must not be told as if this anthropogenically caused change is one tale about humans as a homogenous species acting as one. Rather, the Anthropocene story should tell two different kinds of narratives: the "convergent story" of anthropos's or humanity's legible aggregate impacts on Earth's geophysical systems now and for millennia to come, and the "divergent story" of the widening schism between the rich and the poor that are revealing the immense "inequalities in access to resources and exposures to risk" (Nixon 2014).

Therefore The Archive of Hope and Cautionary Tales is designed to narrate these convergent and divergent stories. Also, as Kyle Powys Whyte emphasizes, this is a "multispecies" tale in the sense that it conveys divergent conceptions of responsibility, agency, and value among various ethnic groups for the plants and animals with which humans interact in different regions around the world (Whyte 2017). Each story describes an environmental justice community project and narrates the story of how that community is working with imagination and creativity to address complex local sustainability challenges. The archive includes one story about an indigenous community of Klamath people working in Oregon to restore their watershed, one about ranchers working in Arizona to restore eroded and desertified grasslands, one about a community in Nepal working to restore a threatened watershed, one about United Farm Workers in the San Joaquin Valley in California, and one about residents in eastern Tennessee carving out a space for public participation in decision making about local waste and pollution.

Another story, by enrolled members of the Little River Band of Ottawa Indians (LRBOI) in Michigan who have designed and implemented a restoration program for a local fish, the Lake Sturgeon—or *Nmé*, as it is called in the language of the Ottawa, an Anishinaabek tribal group—attempts to illustrate one of the H*f*E's common threads, or common aims, which is to make the arts and humanities central to the creation of narratives and projects that "address environmental issues in civil and academic life." This story, titled "Renewing Relatives: *Nmé* Stewardship in a Shared Watershed," is written by Marty Holtgren and Stephanie Ogren of the Little River Band of Ottawa Indians, with support from Michigan State University philosopher (and enrolled member of the Citizen Potawatomi Nation and NAO key researcher) Kyle Powys Whyte. It narrates the design and implementation of a LRBOI restoration program for the Lake Sturgeon.[12] The LRBOI have inhabited the Big Manistee River Watershed for thousands of years and continue to depend on interspecies relationships connecting humans, fish, plants, and animals. Under colonization these relationships were interrupted, and in the Anthropocene, a changing climate and increasing pollutants in the water are endangering the *Nmé*. The *Nmé* conservation program is built on relationships among the LRBOI, federal, and local government officials, nonprofit groups, and settler Americans living in the watershed that is critical to the *Nmé*'s survival.

Readers of the story learn that every September a public release of young *Nmé* brings Indigenous and non-Indigenous community members together for a pipe ceremony and feast. The event can attract up to six hundred attendees. Through narrative and images, visitors to the website can "see" the ways that individuals, whether members of the LRBOI or non-Indigenous residents of the local watershed, come to feel a greater sense of responsibility for *Nmé*, as each pulls a young fish from a bucket, gently places it in the lake and watches it swim away. On their web page, Holtgren, Ogren, and Whyte employ short videos, powerful images, and compelling narrative to record the event digitally and explain how the program they are creating brings indigenous and non-Indigenous residents of the watershed together around distinctive—but compatible—conceptions of sustainability that weave Western scientific and Anishinaabek philosophies together. Jimmie Mitchell, director of natural resources for the tribe, defines sustainability as *baamaadziwin*, which means "living in a good and respectful way." This illustrates how the LRBOI has enriched the term "sustainability" as a multispecies relationality.

The narrative, with its vivid accompanying images, gives web page readers an opportunity to understand better how individual community members, including children, are being guided to feel a greater sense of responsibility for the *Nmé*. The story offers a template for, or one example of, how one community is working to advocate for enriched understandings of sustainability as a flourishing diversity of life for both human children and newly hatched sturgeon.

Together, all the stories in The Archive of Hope and Cautionary Tales work to illustrate how coalitional groups are approaching their work with hope, wonder, and awe. At the same time, the stories in the archive can be read as "cautionary tales" since no one solution is proposed as a panacea. As Mike Hulme, a climate scientist who contributed research to the IPCC reports, has observed, framing complex environmental changes as "mega-problems" necessarily demands "mega-solutions," and this "has led us down the wrong road" (Hulme 2009, 332). In contrast to research that proposes "mega-solutions" to complex sustainability challenges, the archive illustrates how humanists such as Whyte are working with small community-based alliances to seek, not one plan of action, but a range of evidence-based, reasoned, scaled, and culturally diverse responses "reflective of life in a plural world" (Castree et al. 2014, 765–766).

In a reflection on the HfE archive project, Julie Sze, a consultant to the HfE Archive project group, leads a discussion with archive contributors.[13] The group examines evolving praxis in the humanities, explores the processes of collaboration, and reflects on the goals of The Archive of Hope and Cautionary Tales, which is to scale up public information about sustainability and community response to climate change. The implicit question of Sze's discussion with the group is, "How do the humanities [and the archive] contribute uniquely to the promotion of environmental, social and intergenerational justice through storytelling?" (Sze et al., forthcoming). Participants discuss the archive as a carefully curated, and still growing, archive of digital stories that share certain themes and aims. The group reflects on its previous experiences working in digital media, as it outlines what storytelling techniques work well on digital platforms, and the members brainstorm about what they might change in a next iteration of this digital project. The group asserts that the search for sustainability is best served by foregrounding the voices of those most affected by social and environmental inequities.

The archive, then, models new constellations of practice in the humanities by exploring the relationships of digital curation, mapping, short videos, powerful images, and compelling narratives as tools that can be used to reach new communities of readers, government officials, policy makers, and people in other communities who might be searching for ways to respond to their own sustainability challenges. The archive also tests how communities might employ digital tools to make the expertise and evidence that is the usual province of universities, museums, art galleries, and libraries more accessible to nonacademic communities. The stories reflect how the arts and knowledges of stakeholder communities might be made more visible, accessible, and applicable to other communities that may wish to compare, rescale, and analyze the story for its power to transform social values and human behaviors and increase abilities to imagine alternatives and solutions to complex sustainability and social justice challenges.

Life Overlooked

In a second workshop held in February 2014, North American Observatory researchers designed a pedagogically focused project that sought to answer the question, How might we encourage students to think about sustainability, not in terms of "aggregate anthropos," but in terms of "multispecies aggregations" and intergenerational justice for all species? Like The Archive of Hope and Cautionary Tales, this project is easily accessible on the HfE international website and focuses on the diverse life that inhabits what Pope Francis refers to as "our common home."[14] Titled "Life Overlooked," the project experiments with the effectiveness of teaching a template course at multiple universities as a way of "scaling up" public education about rising rates of extinction and death in nonhuman communities.

The course was taught first at the University of Oregon, where Stephanie LeMenager wrote the template syllabus at the undergraduate level and beta tested the course. Joni Adamson at Arizona State University taught a second version of the course at the undergraduate level, and Catriona Sandilands at York University in Canada followed up with a variation taught at the graduate level. Each version of this course was taught as part of an already existing environmental humanities curriculum. A common digital portfolio assignment was inserted into each course focusing on "life overlooked." In her syllabus, Sandilands defined the foci of the courses—"life overlooked"—as attention to "any being that tends for the most part to fly (or swim or creep or crawl or tendril or flit or ooze or flagellate or sit apparently unmoving) under the radar of everyday human attention." Later, the group discovered that, completely independently from (and in advance of) their own work, which began in 2013, the Biodiversity Group, located in Tucson, Arizona, had launched a Facebook page in 2012 to network citizens, scientists, and photographers interested in "citizen science" on behalf of the world's snakes, lizards, and amphibians. Their motto is "Life Overlooked," and therefore they were the first to use the idea.[15]

However, from the first, the HfE Life Overlooked project extended its gaze beyond amphibians to other species, from dust mites to doves to cacti, and especially to those that can be found in urban environments. LeMenager, Adamson, and Sandilands asked their students to employ the arts, sciences, and their own community knowledges to build web pages that sought to empower the public, or members of their own communities, to become more aware of the interrelationships among all species, both those that are charismatic, such a polar bears and dolphins, and those that are not, including those that may even be considered invasive, such as starlings. They challenged their students to become "citizen scientists" who would research scientific understandings of one overlooked species. But they also asked their students to employ the best practices of the humanities, to read and write fiction, poetry, and nonfiction; to take pictures; to make drawings or other artwork; to create short films; and to write narratives or a story about their chosen overlooked species. The goal for the courses would be to identify humanities skills that might enrich how we understand scientific discourses surrounding the chosen species.

The course encouraged students to test and rethink how they might make expertise and evidence that is the usual province of scientists, universities, museums, and libraries more accessible to nonspecialists. Students were asked to explore how these institutions used digital tools to disseminate information. They researched websites focusing on overlooked species, extinction, or species loss and discovered sites such as Maya Lin's "What Is Missing?," Anna Tsing's "Matsutake Worlds," and the Biodiversity Group's "Life Overlooked." Each of these sites offered them ideas about how to employ digital tools and storytelling techniques.[16]

The three versions of the course syllabus can be found on the HfE Life Overlooked web page, where teachers or citizens are invited to download, replicate, adapt, and teach the template ideas at other educational institutions or in other settings. The project explores current research in the humanities about what might constitute a "citizen humanities" that would complement "citizen science" and help disseminate "local ecological knowledge" in new artistic and digital ways" (Adamson 2017a, 108). Other research groups in the environmental humanities have also been exploring and piloting the "citizen humanities." Neimanis, Åsberg, and Hedren (2015) note that the term "citizen humanities" has been popular primarily in digital humanities and information infrastructure contexts, but it offers the environmental humanities suggestive possibilities and challenges as well. If "citizen science" seeks to raise public awareness about the facts and data associated with accelerating environmental change and offers basic scientific understandings of ecological pro-cesses, then a "citizen humanities" might cultivate new environmental "imaginaries" that would be understood to be negotiated, shaped, and contested through stories and narratives and diverse cultures. A citizen humanities might take up the practical cultures of everyday life, for ex-ample, greenwashing or apolitical "green lifestyles." The aim would be to help reengage publics not only as consumers of environmental humani-ties research but as its producers as well. Neimanis, Åsberg, and Hedren point to the work of the Citizen Sense laboratory (http://citizensense .net) as an example of emerging interdisciplinary research strategies that use small-scale do-it-yourself technologies to monitor air or air quality or sensors to monitor the activities of various flora and fauna in the "wild." The aim might be to examine how these kinds of engagements shape an individual's or the public's affective relationships to the envi-ronment and environmental change and potentially lead to behavioral change or increasing awareness.

Like Citizen Sense, Life Overlooked is innovating new humanities constellations of practice that seek to empower everyday citizens and growing publics to complement statistically based or scientifically based scientific understandings of sustainability and nonhuman life with the cultural, affective, literary, historical, and aesthetic.

Dinner 2040: The Future of Food in Maricopa County, Arizona

In the final workshop held in Fall 2014, NAO researchers met to criti-cally reflect on the convergent story of how humans as a species are affecting the planet in ways that are interrupting access to nutritious, culturally meaningful, and sustainably produced foods. The project asks the following questions: Can "aggregate Anthropos" act collectively as a species for the common good? Can a community act collectively to design an environmentally sustainable, socially equitable, and cultur-ally rich food system that can be achieved by 2040, or twenty-five years into the future?[17]

The project group decided to focus on the future of food in Maricopa County, the county in which Phoenix, Arizona, a megacity of four mil-lion people, is located. This focused the project on the complex food sys-tem challenges facing a fast urbanizing and climatically changing desert region. Inspired by "A Future We Want," the project was titled "Dinner 2040" and aimed to experiment with imaginative "arts of futurity" exercises that include futurecasting, backcasting, and scenario planning. These exercises integrate the imaginative strengths of the humanities particularly in relation to risk management, disaster management, and the planning and "production of probable, preferred, or hoped for futures." "Arts of futurity" exercises call attention to the ways in which imagination can give tangible form to "different worlds outside of the constraints of the given present" (Yusoff and Gabrys 2011, 518).

To engage in this visioning exercise, project leaders and researchers gathered a diverse team of Maricopa County community partners from the culinary and gardening arts, food cooperative organizers, local O'odham and Navajo Indigenous communities, farmers, organic farmers, public health, urban planning, and community markets. They planned a "charrette," an exercise often used in urban planning to envision the future of a community. The charrette involved brainstorming and planning for a future food system Maricopa County community residents would want to see in the plausibly near future. Academics with expertise in agricultural technologies, food systems, and architecture and urban planning came together with humanists representing art, philosophy, history, cultural geography, and literature to plan for the next twenty-five years, targeting the year 2040.

In advance of the daylong charrette, project leaders and group participants brainstormed a set of "Values on your Plate" they uploaded to the project web page at the *Humanities for the Environment* website. These principles and values would guide the charrette process. Participants listened to a lecture by the famed seed and agricultural activist, Vandana Shiva, who discussed an array of international instruments, including the UN Declaration on Human Rights and the UN Declaration on the Rights of Indigenous Peoples, which affirm that humans have a sovereign "right to food" (see also Adamson 2011). Often referred to as "food sovereignty," the notion of a sovereign "right to food" covers a range of positions, interventions, and struggles but is "centrally, though not exclusively, about groups of people making their own decisions about the food system" (Grey and Patel 2015, 431). The group agreed that the future of the food system in Maricopa should be guided by (1) best scientific, historical, cultural, and place-based practices; (2) culinary innovations that have emerged in Maricopa County over time; (3) the ecological integrity of the region's ecosystems; (4) cultural traditions, health issues, and just practices in the production, distribution and consumption of food; and (5) attention to ensuring food sovereignty.

The steps of the charrette process are detailed on a graphic and in a short film that is archived on the website.[18] These steps include a "backcasting activity" that filtered the groups' planned outcomes backward through a set of anticipated social and environmental conditions that residents might face over the course of the next twenty-five years. For example, the group reflected on questions such as "What foods might be growing successfully and more sustainably in a drier, hotter Sonoran Desert climate in twenty-five years?" Hoped-for and imagined foods for 2040 included such dishes as tacos made with mesquite flour and cornflour filled with veggies and native chilies and amaranth crepes with verdolagas onion salad, topped with red chili mole and goat cheese.

In a subsequent phase of the project, conducted one year later, in the fall of 2016, a meal featuring some of the dishes envisioned during the charrette was held. Over the various courses of the meal, participants were asked to brainstorm and plot the milestones, policies, and programs that would need to be met and implemented if they hoped to ensure food sovereignty by the year 2040.

Conclusion

The Humanities for the Environment project has now expanded beyond its original funding and its first three Observatories to new locations in Asia (National Sun Yat-sen University and National Chung-Hsing University in Taiwan), Africa (the University of Pretoria in South Africa), the Circumpolar (Mälardalen University), and Latin America (Universidad de Amazonia in Colombia). Throughout the global system, the projects and programming being conducted suggest that, to meet the challenges of the Anthropocene, humans will need the full force of interdisciplinary collaborations among humanists, social scientists, natural scientists, artists, and faith-based and secular community members if they hope to design and build plausible, desirable, and livable futures. The sheer scale of the work that is needed suggests the reasons influential thought leaders on the stage of climate change, including

Pope Francis, have been welcomed as they help scale up the numbers of people willing to fight for "our common home." Along the way, new constellations of humanities practice are calling upon us, in the aggregate, and in all our diversity, to reimagine the meanings of sustainability in terms of survivability, thriveability, and the longue durée, not just for humans but for all life on the planet.

NOTES

1 Future Earth is sponsored by the UN Environmental Program, the International Council for Science, and the International Social Science Council.

2 More information about the Consortium of Humanities Centers and Institutes (CHCI) can be found at www.chcinetwork.org.

3 See the *Humanities for the Environment* website at https://hfe-observatories.org.

4 See "Common Threads," *Humanities for the Environment*, https://hfe-observatories.org.

5 For a history of the growth of the environmental humanities through these various organizations, a listing and links to universities, formal and informal networks, and the global initiatives currently expanding the environmental humanities, see Adamson and Davis (2017), 5–19; and Hartman (2015).

6 The Association for the Study of Literature and Environment alone counts over 1,800 people in forty-one countries among its membership. See ASLE at www.asle.org.

7 See "Welcome to the Anthropocene" (2012).

8 The North American Observatory networked humanists from Michigan State University; Swarthmore College; University of California, Los Angeles; University of California, Davis; University of Illinois Urbana–Champaign; University of Minnesota; University of Oregon; University of Toronto; Clark University; Wake Forest University; and Stony Brook University. See "People" at the *Humanities for the Environment* website, https://hfe-observatories.org.

9 The University of California, Davis, Humanities Institute's Environmental Humanities supercluster is a multidisciplinary research group guided by Louis Warren (with Julie Sze, Mike Ziser, and others) and designed to facilitate faculty study of complex envirocultural problems, support graduate students and postdoctoral scholars working in the field, and collaborate with communities affected by environmental challenges. See the Davis Humanities Institute Supercluster Humanities website at http://environmentalhumanities.ucdavis.edu.

10 Di Chiro (2016) transformed this history and her workshop presentation into an essay, "Environmental Justice."

11 For a full list of consultants, project leaders, and contributors to The Archive of Hope and Cautionary Tales, see *Humanities for the Environment*, https://new.hfe-observatories.org/projects/archive-of-hope-and-cautionary-tales/.

12 See Holtgren, Ogren, and White (n.d.).

13 Sze et al. (forthcoming).

14 See "Life Overlooked," *Humanities for the Environment*, https://new.hfe-observatories.org/projects/life-overlooked/.

15 See the Biodiversity Group's Facebook page at www.facebook.com. The Biodiversity Group website can be found at https://biodiversitygroup.org.

16 Maya Lin, "What Is Missing?," www.whatismissing.net; Anna Tsing, "Matsutake Worlds," www.ucsc.edu; and the Biodiversity Group, https://biodiversitygroup.org.

17 For a full list of consultants and contributors for Dinner 2040, and the "Values That Guide Thinking about the Future of Food in a Particular Place," see the project web page at *Humanities for the Environment*, https://new.hfe-observatories.org/projects/dinner-2040/.

18 See the film "Dinner 2040: Imagining Sustainable Food Practices in Maricopa County, Arizona" at *Humanities for the Environment*, https://new.hfe-observatories.org/projects/dinner-2040/.

REFERENCES

Adamson, Joni. 2011. "Medicine Food: Critical Environmental Justice Studies, Native North American Literature and the Movement for Food Sovereignty." In "Indigenous Studies," edited by Kyle Powys Whyte. Special issue, *Environmental Justice* 4, no. 4 (December): 213–219.

Adamson, Joni. 2016. "Humanities." In *Keywords for Environmental Studies*, edited by Joni Adamson, William A. Gleason, and David N. Pellow, 135–139. New York: New York University Press.

Adamson, Joni. 2017a. "Gathering the Desert: Designing the Citizen Humanities." In *Humanities for the Environment: Integrating Knowledge, Forging New Constellations of Practice*, edited by Joni Adamson and Michael Davis, 106–119. New York: Routledge.

Adamson, Joni. 2017b. "Introduction: Integrating Knowledge, Forging New Constellations of Practice." In *Humanities for the Environment: Integrating Knowledge, Forging New Constellations of Practice*, edited by Joni Adamson and Michael Davis, 3–19. New York: Routledge.

Adamson, Joni, and Michael Davis, eds. 2017. *Humanities for the Environment: Integrating Knowledge, Forging New Constellations of Practice*. New York: Routledge.

Agyeman, Julian, Robert Doyle Bullard, and Bob Evans, eds. 2003. *Just Sustainabilities: Development in an Unequal World*. Cambridge, MA: MIT Press.

Birgersson, Anders, Steven Hartman, and Peter Norrman. 2016. "Bifrost—This Is the Beginning: An Environmental Arts-Research Intervention." *Academia*. www.academia.edu.

Castree, Noel. 2014. "The Anthropocene and the Environmental Humanities: Extending the Conversation." *Environmental Humanities* 5:233–260.

Castree, Noel, et al. 2014. "Changing the Intellectual Climate." *Nature Climate Change* 4 (September): 763–768.

Crutzen, Paul J., and Eugene F. Stoermer. 2000. "The 'Anthropocene.'" *Global Change Newsletter*, no. 41, May, 17–18.

DeLoughrey, Elizabeth. 2015. "Ordinary Futures: Interspecies Worldings in the Anthropocene." In *Global Ecologies and the Environmental Humanities*, edited by Elizabeth DeLoughrey, Jill Didur, and Anthony Carrigan, 352–372. New York: Routledge, 2015.

DeLoughrey, Elizabeth, and George Handley, eds. 2011. *Postcolonial Ecologies: Literatures of the Environment*. Oxford: Oxford University Press.

Di Chiro, Giovanna. 2015. "Environmental Justice and the Anthropocene Meme." In *Oxford Handbook on Environmental Political Theory*, edited by Teena Gabrielson, Cheryl Hall, John M. Meyer, and David Schlosberg, 362–382. New York: Oxford University Press.

Di Chiro, Giovanna. 2016. "Environmental Justice." In *Keywords for Environmental Studies*, edited by Joni Adamson, William A. Gleason, and David N. Pellow, 100–105. New York: New York University Press.

Francis [Pope]. 2015. "On Care for Our Common Home: *Laudato Si'*." Encyclical letter. Washington, DC: United States Conference of Catholic Bishops.

Grey, Sam, and Raj Patel. 2015. "Food Sovereignty as Decolonization: Some Contributions from Indigenous Movements to Food System and Development Politics." *Agriculture and Human Values* 32 (October): 431–444.

Hartman, Steven. 2015. "Unpacking the Black Box: The Need for Integrated Environmental Humanities (IEH)." *Future Earth Blog*, June 3. www.futureearth.org.

Holm, Poul, et al. 2015. "Humanities for the Environment—A Manifesto for Research and Action." *Humanities* 4, no. 4:977–992. Multidisciplinary Digital Publishing Institute. www.mdpi.com.

Holtgren, Marty, Stephanie Ogren, and Kyle Whyte. n.d. "Renewing Relatives: *Nmé* Stewardship in a Shared Watershed." *Humanities for the Environment*. https://hfe-observatories.org.

Howard, Jennifer. 2014. "At Mellon, Signs of Change." *Chronicle of Higher Education*, June 29. www.chronicle.com.

Hulme, Mike. 2009. *Why We Disagree about Climate Change: Understanding Controversy, Inaction and Opportunity*. New York: Cambridge University Press.

Neimanis, Astrida, Cecilia Åsberg, and Johan Hedren. 2015. "Four Problems, Four Directions for Environmental Humanities: Toward a Critical Posthumanities for the Anthropocene." *Ethics and the Environment* 20, no. 1 (Spring): 67–97.

Nixon, Rob. 2014. "The Anthropocene: The Promise and Pitfalls of an Epochal Idea." *Edge Effects* (digital magazine), November 6. Madison: University of Wisconsin, Nelson Institute for Environmental Studies, Center for Culture, History, and Environment. http://edgeeffects.net.

Nixon, Rob. 2015. "The Great Acceleration and the Great Divergence: Vulnerability in the Anthropocene." *Profession*, Presidential Forum. Modern Language Association of America. www.mla.org.

Robin, Libby. 2013. "Histories for Changing Times: Entering the Anthropocene," *Australian Historical Studies* 44, no. 3: 329–340.

Rose, Deborah Bird, Thom van Dooren, Matthew Chrulew, Stuart Cooke, Matthew Kearnes, and Emily O'Gorman. 2012. "Thinking through the Environment, Unsettling the Humanities." *Environmental Humanities* 1:1–5.

Rocheleau, Dianne, and Padini Nirmal. 2016. "Culture." In *Keywords for Environmental Studies*, edited by Joni Adamson, William A. Gleason, and David N. Pellow, 50–55. New York: New York University Press.

Snow, Charles Percy. (1959) 2001. *The Two Cultures*. London: Cambridge University Press.

Suzuki, David. 2013. "Imagining a Sustainable Future: Foresight over Hindsight." Keynote address. University of South Wales, Sydney, Australia, September 22.

Sze, Julie, Julie Anand, Netra Chhetri, and Tracy Perkins. Forthcoming. "Stories from the Field: Public Engagement through the Environmental Humanities and Allied Disciplines." In "The Green Humanities Lab." Special issue, Joni Adamson, guest editor, *Resilience: A Journal of the Environmental Humanities*.

United Nations. 2012. "The Future We Want—Outcome Document." *Sustainable Development Knowledge Platform*. UN Department of Development and Social Affairs. www.un.org.

"Welcome to the Anthropocene." 2012. Film directed by Owen Gaffney and Félix Pharand-Deschênes. London: Planet under Pressure. Posted at Vimeo at https://vimeo.com/39048998.

World Commission on Environment and Development. 1987. *Our Common Future*. Brundtland Report. Oxford: Oxford University Press.

Whyte, Kyle Powys. 2017. "Is It Colonial Déjà Vu? Indigenous Peoples and Climate Injustice." In *Humanities for the Environment: Integrating Knowledge, Forging New Constellations of Practice*, edited by Joni Adamson and Michael Davis, 88–105. New York: Routledge.

Yusoff, Kathryn, and Jennifer Gabrys. 2011. "Climate Change and the Imagination." *WIREs Climate Change* 2, no. 4 (May): 516–534.

Zalasiewicz, Jan, Mark Williams, and Colin N. Waters. 2016. "Anthropocene." In *Keywords for Environmental Studies*, edited by Joni Adamson, William A. Gleason, and David N. Pellow, 14–16. New York: New York University Press.

Zimmerman, Michael E. 2017. "Integral Ecology in the Pope's Environmental Encyclical, Implications for Environmental Humanities." In *Humanities for the Environment: Integrating Knowledge, Forging New Constellations of Practice*, edited by Joni Adamson and Michael Davis, 146–159. New York: Routledge.

3

Situating Sustainability against Displacement

Building Campus-Community Collaboratives for Environmental Justice from the Ground Up

GIOVANNA DI CHIRO AND LAURA RIGELL

Our neighborhoods in North Philadelphia are being torn apart as gentrification from "Temple Town" expands and forces people out; our long-term residents deserve to age-in-place and our youth deserve better opportunities. We want to be able to preserve some *remnants* of a thriving African American community in this part of the city.[1]

—John Bowie, community leader, North Philadelphia

Already frustrated with the seemingly unstoppable forces of gentrification threatening the historically Black neighborhoods of North Philadelphia, long-time resident John Bowie was wary when a group of students and a faculty member from the elite suburban enclave of Swarthmore College showed up at a neighborhood meeting to talk about community gardens and green roofs. John Bowie and others from the North Philadelphia community met with the Swarthmore contingent at Serenity House, a North Philadelphia–based outreach center sponsored by the Arch Street United Methodist Church. Resident Serenity House organizer .O[2] and Swarthmore faculty member Giovanna Di Chiro had co-organized the meeting with the objective to share ideas, skills, and resources to generate "sustainability" initiatives in this North Philly community. In earlier conversations with Serenity House leader Wilhelmina Young, .O had envisioned the Serenity House backyard becoming a community space with the adjoining garage housing a rooftop garden that would supply fresh vegetables for a locally owned food co-op. In the spirit of productive campus-community exchange, and with the belief that local residents would greet such positive sustainability projects with universal endorsement, .O and Giovanna and her students introduced the garden and green roof ideas to the attendees at the meeting.

The response by community residents was less than enthusiastic: "How are flower gardens and fancy roofs going to help our community!?" John Bowie interjected. "Our community needs jobs and decent homes, and our young people need options!" What had started out as a meet-and-greet to discuss possible collaborations between Swarthmore environmental studies students and leaders of Serenity House ended up in a much broader discussion about poverty, unemployment, urban gentrification and displacement, domestic and police violence, and environmental racism. Despite our confidence in the clear environmental "good" of gardens, flowers, food co-ops, and other green projects, many residents at the meeting raised concerns about whether they could trust the students ("Temple college students disrespect our neighborhood, how can we be sure about these students?"). They wanted assurance that there would be positive outcomes from university researchers coming their neighborhoods ("They're always asking us questions and then never come back to show us the results"), and some residents were dubious about the benefits they would see from the purported improvements the city had already implemented in the name of sustainability ("'Temple Town' is grabbing up North Philly property to create 'green' dorms for their students"). These concerns were not unfounded.

Over the last several decades there has been growing interest and expanding participation in efforts to create effective, reciprocal, and sustainable partnerships between institutions of higher education and the communities, cities, and regions in which they reside (Dugery and Knowles 2003; Agyeman 2013; Anguelovski 2014; Beckman and Long 2016). Drawing on the extensive literature on participatory action research and critical education studies, much of this interest and engagement stems from the argument that building bridges and joining forces across domains of education, research, and action will improve educational practices and generate useful knowledge to address the important problems of the day (Forrant and Silka 2006; Hale 2008; Smith et. al. 2010; Greenwood and Levin 2011; Kemmis et al. 2014).[3] The rise in the number of campus-based centers for community partnerships, community-based learning (CBL), community-based research (CBR), community engagement, engaged scholarship, and civic and social responsibility in U.S. institutions demonstrates the perceived value of such partnerships and has even become a branding strategy for many liberal arts colleges. Despite the good intentions, the CBL/community outreach movement (promoted as providing students with real-world experience to prepare them for the global workplace) has become somewhat of a growth industry, with many of its proponents and critics recognizing that "community engagement" presents many challenges and risks.[4] The concerns of the Serenity House community members reflected some of these problems, including the impression that students and faculty from colleges and universities (based on past experiences with neighboring Temple University) were not committed to building a relationship of reciprocity and were there instead to extract data and knowledge without giving back to the community.

Similarly, Serenity House residents' skepticism about the trickle-down benefits of sustainability efforts appearing in their community in recent years was not baseless but grounded in local observations and national trends. Despite evidence to the contrary, mainstream media and the popular imagination have accepted the recent explosion of sustainability initiatives as an unquestioned environmental and social "good" (e.g., see Isenhour, McDonogh, and Checker 2015). Critics have shown that conventional sustainability initiatives (solar technology, green roofs, green buildings, transportation hubs, and community gardens and farmers' markets selling local foods and high-end organics) have contributed to dynamics and outcomes of gentrification and displacement, what some refer to as "green gentrification" (Greenberg, in this volume), as these initiatives tend to increase property values and the desirability of the neighborhoods, thereby pricing out the long-term inhabitants of the region, including both homeowners and renters (Tretter 2015; Gould and Lewis 2016). The promotion of the benefits of green buildings and LEED certification for new dormitories and research laboratories by local colleges and universities (including Temple University's expansion and the newly opened Good Food Flats at nearby Drexel University, a dormitory that displaced a block of affordable housing units; see Heavens 2016), has raised local residents' doubts of the benefits to their communities of the new sustainability craze.[5]

As the Swarthmore College faculty member (Giovanna) and as one of the students (Laura Rigell) who participated in that first meeting at Serenity House, we present in this chapter our experiences of co-creating a campus-community collaboration "from the ground up." In this story, we discuss the steps we took to develop and strive toward an intersectional form of urban "sustainability" grounded in local residents' own interpretations of the term and in the values of racial, economic, and environmental justice. Since that initial meeting with community residents who lived in the neighborhoods served by Serenity House in 2012, we have grappled with the tensions and conflicts reflecting the multiple borders we were crossing and navigating (race, class, gender, sexuality, expertise, age, religion, education, geography) and worked alongside North Philadelphia residents to form the Sustainable Serenity Collaborative (from this point referred to as the Collaborative). The Collaborative, now in its sixth year, embraces a vision of sustainability that resists and contests green gentrification, supports the values of "just sustainability" (Agyeman 2013), and is driven by the needs and dreams of the predominantly Black, low-income residents of North Philadelphia. From these foundations, the Collaborative is working to develop locally owned, culturally relevant, environmentally conscious, and profitable enterprises that would enable the flourishing of *remnants* of African American histories and lifeways in this small section of the city.

Community leaders including John Bowie argue that the preservation of these remnants of Black life *matters*, and not because it preserves and exhibits token displays of times past in an otherwise modernizing eco-city. Rather, the revival of remnants of Black neighborhoods matters because it resists the histories of economic disinvestment, racial segregation, and environmental racism, which many argue lie at the core of North Philadelphia's current dilemmas (Freeman 2006; Rigell 2016). Furthermore, the revival of remnants of Black history and place matters because it reflects an essential *rethinking* of the meaning of "sustainability." Whose lifestyles, landscapes, and communities (human and nonhuman) are to be recognized, valued, and sustained? Perhaps in this era of climate disruptions and displacements all we can reasonably hope for are remnants, or what the anthropologist Anna Tsing has called "patches of sustainability" (2015, 32): small-scale refuges of sustainable communities building relationships of regeneration and resurgence creating

larger biosocial systems that may enable the possibility of earthly survival. This chapter recounts the history, accomplishments, and current
efforts of the Sustainable Serenity Collaborative to re-imagine and re-
create sustainability.

Through our story, we point to some of the "best practices" for
campus-community partnerships that our Collaborative has developed
and embraced, including the importance of relationship and trust building at all stages of the process and by all participants; the establishment
of, and accountability to, a set of norms for working together; the recognition and respect for diverse knowledge systems as central to the
work (academic/ theoretical knowledge, experiential knowledge, cultural knowledge, local knowledge); and the need for greater reciprocity,
collaboration, and accountability in the research process (refusing the
imperialist, "helicoptering" methods of research that extract data from
the community and then depart to the home institution to write up and
publish findings; see Cruz and Giles 2000; Smith 2007; Hoyt 2010).

A Short History of the Sustainable Serenity Collaborative

Sustainable Serenity is a community-college partnership between
community leaders in North Philadelphia and a group of faculty and
students at Swarthmore College. This evolving Collaborative (which
now includes students from University of Pennsylvania and non-profit,
governmental, and business partners from around the city), arose out
of conversations between several Swarthmore faculty and students with
members of Serenity House, a community outreach center serving the
surrounding neighborhoods.[6] Serenity House is located in the Hartranft
section of North Philadelphia, a district that is 93 percent African American with a poverty rate of over 51 percent (compared to a 26 percent
poverty rate in the city at large; see Pew Charitable Trusts 2015). In these
early conversations about how to build trust and develop the practices
of reciprocity and collaboration that would guide our work together,
we delved into difficult discussions about positionality; this involved, in
part, acknowledging our personal interpretations about the race, class,
and gender differences among the members of our two communities. At
the beginning of our partnership, all the participants from North Philadelphia identified as African American, low income, and (the majority)

as male, and most (although not all) of the Swarthmore contingent identified as white, middle class, and female. As of this writing, the racial, class, and gender composition of participants from both places is more diverse.

Early in our process of working together, we explored how these differences in social location—our identities, knowledges, and experiences—would inform our understandings and commitments to the goals of environmental and climate justice and how we could jointly create and facilitate a transition away from fossil fuels toward healthy, thriving, and sustainable communities in North Philadelphia and Swarthmore alike. Our work has been rooted in the idea of *just* sustainability: the theory that a truly sustainable society is one in which all peoples are treated with dignity and have access to healthy environments and secure livelihoods. Having embedded Sustainable Serenity's collaborative approach in these foundational values of social and environmental justice, we have endeavored to produce a model for campus-community engagement that would support interdisciplinary, intersectional, and broadly based sustainability efforts. This is a model that embraces a vision of engaged scholarship and learning committed to real-life, community-driven, and collaborative projects that address the interconnected social, economic, and environmental issues underlying economic disparity, environmental racism, and climate change (Di Chiro 2006; Agyeman 2013; Gibson-Graham, Cameron, and Healy 2013).

Starting a Collaboration: Crossing Borders, Building Relationships

Engaging in bridge-building practices to traverse the academia-community divide, the core faculty member in the Collaborative, Giovanna, was introduced to community leader .O by a mutual colleague in the fall of 2012. In subsequent conversations, .O detailed her work to address pervasive violence (street, domestic, and structural) in the local community and described her theories on how this violence is associated with high rates of incarceration, substance abuse, homelessness, and environmental illnesses. She outlined her strategies to combat these problems, which included introducing men's and women's support groups focusing on restorative justice, "community healing," and capacity-building programs offered through Serenity House, her place of residence and work.

Serenity House is a community ministry and outreach center supported by the Arch Street United Methodist Church, which "serves and provides a sanctuary for the social, spiritual, and human development needs of the predominantly low-income African American residents of our local neighborhoods in North Philadelphia, some of the more economically and environmentally distressed neighborhoods in the city."[7] .O said that the environmental justice framework Giovanna described resonated with her vision for Serenity House, and they both discussed how they could build a productive partnership in this "small place" in the world (Kincaid 1988), joining together the goals of community healing, regeneration, and "just" sustainability (hooks 2003).

After these conversations with .O, Giovanna invited students interested in community-based engagement and environmental justice to help design a sustainability project at Serenity House (originally, a green roof or rooftop garden on the community center's garage). Several students who would later become members of the Collaborative, including Laura, responded and expressed interest in co-designing an independent study course focused on environmental justice and community organizing, which they called "Sustainable Community Action." The students worked with Giovanna to develop a syllabus with readings on decolonial research methodologies, environmental and climate justice, and critical sustainability, and then they met with .O at Serenity House to begin a conversation and a working partnership.

Conceiving Collective Action Research Projects

While visiting Serenity House for the first time in 2013, the students toured the surrounding neighborhood with .O, surveyed the backyard of the house to imagine a vegetable garden, and climbed onto the roof of the garage to investigate the possibilities of installing a green roof. The group began to discuss the action research steps that would be needed to proceed and generated a list of other people who should be at the table and who should be part of the initial conversations and planning steps. This resulted in organizing several community events to bring together community residents from the nearby neighborhoods and Swarthmore College students to collect people's thoughts and concerns about their community. Local resident and activist John Bowie attended these early community meetings and would soon join the emerging college-community partnership. As noted above, it was at the first of these meetings that John voiced his skepticism about the capacity of the proposed "green" projects to meet the needs of North Philadelphia's struggling communities.

Throughout the spring semester of 2013, the students in the Sustainable Community Action independent study course and a growing cohort of new students worked with Giovanna, .O, John and other residents to define relevant and concrete ideas of sustainability and to prioritize action steps to move forward. In the process, the group reached out to local master gardeners and academic researchers, recruited other Swarthmore students to come to North Philadelphia to help with workdays, and secured funding to design and build a community garden in Serenity House's back lot. As the Collaborative expanded and the discussions on what sustainability looks like in an environmental justice community such as North Philadelphia deepened, Serenity House leaders .O and Wilhelmina Young and the members of the organization's men's support group began to envision even greater opportunities for this small place in the neighborhood. Delving into the connections between identity and place, the Serenity House organizers contemplated the following possibilities: Could the Serenity House community garden eventually support a food co-op and a community café? Could the detached garage in the backyard be retrofitted to house a green roof or a rooftop garden to grow vegetables, herbs, and flowers that could be sold at one of the Philadelphia's farmers' markets, thereby supporting small-scale business enterprises? Could the Serenity Garden be transformed into a space to offer community workshops, skills training, and youth programming on organic agriculture, composting, seed saving, beekeeping, and to showcase local African American food cultures and heritages to advance food sovereignty? Could our "small place" create new opportunities for adults and young people and help generate a model for a thriveable and more just sustainability?

Storytelling as Resilience

With these visions about possible futures in mind, the Collaborative organized several community dinners, listening and story circles, and community gatherings bringing residents, young people, and allies together to theorize change, to till the soil, to plant a garden, and to share stories of loss, grief, and renewal in the face of climate change (including a story circle on how people coped during the power outages from Superstorm Sandy in October 2012). Inviting residents to tell their stories in these community meetings emerged as an important tool for the Collaborative's ongoing process and was grounded in the theory that storytelling engenders opportunities for personal experiences to be linked to wider social and political systems, thereby creating "public narratives" that imagine and manifest alternative futures (Canning and Reinsborough 2010). Stories told by members of marginalized communities disrupt official histories of modern development as "progress" and instead help to re-member the lived realities of a community's experiences of social and environmental injustice (Dickinson 2012). Philadelphia-based author and anti-gentrification activist Rasheeda Phillips, the founder and director of Philadelphia's Community Futures Lab, argues that, in the tradition of Afrofuturism, stories told by members of the Black diaspora have served as a liberating practice to re-imagine Black histories and futures. Phillips explains, "Because it provides a perpetual bridge between the past, present and future, Afrofuturism, and the black speculative imagination, can be used as liberation technologies to build future worlds" (Simpson 2016). In the context of the spread of gentrification in neighborhoods across Philadelphia, the Community Futures Lab is collecting peoples' stories, creating remnants of Black histories of place that Phillips argues can help to heal the wounds of displacement and to imagine, create, and act on alternatives. The Sustainable Serenity Collaborative borrows from this Afrofuturist practice: "To value people's stories is healing," explained .O in a conversation at Serenity House. "And it's transformative; it interrupts the power dynamics of people who are disposable. No, these stories are *not* disposable; they are necessary for life."[8] In one of the story circles led by the men's support group, several of the men proposed the idea of planting a butterfly garden at Serenity House. The students in the Sustainable Community Action course responded by soliciting donations of colorful butterfly-attracting plants from the Swarthmore College Arboretum and raising funds to purchase caterpillars. As one men's group member, Myron Reddy, explained, nurturing the butterfly chrysalises throughout the metamorphosis process and releasing them into the blooming butterfly garden had powerful metaphorical significance for the men; it embodied a deeper sense of the concept of social transformation, sustainability, and community resilience.

Sustainable Community Soulutions

With the objective of sustaining these relationships and expanding the action research collaboration, Giovanna offered the second version of the Sustainable Community Action course in the 2013–2014 academic year, engaging another cohort of students. This new cohort invited Swarthmore College engineering professors to assess the capacity of Serenity House's garage to structurally support a roof garden. The engineers determined that the garage would require extensive and expensive structural reinforcements to support the weight of a green roof. One engineering professor suggested installing solar panels on the garage roof instead to power an outdoor charging station for cell phones or lights in the Serenity Garden. Enthusiastic about the prospect of solar panels at Serenity House, members of the men's group imagined this proposition as a scalable idea in support of climate justice and a just transition away from fossil fuels and into secure jobs in the green economy. As climate disruptions worsen, they argued, Serenity House could reduce its use of fossil fuel energy and, in the face of future outages, provide community residents with access to clean, solar-powered electricity. Moreover, this entry point into the solar field could generate new opportunities to enter the workforce in the burgeoning solar economy. The excitement generated in the men's group about the butterfly garden was matched by that of the possible installation of solar panels on the garage roof. Men's group member John Bowie declared: "Bringing solar panels to Serenity House would help our young people to learn how to be on the cutting edge of this new revolution. Sustainability will also be a part of *our* kids' futures."[9]

During the 2014–2015 academic year, Swarthmore engineering professor Carr Everbach volunteered his time teaching community workshops on the science and mechanics of solar energy and solar panels in the Serenity Garden. Community members attended these workshops with enthusiasm, and in September 2014 helped install a solar panel (donated by the College's engineering department) on the garage roof. The solar panel now powers LED string lights on the garage and a security light in the garden. After participating in the solar panel installation and learning that solar technology is rapidly emerging as the future of the coming energy transition, some of the residents inquired about possible training and employment in solar installation. Pointing to the decades of social and economic disinvestment resulting in high unemployment rates and a dearth of living-wage jobs in the area, John and other community members wondered if residents of North Philadelphia couldn't be gainfully employed in the solar industry. Further deliberations on this question with community residents and several Swarthmore students and faculty members gave birth to the idea of "Serenity Soular" as an initiative to promote just sustainability by creating green jobs and expanding access to solar energy production in North Philadelphia. The members of the Collaborative chose the new spelling of "*soula*r" for the name of its new initiative to focus on the *people*, and not just the panels. They would insist that the transition toward a new green economy would need to invent genuinely sustainable solutions—in fact, *soul*utions—to directly address the legacies of slow violence wrought by decades of economic instability and impoverishment, community deterioration and displacement, and now the disproportionate impacts of climate change (Nixon 2011).

The Fruits of a Campus-Community Collaborative

Group Process

Armed with the regenerative vision of the Serenity Soular initiative, the Sustainable Serenity Collaborative has evolved into an intergenerational (students, alums, community partners, new faculty and staff) partnership, which has borne fruit in diverse ways. As the Collaborative has grown, its commitment to the politics of location and to the recognition of social positionality has remained a core value, and it is manifest in the attention to relationship building as an intentional process. The Collaborative seeks to honor the different life experiences and goals that participants bring to the collaboration, although this collective commitment does not prevent conflict from arising. Through many hours spent in meetings and many discussions about group process, racial, gender, and class privilege, and organizing strategy, the Collaborative has evolved an alignment of goals, language, grounding principles, and traditions. Several processes have become institutionalized and, according to many of the members, have enabled the Collaborative to work effectively because of, not in spite of, its members' differences. One such process is the "check-in." The Collaborative starts each meeting with several minutes allocated to each person to share how they are doing and what emotions or concerns they are bringing into the space. This practice has enabled the Collaborative to create what .O calls "a spirit of gentleness" in the work and to recognize each others' humanity. Another practice that has re-inforced the Collaborative's dedication to co-production, reciprocity, and genuine partnership has been the practice of rotating the meeting locations; the bi-weekly meetings have alternated between Serenity House and the Swarthmore College campus. By making the forty-five-minute commute and engaging in geographic border crossings between Swarthmore's verdant college campus and the harder inner-city neighborhoods surrounding Serenity House, our members gain greater understandings of the social, physical, and emotional experiences of place and *dis*placement. The reflections on our "senses of place" (shaped by our lived geographies of home, workplace, school, streets, and green spaces) revealed differing feelings of safety, connections to the "natural environment," and confidence in the *future* (that prospect that sustainability is supposed to protect). Bringing into the open the emotional connections to place and the threats of displacement that those of us living in North Philadelphia have experienced engendered in all of our members a keener sense of the negative impacts of green gentrification and the shortcomings of adopting a version of sustainability that is incognizant of its role in reproducing systems of displacement (Isenhour, McDonogh, and Checker 2015).

Building Traditions and Institutional Structure

Since its beginnings in 2012, the Collaborative has developed into a community institution with honored traditions, consistent leadership, and a focused vision. One tradition initiated by the first Sustainable Community Action course in 2013 has become an annual event: the Mothers & Others Day Celebration. Held in the Serenity Garden, this event celebrates "mothering" figures by inviting young people to paint colorful flowerpots planted with vibrant marigolds and petunias. Throughout the day, youth and adults from the community volunteer to till soil, weed, and plant flowers and vegetables in the backyard garden. This event recalls Sustainable Serenity's beginnings, which was rooted in gardening, a culture of reciprocity, a respect for the role of "mothering" (the responsibilities associated with caregiving, not the exclusively female-gendered identity), and honoring and nurturing our connections to each other and to the Earth. An effective community-building strategy, the annual Mothers & Others Day garden event draws a large crowd of children and adults from the neighborhoods and a wide swath of Swarthmore students eager to put their knowledge of growing plants and growing community into practice.

The Collaborative has become a recognized and valued partner in the environmental studies courses at Swarthmore that incorporate community-based learning and engaged scholarship methods. First offered in 2013 as an independent study course, Sustainable Community Action is now an official course (now called Urban Environmental Community Action) in the environmental studies curriculum and attracts students from a wide variety of disciplinary backgrounds and experiences. The Collaborative's status as an acknowledged community partner at the college promises that there will be an ongoing commitment to the work in North Philadelphia with an expanding base of young college students learning about and engaging in socially critical approaches to sustainability. Working with the Sustainable Serenity Collaborative as a community partner in their environmental studies course, students describe feeling that their research is "more meaningful" because it can support the goals of a community struggling to improve the lives of its members. For example, one of the students in Giovanna's Sustainable Community Action course worked with local community leaders to generate GIS maps tracing how the racial, class, home-ownership, profession, land-use, and age profiles of the neighborhood have changed over the last forty years, providing evidence for the residents' claims of accelerating displacement and the erosion of the historically Black neighborhoods in the Hartranft district of North Philadelphia. Other students in the course with backgrounds in economics and computer science met with John Bowie and other residents to identify goals for enterprise development. They researched national models for solar workforce development and training and the legal and business structures most effective for incorporating Serenity Soular as a 501(c)(3) organization or worker-owned solar cooperative. This ongoing research has expanded bringing new partners with legal and non-profit expertise to the Collaborative to support Serenity Soular's capacity to apply for funding and resources from public and private entities, to invest in local enterprises and jobs in the local region, and to counteract the trend of disinvestment in North Philadelphia.

The experience of building community and local approaches to just sustainability in North Philadelphia led some Swarthmore College alumni (including several students in the first Sustainable Community Action course in 2013) to settle in Philadelphia after graduating and establish an environmental justice organization in the city: the Maypop Collective for Climate and Economic Justice, an organizing collective that aims to generate solutions to the climate crisis centered on racial and economic justice. Members of the Maypop Collective partnered with community residents to start Philly Thrive, a climate justice group that in 2016 organized the Right to Breathe campaign, an initiative focusing on stopping the incursion of oil and gas industries in Philadelphia.[10] Contributing to the growth of environmental and climate justice organizing in Philadelphia, the Maypop Collective has acted as the fiscal sponsor for Sustainable Serenity's initiatives and has led training in community organizing for climate and economic justice at Serenity House. While now engaging in different wings of Philadelphia's flourishing climate justice movement, these groups remain connected through their mutual vision working toward a more just, sustainable, and thriving city.

Widening the Circle: Partnership and Network Building

In early 2015, members of the growing Sustainable Serenity Collaborative met with local organizations and potential allies and stakeholders, including organizers with the Energy Coordinating Agency (ECA), a North Philadelphia–based green-energy-training organization. To start the community education process and to generate community interest in energy conservation issues, ECA held a workshop at Serenity House introducing residents to the theory and practice of home weatherization and saving on energy costs. The Sustainable Serenity team also learned about the city's Coolest Block Contest through ECA. This annual competition allows low-income homeowners living on the same block to apply to become the "coolest block" and, if successful, receive weatherization retrofits for the entire block. To support the expansion of Sustainable Serenity, John Bowie worked with a nearby homeowner's association on the 1200 block of Seltzer Street to apply for and win the contest. Once the Seltzer Street block was selected, the Collaborative supported the Seltzer Street block captain, Darlene Pope, to collect the required information from homeowners (deeds, social security numbers, utility bills) in order to approve the retrofits to their homes. Because the members of the Collaborative had built trust with the community, local residents were willing to share this personal information, and Sustainable Serenity enabled eighteen low-income homeowners on Seltzer Street to receive full energy-efficiency retrofits (energy audits, weatherization, sealing, new windows, white roofs, energy star appliances, and HVAC systems) from ECA.

The home improvements for long-term, low-income African American residents on this single block have already resulted in significant positive outcomes, including lower electricity and gas bills. As the city of Philadelphia's most recent "coolest block," Seltzer Street has emerged as a symbol of community resilience: By improving the durability and energy efficiency of these houses, the retrofits have also increased the neighborhood's adaptive capacity in the face of increasing weather extremes, including hotter summers and cold, damp winters. The lower energy costs and durability of the houses on the block also enable homeowners to afford to remain in their homes, defying the encroaching trend of gentrification, which has already displaced hundreds of historically Black residents throughout the city.[11] By promoting local sustainability initiatives such as this one, the Collaborative strives to implement one of the core values of climate justice: sustainability without displacement.

To build on the success of the Seltzer Street energy retrofits, the Collaborative partnered with Morris Chapel Baptist Church, one of Philadelphia's oldest historically Black churches located across the street from Serenity House, to organize several community forums during which we asked residents to share their hopes for the community. In line with the findings of the growing, national "Green the Church" movement, which argues that the history of the power and purpose of the Black church should provide "moral and social leadership on climate issues" (Abrams 2015), attendees voiced their desires for living-wage jobs, healthy food, and safe, clean streets. Members of the Sustainable Serenity Collaborative perceive these desires as central to the realization of a more "sustainable" North Philadelphia.

Adding momentum to the project, in May 2015, the Collaborative entered into a new partnership with RE-volv, a San Francisco–based organization whose mission is to empower people and communities to invest collectively in renewable energy. RE-volv, an inaugural member of the White House's Initiative on Community Solar Partnerships,[12] sponsors selected teams of college students and community organizations from across the country as "solar ambassadors" to spearhead a solar project in their community using RE-volv's innovative solar financing model. Three student leaders of the Collaborative, under the auspices of Serenity Soular, applied for, and were selected as, one of five national solar

Figure 3.1. Completed installation of 9.0 kilowatt solar array on the roof of Serenity House. Photo credit: Laura Rigell.

ambassador teams. In the spring of 2016, RE-volv leaders trained and supported the students to develop a high-impact crowdfunding campaign to cover the cost of the solar installation. After our successful fundraising campaign, in July 2016, a 9.0 kilowatt solar system was installed onto the roof of Serenity House. Arch Street United Methodist Church, as the owner of Serenity House, signed a twenty-year lease with RE-volv and submits monthly payments to RE-volv in exchange for the clean energy; these payments are lower than Serenity House's previous electric bills. RE-volv leverages the incoming lease payments to support the future expansion of solar in other community-supporting organizations across the country. As an outcome of Serenity Soular's partnership with RE-volv, 100 percent of Serenity House's electricity usage is now offset by power from the sun.

Partnering with RE-volv to solarize Serenity House allows the organization to share some of the savings it reaps from investing in solar with other nonprofits that want to do the same. A dollar donated to install panels on Serenity House will have an amplified impact, adding momentum to the nationwide transition to renewables. Although the Collaborative's work on 12th and W. Lehigh Avenue might seem small, our attempts to advance climate, racial, and economic justice have profound implications for other communities. Sustainable Serenity and Serenity Soular's collaboration with RE-volv helps to broadcast local stories of "patchy sustainability" (Tsing 2015), demonstrating how efforts to improve and preserve a "small place," a local neighborhood, a remnant of Black community resilience, can have ripple effects across the country.

Early in the Collaborative's partnership with RE-volv, John Bowie raised the question of how the installation of solar technology would build genuine sustainability for North Philadelphia. He was concerned about how our model would stay committed to building local capacity and self-determination in the growing solar industry without exclusively relying on contracting with white-owned solar-installation companies. In response to these concerns, the Collaborative (in partnership with the chosen solar-installation company, Solar States) explored the possibility of developing a solar apprenticeship program for local young people interested in job-training opportunities that would run parallel with the solar array installation on Serenity House. To support these efforts, in the fall of 2015, students in Giovanna's Sustainable Community Action course worked in collaboration with Sustainable Serenity members to research existing apprenticeship programs and worker-owned business models across the country.[13]

As a result of these conversations and research, the Serenity Soular initiative, in consultation with Solar States, distributed applications for a solar apprenticeship program in the local community and selected two young people from the neighborhood to attend a solar-installation course and job shadow the installers during the Serenity House panel installations. The Sustainable Serenity team had earlier conducted a crowdfunding campaign in the fall of 2015,[14] raising over $8,000 to support the research and organizing to lay the groundwork for the Serenity Soular initiative. Speaking in the crowdfunding video, John Bowie explains the clear connections between the work of Serenity Soular and the goals of a just transition:

> Out of our work for the past two years, we have come to an idea that will provide a model for a just transition away from fossil fuels and towards community resilience. We want to create a cooperative business that will employ neighborhood residents to install solar panels. We will call the business Serenity Soular, to indicate our commitment to a triple-bottom-line model: a model that prioritizes a profitable business along with a commitment to the well-being of people and the well-being of the environment. We insist that this business be based in the neighborhood, and owned by its workers, so that we are building, rather than extracting, wealth and knowledge within the community.[15]

A portion of this crowdfunded money was earmarked as stipends for the two young apprentices to compensate them for their time attending the solar-energy classes and shadowing the installation process with Solar States. Impressed by the apprentices' enthusiasm and commitment to the vision of the solar energy revolution, at the end of the apprenticeship and installation process, Solar States hired both trainees as full-time solar installers. This success reinforced the triple-bottom-line promise: to support and stay in the local community, provide economic security, and protect the Earth and the climate. In addition to getting two young people from North Philadelphia gainfully employed in the solar economy, according to RE-volv's energy audit of Serenity House, this *local* solar project successfully implemented by Serenity Soular will have also prevented 92,141 lbs of CO_2 from being emitted into the atmosphere.[16] Moreover, it may have moved us just a little bit closer to preserving this "small place" or remnant of the 12th and W. Lehigh block of the historically Black Hartranft neighborhood in North Philadelphia.

To build on the Collaborative's theme of sustainable development without displacement, in August 2016, the students involved with Serenity Soular applied again to work with RE-volv and this time to partner with Morris Chapel Baptist Church. Having successfully completed another round of fundraising, outreach, and community green-jobs training, the Collaborative continues to scale up the community-based solar economy in the region.[17] Serenity Soular's goal is to build a local hub of locally generated sustainability initiatives that enable the flourishing of *remnants*, or patches, of thriving African American neighborhoods, productive urban gardens, solar-fitted homes and buildings, and successful clean-energy businesses training and the hiring of local residents to conduct energy audits, retrofit homes and buildings for energy efficiency, and install solar panels in Philadelphia's low-income neighborhoods.

Figure 3.2. Solar installers Kylonda Sanders and Robert Crawford, celebrating the solar installation on Serenity House. Photo credit: Laura Rigell.

Moving Forward: Financing Patchy Sustainability

The issue of how to financially sustain sustainability initiatives, including those of Sustainable Serenity and Serenity Soular after six years of working together, is inevitably a major concern. Over the years, our Collaborative has been supported by several grants and fellowships through Swarthmore College's Lang Center for Civic and Social Responsibility, Pericles Fund monies, faculty research grants, a Penn Praxis Social Impact grant through the University of Pennsylvania, crowdfunding campaigns and other private donations, and an award from the Energy Sprout grant program through Pennsylvania State University's Energy Path program.

In moving toward this vision, the Serenity Soular initiative has engaged in dialogue and collaboration with other organizations, the local energy utility, and the City of Philadelphia. We have engaged with the Earth Quaker Action Team's (EQAT) political campaign to push the electric utility PECO to subsidize local green jobs[18] and have met with climate-friendly city council members in city government and the Philadelphia Energy Authority, a state authority working to support workforce development and solar-energy opportunities for Philadelphia's low-income communities. Additionally, Serenity Soular has participated in the Philadelphia Area Cooperative Alliance's (PACA) community trainings focusing on the history and structure of cooperative businesses. Building on the success of the PACA trainings, in 2017 Serenity Soular members started to develop a cooperative business model with technical support from the organization.[19] This learning process has provided Serenity Soular with the expertise to advance the goal of launching a triple-bottom-line enterprise that would support local solar workforce development as well as build healthy, sustainable, and community-driven income-generating opportunities.

Conclusion: University-Community Partnerships as Co-production

We have examined the establishment of the Sustainable Serenity Collaborative, the expanding campus-community collaboration between community leaders and Swarthmore College committed to advancing a just transition in North Philadelphia. The Sustainable Serenity Col-laborative views collaboration and the co-production of sustainable futures across difference as key to its success, both strategically and procedurally.[20] As a new organization, the Collaborative has unsurpris-ingly depended on many allies to achieve initial outcomes. However, the Collaborative values collaboration beyond its measurable benefits, not only for the transactional value that comes from partnering with other groups. The Collaborative aims to interrupt the culture of competition so common in institutions of higher education (like Swarthmore College and the University of Pennsylvania) and to demonstrate that working together interrupts the neoliberal logic of success as an individualistic accomplishment. Rather, the Sustainable Serenity Collaborative hopes to model that collaboration amplifies our power and capacity to enact social and environmental transformations. In bringing together a very diverse group of individuals, coming from different racial and class backgrounds, sexual and gender identities, and ranging from teenagers to retirees, the Sustainable Serenity Collaborative is demonstrating the power that can come from working through the conflicts and messi-ness that inevitably arise in diverse coalitions. By creating space to address conflicts, allowing time for respecting and processing emotions, and emphasizing the values of a caring community, the Collaborative has maintained a solid group of leaders who continue to show up and contribute their ideas, their labor, and their hearts to create genuinely sustainable *soul*utions in North Philadelphia.

The Sustainable Serenity Collaborative and the Serenity Soular initiative have already helped to amplify the voices of local residents who are calling for local economic development that is environmen-tally sustainable, generates community resilience and prosperity, does not enable displacement, and contributes to reducing the dangerous impacts of climate change. Local elected officials, local business lead-ers, and local social justice organizations (e.g., EQAT, POWER, and Philly Thrive) have joined with the Collaborative to support this "small place" effort, recognizing its more "globalized" implications and pos-sibilities.[21] Moreover, the work of the Sustainable Serenity and Serenity Soular campus-community collaborations has influenced Swarthmore College's discourse and decision making on the relationship between climate change and social responsibility. Although the college's board

Figure 3.3. Youth members of the Sustainable Serenity Collaborative. Photo credit: Giovanna Di Chiro.

of managers has to date rejected student activists' call to divest its large endowment from fossil fuel companies, the Board and members of the administration have for the first time enacted a "carbon charge" on the college's operating budget, generating close to $300,000 in a green reinvestment fund that will support campus-based sustainability efforts and, in the Quaker spirit of social responsibility, could also offer grants or loans for local energy efficiency and just sustainability initiatives to the college's struggling "neighbors," like Philadelphia and Chester. Several faculty members at the College have hired Solar States to solarize their private homes, and they praised the work of Ky and Robert, the two newly hired solar installers who graduated from the Serenity Soular apprenticeship program. Proactive and successful initiatives like Serenity Soular have sparked these new conversations and encounters.

The Sustainable Serenity Collaborative is poised to move forward from the successful track record of our college-community partnership. Partners from Swarthmore College and North Philadelphia remain committed to working together for social, environmental, and climate justice. Drawing on the diverse resources and skills of the group,

Sustainable Serenity holds great promise to generate a more just sustainability for all communities in the Philadelphia metropolitan area and beyond.

NOTES

1 Temple Town is the term (some say a euphemism) that refers to the expansion of Temple University into historically Black neighborhoods in North Philadelphia by buying up land to build new dorms, classrooms, and research space. See Moskowitz (2014); and Pew Charitable Trusts, 2016.

2 ".O" is the chosen name and spelling of the community activist, Serenity House resident, and co-founder of the Sustainable Serenity Collaborative.

3 With respect to community-based learning (CBL), much of the literature focuses on how out-of-classroom learning can enhance the curriculum (providing students with "practical" knowledge to supplement their more theoretical studies); contribute to citizenship education (learning to be effective citizens through "civic engagement"); better prepare students for course-related activities in the community; encourage students to address their own class, racial, gender, and cultural "positionality"; and support students to reflect on these experiences when they return to the classroom. With respect to discussions focused on the benefits and difficulties of building campus-community partnerships, the writing has detailed the many challenges and obstacles (making the argument that colleges and universities should see themselves as citizens responsible to the larger geographic area in which they reside) and has examined the role and contributions of colleges and universities in addressing broader social problems.

4 Some of the challenges and obstacles include the lack of preparation of faculty and students to work with a community with different racial, class, and cultural background; the lack of recognition of the labor required for community-based organizations (CBOs) to work with students and faculty; the differing time horizons of colleges and communities; the lack of coordination among institutions working with the same CBOs; the lack of reciprocity (students and/or faculty doing their research and never returning reports or outcomes to the community); the problem of the "service" or "charity" standpoint (i.e., the lack of recognition and understanding of the resources, knowledge, expertise that exist in the community); and the discrepancies of power and resources between academic institutions and community partners that can lead to assumptions in agenda setting and control of the research and initiatives undertaken.

5 The U.S. Green Building Council offers the Leadership in Energy and Environmental Design (LEED) program as a green building design certification.

6 An earlier version of sections of this history is found in Di Chiro (2015).

7 Giovanna's interview with .O, January 24, 2014.

8 Interview with .O by Swarthmore student Kathryn Wu, April 19, 2014.

9 Giovanna's interview with John Bowie, April 19, 2014.

10 *Philly Thrive: Right to Breathe Campaign*, www.phillythrive.org.

11 *Philadelphia Daily News* (n.d.).

12 White House Initiative on Community Solar Partnerships, www.energy.gov.

13 Zavez et al. (2015).

14 Nora Kerrich, "Jumpstart Serenity Soular," *Crowdrise*, www.crowdrise.com.

15 Ibid.

16 See the RE-volv website at www.re-volv.org.

17 As of this writing, Serenity Soular has contracted with a third RE-volv–Solar Ambassadors partnership with the Village of Arts and Humanities, http://vil lagearts.org, a well-established community organization that draws on the arts and cultural work to build community capacity and to generate local economic development.

18 See the Earth Quaker Action Team, PECO campaign web page and green jobs campaign webpage, "Walk for Green Jobs and Justice," at www.eqat.org.

19 See the Philadelphia Area Cooperative Alliance's 20 by 20 Initiative at www.phila delphia.coop.

20 Julian Agyeman draws on Duncan McLaren's work to define the concept of co-production as a social and economic model that draws on people's capabilities. "It sees people as assets not as burdens, invests in their capacities, promotes mutuality and reciprocity, facilitates rather than delivering and uses peer-support networks in addition to professionals to transfer knowledge and capabilities. In narrower, economic terms co-production refers to the involvement of the consumer in the manufacture of the goods and services they consume thereby blurring the distinction between producer and consumer" (Agyeman 2013, 43). Agyeman argues that "co-production is already emerging in several diverse arenas. While some of the trends (e.g. greater self-assembly of furniture) offer little benefit, others (e.g. domestic energy generation, timebanking/time-dollar schemes, self-build co-housing, open source software) exhibit key benefits in that people are reclaiming and reinventing work, refusing to be directed by the logic of capital, engaging their individual and collective capacities to invent, create, shape and co-operate without monetary incentive" (45).

21 POWER (Philadelphians Organized to Witness, Empower & Rebuild) is an inter-faith organization whose mission is to empower local communities to strengthen and mobilize networks to engage in local politics so the needs and priorities of all Philadelphians are reflected in the city's systems and policies. POWER has recently launched an initiative to address poverty, unemployment, and sustainable development through green jobs training in Philadelphia. See POWER's new project, *Black Work Matters: The Green Jobs Report*, at https://powerinterfaith.org.

REFERENCES

Abrams, Lindsay. 2015. "'For Far Too Long, People of Color Have Been at the Bottom of the Pile': Why Black Churches Are Embracing the Clean Energy Revolution." *Salon*, August 23. www.salon.com.

Agyeman, Julian. 2013. *Introducing Just Sustainabilities: Policy, Planning and Practice.* London: Zed Books.

Anguelovski, Isabelle. 2014. *Neighborhood as Refuge: Community Reconstruction, Place Making, and Environmental Justice in the City.* Cambridge, MA: MIT Press.

Beckman, Mary, and Joyce F. Long, eds. 2016. *Community Based Research: Teaching for Community Impact.* Sterling, VA: Stylus Publishing.

Canning, Doyle, and Patrick Reinsborough. 2010. *Re: Imagining Change: How to Use Story-Based Strategy to Win Campaigns, Build Movements, and Change the World.* Oakland, CA: PM Press.

Cruz, Nadine, and David Giles. 2000. "Where's the Community in Service-Learning Research?" *Michigan Journal of Community Service Learning* 7 (Fall): 28–34.

Di Chiro, Giovanna. 2006. "Environmental Studies and the Pedagogy of Intersectionality: Teaching Urban Ecology." *Feminist Teacher* 16, no. 2 (2006): 98–109.

Di Chiro, Giovanna. 2015. "A New Spelling of Sustainability: Engaging Feminist-Environmental Justice Theory and Practice." In *Practicing Feminist Political Ecologies: Moving beyond the "Green Economy,"* edited by Wendy Harcourt and Ingrid Nelson, 211–237. London: Zed Books.

Dickinson, Elizabeth. 2012. "Addressing Environmental Racism through Storytelling." *Communication, Culture, and Critique* 5:57–74.

Dugery, John, and J. Knowles, eds. 2003. *University and Community Research Partnerships: A New Approach.* Charlottesville, VA: Pew Partnership for Civic Change.

Forrant, Robert, and Linda Silka, eds. 2006. *Inside and Out: Universities and Education for Sustainable Development.* Amityville, NY: Baywood Publishing.

Freeman, Lance. 2006. *There Goes the 'Hood: Views of Gentrification from the Ground Up.* Philadelphia: Temple University Press.

Gibson-Graham, J. K., Jenny Cameron, and Stephen Healy. 2013. *Take Back the Economy: An Ethical Guide for Transforming Our Communities.* Minneapolis: University of Minnesota Press.

Gould, Kenneth, and Tammy L. Lewis. 2016. *Green Gentrification: Urban Sustainability and the Struggle for Environmental Justice.* New York: Routledge.

Greenberg, Miriam. 2018. "Situating Sustainability in the Luxury City: Toward a Critical Urban Research Agenda." In this volume.

Greenwood, Davydd J., and Morton Levin. 2011. "Reconstructing the Relationships between Universities and Society through Action Research." In *Handbook of Qualitative Research,* edited by Norman Denzin and Yvonna Lincoln, 85–106. Thousand Oaks, CA: Sage Publications.

Hale, Charles. 2008. *Engaging Contradictions: Theory, Politics, and Methods of Activist Scholarship.* Berkeley: University of California Press.

Heavens, Alan. 2016. "Good Food Flats: Off-Campus Housing for 'Foodies' at Drexel." *Philadelphia Inquirer,* February 16. www.philly.com.

hooks, bell. 2003. *Teaching Community: A Pedagogy of Hope.* New York: Routledge.

Hoyt, Lorlene. 2010. "A City-Campus Engagement Theory from, and for, Practice." *Michigan Journal of Community Service Learning,* Fall, 75–88.

Isenhour, Cindy, Gary McDonogh, and Melissa Checker, eds. 2015. *Sustainability in the Global City: Myth and Practice*. New York: Cambridge University Press.

Kemmis, Stephen, et al. 2014. *The Action Research Planner: Doing Critical Participatory Action Research*. Singapore: Springer Publications.

Kincaid, Jamaica. 1988. *A Small Place*. New York: Farrar, Straus, & Giroux.

Moskowitz, Peter. 2014. "Philadelphia Universities' Expansion Drove Wider Gentrification, Tension." *Aljazeera America*, December 31. www.america.aljazeera.com.

Nixon, Rob. 2011. *Slow Violence and the Environmentalism of the Poor*. Cambridge, MA: Harvard University Press.

Pew Charitable Trusts. 2015. *Philadelphia 2015: The State of the City*. March. www.pewtrusts.org.

Pew Charitable Trusts. 2016. "Gentrification and Neighborhood Change in Philadelphia." May 19. www.pewtrusts.org.

Philadelphia Daily News. n.d. "The Problems and the Promise: Gentrification in Philadelphia." www.philly.com.

Rigell, Laura. 2016. "A History and Future of Neighborhood Change in North Philadelphia." Senior thesis, Swarthmore College.

Simpson, Melissa. 2016. "Race against Time: A North Philly Artist Aims to Document Her Disappearing Community." *PhillyVoice*, June 16. www.phillyvoice.com.

Smith, Laura, et al. 2010. "Between Idealism and Reality: Meeting the Challenges of Participatory Action Research." *Action Research* 8, no. 4:407–425.

Smith, M. K. 2007. "Action Research." In *The Encyclopedia of Informal Education*, edited by Mark K. Smith. www.infed.org.

Tretter, Eliot. 2015. "The Environmental Justice of Affordable Housing: East Austin, Gentrification, and Resistance." In *Sustainability in the Global City: Myth and Practice*, edited by Cindy Isenhour, Gary McDonogh and Melissa Checker, 350–375. New York: Cambridge University Press.

Tsing, Anna Lowenhaupt. 2015. *The Mushroom at the End of the World: On the Possibility of Life in Capitalist Ruins*. Princeton, NJ: Princeton University Press.

Zavez, K., D. Ranshous, E. Gluck, Z. Peyton Jones, C. Ren, and S. Worlanyo. 2015. "Proposing a Business Model and Apprenticeship Program for Serenity Soular." Community-based learning project for the class ENVS 004: Sustainable Community Action, Swarthmore College, December.

4

Situating Global Policies within Local Realities

Climate Conflict from California to Latin America

TRACY PERKINS AND AARON SOTO-KARLIN

In 2010, the state of California became involved in an international debate that speaks to the deep conflicts surrounding climate politics. State officials began contemplating how to link California's carbon market to international programming designed to use money from industrialized countries to preserve forests in developing countries. This system is called REDD, short for Reducing Emissions from Deforestation and forest Degradation. Small REDD projects are being developed in multiple locations around the world, but none has yet been implemented by an entire state, as California proposes to do. The program is meant to be environmentally beneficial, but not all environmentalists favor it.

Among the skeptics are indigenous activists from Latin America who oppose a proposed REDD program that includes California, Chiapas (Mexico), and Acre (Brazil). In 2012, representatives of some indigenous groups from these states undertook a political tour through California. Friends of the Earth and the Indigenous Environmental Network convened a public event called "Indigenous Peoples Confront False Climate Change Solutions." On one side of the room at the event, black T-shirts with "REDD + Indigenous Peoples = GENOCIDE" in red letters were displayed and available for purchase. Two large posters behind the speakers' table showed the early twentieth-century Mexican revolutionary Emiliano Zapata and an indigenous man from the Amazon forest with the letters REDD printed on their foreheads in a circle with a line through it. The rear tables were covered with reports and letters with titles such as "Letter from the State of Acre: In Defense of Life and the Integrity of the Peoples and Their Territories against REDD and the

Commodification of Nature," and "Open Letter of Concern to the International Donor Community about the Diversion of Existing Forest Conservation and Development Funding to REDD+" (Assentamento de Produção Agro-Extrativista Limoeiro-Floresta Pública do Antimary et al. 2011; The No REDD Platform and Rising Tide et al. 2011).

What factors led to this conflict between California climate policy and some of its intended beneficiaries? When abstract global policy lands in the messy reality of local context, people respond in ways that policy makers may not expect but that are understandable, nonetheless. The interface between global policy and the politics, history, economics, and cultural meanings experienced in actual places can mean the difference between continuing to live on ancestral lands or being relocated, between improved or worsened air quality in one's neighborhood, and between gaining or not gaining a vital addition to one's income. While policy makers think in terms of the big picture, local realities can make or break the success of their efforts.

This chapter presents the global policy debate over forest carbon offsets as it plays out on the ground. More specifically, it analyzes the first sub-national international memorandum of understanding (MOU) on forest carbon offsets,[1] that is, the first international MOU agreed to directly between states within different countries, rather than between their national governments (Schwarzenegger, Marques de Almeida Júnior, and Guerrero 2010). The California-Chiapas-Acre agreement represents an innovative effort in multi-level governance, and it would link carbon reduction efforts in states within three different countries.[2] This chapter situates global policy within local reality by demonstrating how support for and against the MOU is affected by preexisting political conflict in two of the three participating jurisdictions: California and Chiapas. To do so, it presents the historical and political context of the REDD debate in each location. Our analysis draws on interviews, policy, and legal research.[3]

International carbon offsets are one of many policy tools that fit within broader global debates about sustainability. However, not all of the key actors in our case focus on "sustainability" in their work. Representatives of the California Air Resources Board often speak about the broad benefits and inherent good of sustainability, with a focus on mitigating global warming. California environmental justice activists, in contrast, speak most frequently in terms of pollution, health, social justice, and climate justice. Many of the indigenous opponents in Chiapas use the language of cultural survival, rural development, and access to land and forest products.

The divergent language used by the many actors involved in this case reflects the different interests and values that they bring to the table, which are themselves situated within different geographic and social spaces. This underscores Sze et al.'s emphasis in this volume's introduction that sustainability is not "neutral or universal," and that "environmental crises and social inequality are in fact twins, born of coexisting political and economic processes." The rest of this chapter tells the story of how these divergent interests and values collided in the California-Chiapas-Acre MOU process.

California and the Memorandum of Understanding

The 2012 anti-REDD event that opens this chapter took place at a fitting time for a panel on climate change. The 2006 California Global Warming Solutions Act (AB 32) requires businesses and government agencies to reduce greenhouse gas emissions to 1990 levels by 2020 and to 80 percent below 1990 levels by 2050. Because of this ambitious goal, the law is widely regarded as a national model for tackling climate change.

A goal of this magnitude requires an intricate and still evolving process to implement. The anti-REDD event focused on one proposed component of the Global Warming Solutions Act's implementation that has yet to be put into practice: international carbon offsets. The law requires California industries to reduce their greenhouse gas emissions over time. A memorandum of understanding signed in 2010 between California, Chiapas, and Acre proposes that California polluters be allowed to purchase carbon "offsets" in Chiapas and Acre as a substitute for reducing some of their greenhouse gas emissions in California. It was the first sub-national government-to-government carbon-offset agreement in the world. The idea is that, when a California company purchases an offset, it pays someone in Chiapas or Acre to not cut down a portion of a forest that they would have cut down in the normal course of events. Forests absorb carbon dioxide, which is a key contributor to climate change. So when forests are cut down, carbon dioxide levels go up. But cutting down forests produces economic value through the production of timber, paper products, or land for ranching or agriculture, so forests are cut down in spite of their environmental importance.

The intent of paying to prevent forests from being cut down is that global society retains the environmental value of forests, while the people who would have cut them down still receive their economic value. In theory, it is a win-win solution in which reducing actual carbon dioxide output from a California polluter and preventing the loss of carbon-absorbing forests contribute roughly equally to slowing climate change. Offsets also give California industries flexibility in choosing what is most cost-efficient—they can invest in local improvements to lower their own carbon emissions or pay to save trees elsewhere.

This, at least, is how the model is described by the California Air Resources Board, which is responsible for implementing the Global Warming Solutions Act and its attached international offsets proposals. It is also how the model is described by a wide array of pro-market environmental organizations and the Governor's Climate and Forest Task Force, which helped create the agreement between the three states. But some critics see international offsets as a threat to local autonomy, values, and health. Critics of the agreement include an array of scholars, international environmental and social justice organizations, and some Latin American forest-dwelling communities that policy makers saw as intended REDD beneficiaries (Activist San Diego et al. 2012; Assentamento de Produção Agro-Extrativista Limoeiro-Floresta Pública do Antimary et al. 2011; Conant 2011a, 2011b; Conselho Indigenista Missionário Regional Acre 2012; Council of Traditional Indigenous Doctors and Midwives from Chiapas 2011; McAffee 2013; Sanchez 2012).

REDD and the Cap-and-Trade Conflict

The plan to create an international carbon-offset program among California, Chiapas, and Acre meant that international conflict about REDD programs merged with conflict in California about how to implement the state's Global Warming Solutions Act. One conflict concerned the state's choice of cap-and-trade as the central mechanism to reduce carbon emissions from industrial sources. Under a cap-and-trade plan, the state limits the amount of greenhouse gas emissions that companies are allowed to produce as a by-product of their businesses—this is called the "cap." The state does not require reduced emissions at any particular point of origin at a plant, industry, or region, as other pollution regulation sometimes does. Rather, the emissions cap is set at the state level. The government creates a market in which greenhouse gas emission reductions are bought and sold. To comply with the cap, individual companies can either reduce emissions on site, purchase emission reduction credits from other emitters who have unused emission reduction credits (the "trade" part of cap-and-trade), or purchase offsets. Both offsets and cap-and-trade are built on the premise that as long as emissions reductions happen, it doesn't matter where they happen.

California's Global Warming Solutions Act mandated emissions reductions but left many decisions about how to achieve those reductions up to the California Air Resources Board. According to the board, cap-and-trade allows businesses to decide where in their energy production system they can most cost-effectively reduce emissions, thereby providing incentives for a company to get rid of its dirtiest energy first. Reasoning that companies know their facilities much better than regulators do, the California Air Resources Board decided that each company could best identify how to minimize their own greenhouse gas emissions. Ideally, this approach provides both industry and society with the biggest bang for its reduction buck.

However, the inclusion of cap-and-trade in California's plan to address global warming drew intense criticism from the state's environmental justice activists (Hanemann 2007; Kaswan 2014; London et al., 2013; Perkins 2015; Sze et al. 2009). Environmental justice activists work on environmental issues primarily in low-income communities of color and often conceive of themselves as distinct from the broader environmental movement. Their communities live with a disproportionate burden of pollution compared to wealthier, whiter areas. The link between poor people, people of color, and pollution is due, in part, to market forces that result in both poor people and polluting industries locating in places with cheap land and to other ways that markets have been bound together with deeply embedded structures of racism (Cole and Foster 2001; Pulido 1996; Rechtschaffen, Guana, and O'Neill 2009). As a result, environmental justice activists have long critiqued market-based approaches to environmental governance. They often see markets as part of the problem, rather than part of the solution.

In addition to their general concern about market-based environmental governance, California environmental justice activists also opposed cap-and-trade because of the fear that it would deprive low-income communities and communities of color of the air pollution reductions and health benefits they might receive if the state required cuts in emissions at all industrial sites. The logic behind this is as follows: Facilities that emit greenhouse gases also typically emit other kinds of more immediately health-threatening air pollutants such as particulate matter and nitrogen oxides. These air pollutants are associated with asthma, acute bronchitis, and premature death (Shonkoff et al. 2009). Reducing greenhouse gas emissions usually also entails reducing these other forms of pollutants. If, instead of reducing their own emissions, industries in low-income communities of color repeatedly choose to purchase credits from other facilities located in places that have more political pressure from wealthy residents, low-income communities of color could miss out on the local benefits of pollution reduction. Activists also raised the possibility that this same process could not only create uneven pollution reductions but also potentially increase greenhouse gas emissions and their accompanying air pollutants in industrial "hot spots," even while reducing the level of greenhouse gases emitted by the state as a whole.

Preliminary research evaluating equity outcomes of cap-and-trade highlights concerns similar to those environmental justice activists raised years before. Cushing and colleagues found that "in-state [greenhouse gas] emissions from regulated companies have increased on average for several industry sectors and that many emissions reductions associated with the program were linked to offset projects located outside of California." Of particular concern to the low- income communities most exposed to the health-threatening pollutants associated with greenhouse gas emissions, the authors also found that "Large [greenhouse gas] emitters that might be of most public health concern were the most likely to use offset projects to meet their obligations under the cap-and-trade program" (Cushing et al. 2016, 10).

Activists argued that the state could have done better for disadvantaged populations by prioritizing places with the highest greenhouse gas emissions, which are disproportionately low-income communities of color (Pastor et al. 2013), for the steepest reduction requirements. This would lower greenhouse gas emissions and improve local health outcomes at the same time.

California environmental justice activists opposed the agreement to create an international carbon-offset program between California, Chiapas, and Acre for many of the same reasons that they opposed cap-and-trade in California (Perkins 2015). For example, this California activist, who lives in close proximity to a Chevron refinery, links the two programs as follows:

> It's a constant fight. That's pretty much the situation where we're at right now with this, a major modernization project that Chevron is taking through the environmental review process now, where they're saying that the project would not result in a net increase of greenhouse gas emissions. Well, that's all good, but in order to achieve that, they're going to have to buy some pollution credits. So technically it really won't result in zero net emission impact because the emissions will increase at the refinery here in Richmond, because they'll be buying some pollution credits that may benefit somewhere else, where they may plant some trees or whatever. But it would allow the emissions to increase here in Richmond.

Activists also argued that the offset system was vulnerable to abuse. It might not actually result in reductions to greenhouse gases if the state allowed offsets that did not truly reduce carbon emissions. Offsets fail, for example, when they are allocated to conservation projects already planned that would happen even without the offset. Offsets also fail when they are allocated to avoid forest destruction in one location but result in forest destruction simply moving elsewhere. In policy language such failures are referred to as problems of "additionality" and "leakage" (Wara and Victor 2008). For REDD systems to work, offsets also need to last forever, even as the world around them changes.

For all these reasons, environmental justice activists opposed the California-Chiapas-Acre memorandum of understanding even as the California governor and the California Air Resources Board promoted it as a win-win agreement for all. Pro- and anti-offset camps in California draw on different values and goals to support their positions. The California Air Resources Board speaks about the broad benefits and inherent good of sustainability, with a focus on mitigating global warming. California environmental justice activists, however, speak most frequently in terms of local pollution levels, social justice, health, and climate justice.

Chiapas, Mexico

In California, conflict over international carbon offsets was tightly linked to the cap-and-trade debate, but in Chiapas it arose instead from a heated, multi-decade dispute between government and peasant-farmers over land ownership. Here again, for offsets to be effective, a number of conditions must be met. For example, the forest land to be "saved" needs to be owned by a person or group with clear and undisputed title to the land. Without clear legal ownership of the land, an offset credit cannot be legal or effective. After all, if one purported owner of the land accepts payments in order to not cut down the trees, but another purported owner does not and continues to use the land as it sees fit, the environmental purpose of the offset fails.

Shortly after the California-Chiapas-Acre memorandum of understanding was signed, the governor of Chiapas, Juan Sabines, chose to pilot a Chiapas REDD program in his state's Lacandon Jungle. But the Lacandon Jungle exists in a web of institutional ambiguity and conflict. An array of competing interests vie for government, nonprofit, and international development aid amid scarce access to markets, schools, health care, and other services (Howard 1998; Sanchez Perez 2006). Such factors complicated land ownership in ways that ensured little chance of success for Governor Sabines's choice of a REDD pilot site.

Historical and Political Context

The social and political landscape of the Lacandon region of Chiapas is marked by a long history of land tenure ambiguity and conflict. By the middle of the twentieth century, the existing hacienda system had started to crumble. Large landowners had used indebted farm laborers to work their land. In exchange, the laborers were often allowed a portion of land on which to grow their own crops. As cattle ranching replaced this system, the peasants were forced off of the hacienda lands (or fincas, as they are known in Chiapas). These now landless peasants needed new lands on which to live and grow food, and many moved into the Lacandon Jungle to find them.

Over time, more and more people colonized that region of the state as they lost access to hacienda lands, fled religious and other forms of conflict, or were relocated there by the government, which saw the publicly owned lands of the Lacandon Jungle as a "wasteland" at that time. A government program to colonize the jungle offered Chiapas a momentary path of least resistance for solving the problem of landless farmers without breaking up and redistributing large estates owned by powerful families. Populating the jungle with Mexican citizens also served the federal government's interests by strengthening the porous border with Guatemala in the context of long-standing border disputes (De Vos 2002).

But Mexican authorities often gave colonists land that was already occupied. They also gave the same land to multiple new colonist groups. Often the new colonists tried to file title to the land over and over without ever receiving actual title to the land. As a result of these and other problems, twentieth-century colonization of the Lacandon region created ambiguity and conflict over land ownership (De Vos 2002). Consequent government efforts to bring order to conflicting land tenure and use regulations have dragged on for over forty years. Significant progress toward tenure clarity has been made over the last two decades, but it has proceeded piecemeal, usually favoring individuals and communities in a "you scratch my back, I'll scratch yours" relationship with government officials (Ascencio Franco 2008).

To further complicate the political landscape, an uprising by a militant indigenous organization called the Zapatista National Liberation Army took place in 1994. The Zapatistas rallied against racism, oppression, and the inequities of globalization and advocated for autonomy and dignity. Images of peasants holding guns and wearing black masks over their faces circulated the globe and brought international attention to the region. Large landowners were forced off their land by Zapatista militants looking for more land to farm. And both large landowners and peasant farmers alike were displaced in the wake of the violent confrontation between the Zapatistas and the Mexican military. The Zapatista uprising brought an influx of new actors to the Lacandon region:

Government social development programs intended to lure residents away from the Zapatista resistance, international development initiatives, anti-globalization solidarity groups, and many national and international nonprofit organizations (Ronfeldt et al. 1998). The arrival of these new social actors coincided with the arrival of environmental conservation and activism in the region.

Over the last twenty years, the debate about who owns the Lacandon Jungle has been inseparable from the debate about how to care for it sustainably. Government and conservation organizations cite that the jungle holds the greatest biodiversity in Central America. Beginning in 1978, the government quietly created seven Natural Protected Areas in the region (Mendoza and Dirzo 1999). Hunting and farming was limited in these protected areas, even though indigenous peoples already lived, hunted, or farmed there. The change in the status of the lands was made with little consultation with the existing residents. As a result, the reserves deepened existing land tenure conflicts as residents sought continued access to the land (Durand, Figueroa, and Trench 2014).

The most recent era of conflict between indigenous farmers and conservation groups began in 1998, when the worst forest fires in decades swept through the Lacandon Jungle. Conservation organizations blamed the loss of the rainforests on the indigenous people who use fire to clear vegetative waste in their fields and fertilize the soil in order to grow food for their families (Lara Klahr 2000). These claims generated controversy among social justice groups, who argued that the fires were not started by the indigenous farmers but, rather, by natural causes. The fires also led to a government effort to update land-use planning in the Lacandon region in order to better manage natural resources newly recognized as valuable. This newfound value stemmed from a discovery of the importance of natural resources to scientific research and air and water quality protection, as well as from recognition that ecotourism and climate change mitigation projects would make preserving these natural resources profitable.

In 2000, the Mexican government recommitted its land-use planning to removing communities that did not have formal title to the land on which they lived. Indigenous communities were removed from land in protected areas that the government had invited them to colonize thirty to forty years prior. The state negotiated the relocation of some communities to settlements elsewhere, paid others to leave, and forcibly evicted others without resettling them or paying them (Cortez and Paré 2006). The abandoned land was left to regenerate into forests. The government relocation policy provoked pockets of vehement resentment and a belief that conservation organizations were collaborating with military efforts to control the Zapatistas (Castro Soto 2004). Later, after the carbon-offset agreement among California, Chiapas, and Acre had been signed, Governor Sabines pointed to the "success" of these relocation programs in clarifying land tenure and removing people from lands to be preserved, saying that this was key to the viability of REDD in Chiapas. The Sabines administration saw some indigenous communities as obstacles to the forest conservation necessary for REDD.

This history of denying indigenous peoples access to their lands as part of the creation of protected reserves has led to widespread disagreement about both the meaning of sustainability and the appropriate relationship between environmental and social justice goals. In Chiapas civil society, environmentalism is often seen as conflicting with social justice. Environmental management projects there are routinely criticized as designed by outsiders to benefit outsiders and spread capitalist ideology. For example, the U.S. National Institutes of Health supported a project (through the International Cooperative Biodiversity Group–Maya) to develop pharmaceutical products with plants sustainably collected by local indigenous healers. Some in Chiapas saw this project as biopiracy—the theft of local plant knowledge, which is then turned into privately owned intellectual property in the form of pharmaceutical patents (Castro Soto 2004). Other environmental projects are denounced as counterinsurgency efforts to undermine Zapatista militants. For example, some conservation organizations conduct environmental monitoring activities in rebel territories that involve collecting data about where people are and how they use the land.[4] In addition to its utility for conservation activities, this information could be useful to government efforts to suppress insurgent politics. The Mesoamerican Biological Corridor funded by the Global Environment Facility trains and employs locals in conservation monitoring and management and is accused of both biopiracy and covert counterinsurgency. These suspicions also inform local skepticism about new REDD programming.

Launching the REDD Pilot Project

Californians were not the only ones interested in using the jungles of Chiapas for REDD and other projects that would pay local land owners for environmental preservation goals. In 2008, two years prior to the REDD MOU, which is the focus of this chapter, the Chiapas state environmental agency and a group of local, national, and international conservation nonprofits began to promote similar projects to jungle communities there. During the same time period, CONAFOR, the Mexican federal forestry agency (as opposed to the Chiapas state government), began articulating its own plans for forest carbon credit programs, with the Lacandon Jungle once again listed as a potential pilot site.

By the time of the 2010 UN Climate Change Conference in Cancún, Mexico, the Chiapas forests had become the focus of domestic and international attention. A rivalry had developed between Chiapas state and Mexican federal governmental entities, which prompted Governor Sabines to unexpectedly commit to paying jungle residents two thousand pesos per month, beginning in January 2011.[5] After the governor's public commitment before the international press, the Chiapas state environmental agency was obliged to follow through on what they called a pilot REDD program. In doing so, the Sabines administration scrapped years of community outreach and consultation that was intended to form the basis of a viable long-term community payment program to conserve the forests. These actions were not sanctioned by the California Air Resources Board. However, the Sabines administration explicitly linked the agreement with California as part of the impetus behind the pilot Lacandon Jungle REDD program. And, upon Sabines's invitation, members of the California REDD Offsets Working Group (ROW) visited Chiapas to observe the delivery of "REDD payments" to Lacandon Jungle residents. One California-based activist described the links between the California-Chiapas-Acre MOU and the program that was unilaterally implemented by Governor Sabines as follows:

> They were using some public money in Chiapas to pay for the implementation of that program in Chiapas as they awaited funds from California. So California had never promised money to pay for that program, but it was basically what economists call a price signal, where California said,

"If you do things right, there will be money later," and [Sabines] just went ahead and started doing stuff. So to that extent, California technically has no culpability, but in the larger framework, I would say California created the environment where a corrupt governor created a really problematic program with no accountability.

The Sabines monthly payment program was allotted to only three of the over eighty communities living in and around the Lacandon Jungle protected areas, and it was canceled as soon as Sabines left office at the end of 2012. So in the end, his program had little impact on conservation or local communities. The program has been consistently criticized as an opportunistic way for Governor Sabines to leapfrog onto the international stage through the prestige of REDD programming. Proponents of REDD dismissed it as having none of the components of an effective REDD program, while REDD critics pointed to it as a tool that, if fully implemented, would have perpetuated existing inequalities by restricting community access to the natural resources on which they depend.

In Chiapas, international carbon offsets are situated within concerns about access to land and forest products, racism, cultural survival, and rural development. These divergent experiences are the background for conflict over international carbon offsets and illustrate the way in which sustainability efforts are situated within diverse local contexts that shape their meaning and interpretation.

Beyond the Memorandum of Understanding

Since the 2010 announcement of the California-Chiapas-Acre MOU, there has been contentious public debate between opponents and advocates of the inclusion of forest carbon credits in California's cap-and-trade program. The formal aspects of the debate took place in state agency hearings and three public engagement meetings and in the alternative press, where it became especially heated in the comments section of two online environmental publications (Gonzalez [2014]; Mitra 2013).

Under the banner of broadening participation in the debate, ROW hosted three stakeholder engagement fora on three distinct REDD design aspects at prominent California universities. The conversation at all three events was unusually emotional for a technical advisory workshop discussing a policy mechanism little known to the general public. As one participant described a particularly tense exchange that took place at a public workshop over a basic point of fact: "It became another in an endless series of 'he said, she said,' in the REDD debate, where we seem to experience different realities."

Each forum brought together experts for panels, as well as question-and-answer sessions with onsite attendees and online participants. All of the panelists save one were actively engaged in implementing international offset projects. The lone critic invited to speak was Friends of the Earth's Jeff Conant. Leaders from both local and international environmental justice organizations formed a sizable minority at the workshops, although they were not official speakers.

Conant's work, along with the steady public messaging of several local environmental justice organizations, significantly marred the reputation of both REDD and Chiapas as a potential California REDD site (Brunello 2012; Young 2014). However, both avowed REDD opponents and boosters agreed on the importance of the message that California's stance on REDD was sending to the world. Participants from all political perspectives in countless meetings, protests, and press events agreed, "All eyes are on California."

After the workshops, ROW quietly culminated its work with the public release in the summer of 2013 of its recommendations on international REDD. The group recommended a number of legal, policy, and financial reforms to facilitate moving forward with the REDD programming in Chiapas and Acre. Thereafter the group just as quietly disbanded and, as of this writing, the ROW website is no longer available online.

Subsequently, California governor Arnold Schwarzenegger's successor, Jerry Brown, and the California Air Resources Board surpassed Schwarzenegger's state-level California-Chiapas-Acre agreement by establishing a direct collaboration with the Mexican federal government.[6] In July 2014 Brown led a trade mission of over one hundred fifty leaders from California government, business, and academia to broker deals with Mexican president Enrique Peña Nieto and his cabinet. That trip resulted in a new memorandum of understanding between the Brown administration and Mexico's Environment Ministry that emphasized their shared effort to put a price on carbon emissions. In 2014, the California Air Resources Board began holding meetings again to work toward creating an international, sub-national, jurisdiction-wide carbon-offset agreement. The meetings used the work put into the California-Chiapas-Acre MOU as a starting point without restricting future plans to just those locations.

In the aftermath of the widely acknowledged REDD debacle under former Governor Sabines, the Governor's Climate and Forest Task Force, the Mexican Environment Ministry, and the Chiapas state government formed a council of experts, government officials, and non-profit organizations whose purpose was to design a long-term vision of REDD for Chiapas. The group includes major state, national, and international nonprofit organizations, university experts, consultants, state and federal government officials, development professionals, and local and international graduate students. The council's primary focus and responsibility is to align the Mexican federal REDD policy process with state-level realities in Chiapas and to serve as an intermediary between the national policy community and ground-level forest realities. However, the technical council includes few participants from a crucial stakeholder group, forest inhabitants.

Conclusion

State government officials, environmental and environmental justice activists, nonprofits, and forest dwellers in California, Chiapas, and Acre approached the carbon-offset agreement from very different social and political contexts. These contexts diverge both between the states and within them.

This case shows that there are good reasons that people who share broad, pro-environmental values are in deep conflict with each other about how to address climate change. Better understanding the local contexts that influenced responses to the California-Chiapas-Acre MOU has the potential to promote more constructive discourse on these conflicts and on associated policy trade-offs by taking seriously the motivations of REDD opponents and integrating their concerns into the policy-making process. If we understand the local contexts of all these groups, we could create better REDD programs.

Although the state governments in California and Chiapas stumbled in their efforts to understand these important local concerns and the contexts that underpin them, many promoters of international offsets are trying to make their systems accomplish exactly these goals. But activists who have moral concerns about the commodification of nature are unlikely to be satisfied by improving the details of how REDD works. Neither is an impeccably run international offsets program likely to fulfill the desire of California environmental justice activists to see concrete pollution reduction in the low-income communities of color in which they work and live.

The offsets program among California, Chiapas, and Acre has not yet come to pass. But the conflicts about the proposal illustrate broad tensions around designing market-based climate change interventions that exist beyond the limitations of this case. Indeed, REDD and similar market-based environmental interventions have been alternately embraced, adapted, and contested around the globe (Hiraldo and Tanner 2011; McAfee and Shapiro 2010; Milne et al. 2016; Mulyani and Jepson 2013; Shapiro-Garza 2013a, 2013b; Suiseeya and Caplow 2013; Walbott 2014). These conflicts illustrate how environmental interventions are situated in complex sociopolitical environments that shape how they are received. California occupies a key place in the United States and the global economy; the state has the most ambitious climate-change policies in the nation and is widely seen as an environmental trendsetter. The outcome of its policy debates will have significance beyond the state's borders.

Actor Table

Jerry Brown: Governor of California, 2011–present. Inherited California-Chiapas-Acre REDD memorandum of understanding from predecessor Arnold Schwarzenegger, made no public action on the memorandum of understanding. His administration has strengthened environmental cooperation with the Mexican federal government.

California Air Resources Board: California state government agency responsible for air quality and climate policy, including the Global

Warming Solutions Act of 2006 and its cap-and-trade program: The board will decide whether or not to include international forest carbon offsets into cap-and-trade.

CONAFOR: The National Forestry Commission of Mexico (Comisión Nacional Forestal).

Friends of the Earth: International environmental nonprofit actively advocating against REDD and international forest carbon offsets in California.

Governors Climate and Forest Task Force: International non-profit organization formed by affiliates of the Schwarzenegger administration to broker forest carbon-offset agreements between California and other states.

Enrique Peña Nieto: President of Mexico, 2012– present.

REDD Offsets Working Group: Technical advisory group to the three governments that signed the memorandum of understanding (California, Chiapas, and Acre), made up of seasoned leaders from nonprofit organizations, government, and academia advocating for and implementing REDD projects.

Juan Sabines: Governor of Chiapas, Mexico, 2006–2012. His administration brokered the REDD memorandum of understanding with California and Acre and launched the REDD program in Lacandon Jungle, 2011–2012.

Arnold Schwarzenegger: Governor of California, 2003–2011. His administration launched the Governors Climate and Forest Task Force and presided over the REDD memorandum of understanding among California, Chiapas, and Acre.

UN Climate Change Conference: Annual Conference of the Parties (COP) meeting for participants in the UN Framework Convention on Climate Change (UNFCCC), an international environmental treaty adopted in 1992. The 2010 meeting was held in Cancún, Mexico.

NOTES

1   For the purposes of this chapter, we use the term "REDD" interchangeably with forest carbon offsets.

2   After California Governor Schwarzenegger put out a call for partnership with tropical forest governors, representatives from Chiapas and Acre articulated the most compelling proposals, resulting in the agreement between the three states.

3   Specifically, this chapter draws selectively from ninety-four interviews that Tracy Perkins conducted between 2007 and 2015 with California environmental justice activists and their allies. It also draws on her participant observation in California environmental justice activism during the same time, as well as her policy and legal research on environmental justice activists' involvement with the passage and ongoing implementation of the California Global Warming Solutions Act of 2006. Although the majority of her interviews did not speak directly to the MOU we cover here, we use them to help analyze the California context in which the MOU took place. We also use her interviews to understand the logic of California environmental justice activists' opposition to both the MOU and the cap-and-trade program that was implemented as part of the Global Warming Solutions Act, as their opposition to cap-and-trade helps explain their critique of REDD. This chapter also draws on forty-five interviews with farmers, conservationists, social activists, government officials, development practitioners, and policy analysts conducted by Aaron Soto-Karlin between 2008 and 2015 in Chiapas, Mexico. These interviews allow us to analyze how divergent attitudes toward REDD are shaped by social status and power. They also show how a long history of sustainable rural development initiatives affects the way in which REDD is viewed by local practitioners. Additionally, we draw on his twelve interviews, conducted in California between 2012 and 2015, with California agency staff, industry representatives, and analysts of the California-Chiapas-Acre memorandum of understanding. We compare these with Perkins's interviews with environmental justice activists to show how attitudes toward REDD diverge according to position in society.

4   A U.S. Agency for International Development ecotourism project has suffered from similar concerns (Conservation International 2004).

5   This announcement came immediately after federal forestry representatives touted their own forest conservation pilot programs in Chiapas and challenged the ones developed by the state government. Chiapas governor Sabines responded by one-upping the federal representatives. He said that, while they were paying jungle residents one thousand pesos per month for conserving ecosystems, he would pay them two thousand pesos per month and committed to beginning payments in January 2011 (Monfreda 2015).

6   See Osborne, Bellante, and vonHedemann (2014) for a critical overview of REDD programming and its impact on indigenous peoples in Mexico.

BIBLIOGRAPHY

Activist San Diego et al. 2012. "Re: Climate Change Policy—International Forest Offsets in California's Cap and Trade." Posted at Amazon Web Services. https://aws .amazon.com.

Ascencio Franco, Gabriel. 2008. *Regularización de la propiedad en la Selva Lacandona: Cuento de nunca acabar*. Tuxtla Gutiérrez: Universidad de Ciencias Artes de Chiapas.

Assentamento de Produção Agro-Extrativista Limoeiro-Floresta Pública do Antimary et al. 2011. "Letter from the State of Acre: In Defense of Life and the Integrity of the Peoples and Their Territories against REDD and the Commodification of Nature." Accessed May 25, 2015. Posted at *Carbon Trade Watch*. www.carbontradewatch .org.

Brunello, Anthony. 2012. In-person interview with Aaron Soto-Karlin. San Cristóbal de Las Casas, Chiapas, September 29.

Castro Soto, Gustavo. 2004. "El Pukuj Anda Suelto en Montes Azules: Biopiratería y Privatización de la Vida." San Cristóbal de las Casas, Chiapas. June 14, 2004. *EcoPortal.net*. www.ecoportal.net.

Cole, Luke, and Sheila Foster. 2001. *From the Ground Up: Environmental Racism and the Rise of the Environmental Justice Movement*. New York: New York University Press.

Conant, Jeff. 2011a. "Do Trees Grow on Money?" *Earth Island Journal* 26, no. 3. www .earthisland.org.

Conant, Jeff. 2011b. "Global Warming Law Shifts Responsibility from Polluters to Communities." *AlterNet*. www.alternet.org.

Conselho Indigenista Missionário Regional Acre. 2012. "Dossiê Acre: O Acre Que Os Mercadores Da Natureza Escondem." Brasilia: Conselho Indigenista Missionário. www.cimi.org.br., retrieved May 25, 2015.

Conservation International. 2004. "Biodiversity Corridor Planning and Implementation Program." Usumacinta Watershed for Economic Development and Environmental Sustainability. Associate Cooperative Agreement No. 523-A-00-03-00047-00. "Mid-year Report: From October 1, 2003 to March 31, 2004." Tuxtla Gutiérrez, Chiapas: Conservation International and U.S. Agency for International Development. www.pdf.usaid.gov.

Cortez, Carlos, and Luisa Paré. 2006. "Conflicting Rights, Environmental Agendas and the Challenge of Accountability: Social Mobilization and Protected Natural Areas in Mexico." In *Rights, Resources and the Politics of Accountability*, edited by P. Newell and J. Wheeler, 101–121. London: Zed Books.

Council of Traditional Indigenous Doctors and Midwives from Chiapas. 2011. "Communique from the Communities of the Amador Hernandez Region, Monte Azules, Lacandon Jungle." *Climate Connections*. www.climate-connections.org.

Cushing, Lara J., Madeline Wander, Rachel Morello-Frosch, Manuel Pastor, Allen Zhu, and James Sadd. 2016. "A Preliminary Environmental Equity Assessment of

California's Cap-and-Trade Program." Los Angeles: University of Southern California, Dornsife College of Letters, Arts, and Sciences. www.dornsife.usc.edu.

De Vos, Jan. 2002. "Una tierra para sembrar sueños: Historia reciente de la selva
Lacandona, 1950–2000." México, D.F.: Centro de Investigaciones y Estudios Superi-
ores en Antropología Social.

Durand, Leticia, Fernanda Figueroa, and Tim Trench. 2014. "Inclusion and Exclusion in Participation Strategies in the Montes Azules Biosphere Reserve, Chiapas,
Mexico." *Conservation and Society* 12, no. 2:175–189.

Gonzalez, Gloria. [2014]. "Could California Make or Break REDD?" *Forest Carbon
Portal.* www.forestcarbonportal.com.

Hanemann, W. Michael. 2007. "How California Came to Pass AB 32, the Global
Warming Solutions Act of 2006." Berkeley: University of California, Department of
Agricultural and Resource Economics.

Hiraldo, R., and Tanner, T. 2011. "Forest Voices: Competing Narratives over REDD+."
IDS Bulletin 42, no. 3:42–51.

Howard, Philip. 1998. "The History of Ecological Marginalization in Chiapas." *Environmental History* 3, no. 3 (July): 357–377.

Kaswan, Alice. 2014. "Climate Change and Environmental Justice: Lessons from the
California Lawsuits." *San Diego Journal of Climate and Energy Law* 5, no. 1:1–42.

Lara Klahr, Marco. 2000. "La Lacandona Devastacion: Chiapas sin Reservas. Incendios
e invasiones consumen la selva." *El Universal*, May 18. www.eluniversal.com.

London, Jonathan, Alex Karner, Jule Sze, Dana Rowan, Gerardo Gambirazzio, and
Deb Niemeier. 2013. "Racing Climate Change: Collaboration and Conflict in
California's Global Climate Change Policy Arena." *Global Environmental Change*
23:791–99.

McAfee, Kathy. 2013. "Including Offsets from Latin America in California's Cap-and-
Trade Plan Is a Bad Idea." Tucson: University of Arizona, Public Political Ecology
Lab. www.arizona.edu.

McAfee, Kathleen, and Elizabeth N. Shapiro. 2010. "Payments for Ecosystem Services
in Mexico: Nature, Neoliberalism, Social Movements, and the State." *Annals of the
Association of American Geographers* 100, no. 3:1–21.

Mendoza, E., and R. Dirzo. 1999. "Deforestation in Lacandonia (Southeast Mexico):
Evidence for the Declaration of the Northernmost Tropical Hotspot." *Biodiversity
and Conservation* 8:1621–1641.

Milne, S., M. Milne, F. Nurfatriani, and L. Tacconi. 2016. "How Is Global Climate
Policy Interpreted on the Ground? Insights from the Analysis of Local Discourses
about Forest Management and REDD+ in Indonesia." *Ecology and Society* 21, no.
2:6.

Mitra, Nandini. 2013. "California's Interest in Overseas Carbon Offsets Schemes Makes
Some Greens See Red." *Earth Island Journal*, July 24. www.earthisland.org.

Monfreda, Chad. 2015. "Green Economy Governance: Transforming States and Markets through the Global Forest Carbon Trade in California and Chiapas." PhD diss.,
Arizona State University.

Mulyani, M., and P. Jepson. 2013. "REDD+ and Forest Governance in Indonesia: A Multistakeholder Study of Perceived Challenges and Opportunities." *Journal of Environment and Development* 22, no. 3: 261–283.

The No REDD Platform and Rising Tide et al. 2011. "Open Letter of Concern to the International Donor Community about the Diversion of Existing Forest Conservation and Development Funding to REDD+." World Rainforest Movement. http://wrm.org.uy.

Osborne, Tracey, Laurel Bellante, and Nicolena vonHedemann. 2014. "Indigenous Peoples and REDD+: A Critical Perspective." November. Cusco: Indigenous People's Biocultural Climate Change Assessment Initiative; Tucson: University of Arizona, Public Political Ecology Lab.

Pastor, Manuel, Rachel Morello-Frosch, James Sadd, and Justin Scoggins. 2013. "Risky Business: Cap-and-Trade, Public Health, and Environmental Justice." In *Urbanization and Sustainability: Linking Urban Ecology, Environmental Justice and Global Environmental Change*, edited by Christopher G. Boone and Michail Fragkias, 75–94. New York: Springer.

Perkins, Tracy. 2015. "From Protest to Policy: The Political Evolution of California Environmental Justice Activism, 1980s–2010s." PhD diss., University of California, Santa Cruz.

Pulido, Laura. 1996. "A Critical Review of the Methodology of Environmental Racism Research." *Antipode* 28, no. 2:142–159.

Rechtschaffen, Clifford, Eileen Guana, and Catherine A. O'Neill. 2009. *Environmental Justice: Law, Policy, and Regulation*. Durham, NC: Carolina Academic Press.

Ronfeldt, David, John Arquilla, Graham Fuller, and Melissa Fuller. 1998. *The Zapatista "Social Netwar" in Mexico*. Santa Monica, CA: RAND Corporation. www.rand.org.

Sanchez, Eufemia Landa. 2012. "Statement Opposing REDD Offsets Read to Governors' Climate Change Task Force in Chiapas, Mexico." Mexico: San Cristóbal de Las Casas.

Sanchez Perez, Hector Javier. 2006."Excluded People, Eroded Communities: Realizing the Right to Health in Chiapas, Mexico." Boston: Physicians for Human Rights; Campeche: El Colegio de la Frontera Sur.

Schwarzenegger, Arnold, Gov., Gov. Arnóbio Marques de Almeida Júnior, and Gov. Juan Sabines Guerrero. 2010. "Memorandum of Understanding on Environmental Cooperation between the State of Acre of the Federative Republic of Brazil, the State of Chiapas of the United Mexican States, and the State of California of the United States of America." Accessed May 22, 2015. Boulder, CO: Governors' Climate and Forests Taskforce. www.gcftaskforce.org.

Shapiro-Garza, Elizabeth. 2013a. "Contesting Market-Based Conservation: Payments for Ecosystem Services as a Surface of Engagement for Rural Social Movements in Mexico." *Human Geography* 6, no. 1:134–150.

Shapiro-Garza, E. 2013b. "Contesting the Market-Based Nature of Mexico's National Payments for Ecosystem Services Programs: Four Sites of Articulation and Hybridization." *Geoforum* 46:5–15.

Shonkoff, Seth B., Rachel Morello-Frosch, Manuel Pastor, and James Sadd. 2009. "Minding the Climate Gap: Environmental Health and Equity Implications of Climate Change Mitigation Policies in California." *Environmental Justice* 2 (2009): 173–77.

Suiseeya, K. R. Marion and S. Caplow. 2013. "In Pursuit of Procedural Justice: Lessons from an Analysis of 56 Forest Carbon Project Designs." *Global Environmental Change* 23:968–979.

Sze, Julie, Gerardo Gambirazzio, Alex Karner, Dana Rowan, Jonathan London, and Deb Niemeier. 2009. "Best in Show? Climate and Environmental Justice Policy in California." *Environmental Justice* 2, no. 4:179–184.

Wallbott, L. 2014. "Indigenous peoples in UN REDD+ negotiations: 'Importing power' and lobbying for rights through discursive interplay management." *Ecology and Society* 19, no. 1:21.

Wara, Michael W., and David G. Victor. 2008. "A Realistic Policy on International Carbon Offsets." Working Paper no. 74. Palo Alto, CA: Stanford University Program on Energy and Sustainable Development.

Young, Stanley. 2014. In-person interview with Aaron Soto-Karlin. Sacramento, CA, June 6.

5

Situating Urban Drought Resilience

Theory, Practice and Sustainability Science

LAWRENCE BAKER

Six hundred years ago, the accepted knowledge was that the sun revolved around the Earth. Then in 1543, Copernicus proved that it was the other way around: The Earth revolved around the sun. The heliocentric theory became conventional wisdom, changing our cosmology forever. Today we are going through another cosmological rupture, as we discover that humans do not reign over nature but are an integral part of ecosystems; humans both alter ecosystems and are affected by these alterations. Nowhere is this perspective more important than in thinking about the resilience of cities to droughts, with droughts being conceptualized not only as a hydrologic phenomenon but also as a socioecological problem. From this perspective, building resilience to urban droughts requires both adaptive physical *and* social infrastructures.

The idea of *anthropocentric ecosystems* was first presented in the same publication that defined the word *ecosystem* (Tansley 1935), but the concept was largely forgotten for the next half century, during which ecologists nearly always focused on natural ecosystems. To the extent that humans were included in ecosystem studies they were invariably considered in the context of impacts. Moreover, nearly all ecological studies were conducted in the hinterlands, rarely in cities. This narrative changed abruptly with the inception of two major urban ecosystem studies in the National Science Foundation's Long-Term Ecological Research Program (LTER) in 1998. These two programs, the Baltimore Ecosystem Study (BES-LTER) in Maryland (U.S.) and the Central Arizona-Phoenix Ecosystem Study (CAP-LTER) study in Phoenix, Arizona, have been catalysts for rethinking "the urban." As a member of the founding team of CAP-LTER eighteen years ago, I have argued the validity of urban ecosystems research and have observed the transition of the phrase "urban ecosystems" from an oxymoron to a valid focus of research, one that enriches ecology generally. We also now speak of *human well-being* without evoking groans from audiences of ecologists. Many of us who study urban ecosystems now focus not only on the influence of human actions on the environment but also equally on the reciprocal effects of these actions on human well-being, especially the differentiation of impacts on various social groups. For example, in Phoenix, wealthy households benefit from more trees and greater vegetation diversity (Hope et al. 2003); the poor often live in the hottest parts of cities and are at greater risk from heat waves (Harlan et al. 2006). This research often involves interdisciplinary teams that have become imbued with the idea of transdisciplinary research, research based on "interpenetrating epistemologies" (Gibbons et al. 1994), to approach socioecological questions, not always comfortably (Baker 2006). We are temporally situated at the beginning of a "Copernicus moment"; within a decade or two our cosmology will shift to the point that consideration of the ecosystem function of cities will become deeply embedded into the thought processes of citizens and a well-accepted point of discussion in city council meetings.

This chapter examines one vital part of urban ecosystems, the *water environment*, in particular, the idea of urban drought resilience as a way to advance the integration of theory-driven ecosystem science with sustainability science, a field driven by practical problems (Clark 2007). Because our knowledge regarding urban drought resilience has received very little study, the chapter develops several hypotheses regarding drought resilience and proposes a research agenda to address them. My perspective is informed by my extensive research in the dry/rich city of Phoenix, Arizona, and a brief but enlightening experience in the dry/poor city of Ouagadougou, Burkina Faso, where I served as a Fulbright Senior Specialist. Both cities have extremely dry seasons with maximum daily maximum temperatures greater than 30°C, but the average per capita income of the Phoenix area is seven times higher than that of Ouagadougou (US $42,000 vs. US $615). This chapter is thus situated in these two extreme case studies.

The Water Environment of Cities

Before exploring the topic of urban drought, we need to understand the urban hydrologic cycle and our relationship to it. Precipitation within the city boundary is rarely sufficient for urban water needs; hence the urban water environment generally extends far beyond the urban area itself. This *hydroshed* includes not only the natural topographic watershed but also watersheds outside the natural drainage area, connected to the city by canals, aqueducts, or pipes. Because the natural flow of water from watersheds rarely matches urban water demand temporally, natural lakes or dammed reservoirs are used to store water, which is released as needed. Water may be stored in reservoirs along the river (in-stream reservoirs) or diverted to off-stream reservoirs, which may be located some distance from the river. Cities often withdraw groundwater from underground aquifers, either those underlying the city or those located outside the city boundaries, again transporting water via constructed conduits. Aquifers are composed of porous materials— sand, gravel, or porous rock—with water contained in the open spaces (pores). Cities often prefer to use groundwater rather than surface water because it is often less polluted and can be used without extensive treatment. Surface water always requires treatment for municipal use. (See fig. 5.1.)

Water exits cities by three pathways: evapotranspiration, surface drainage, and groundwater recharge. Evapotranspiration includes transpiration (the water that is evaporated through the leaves of plants) and evaporation, which occurs from lakes, wetlands, impervious surfaces, and cooling towers. Water moves from cities to surface water via surface drainage (stormwater pipes, ditches, and streams), sanitary sewers (for sewage only), or combined sewers (which transport both sewage and runoff). Urban water can also move downward into aquifers, recharging them and, in some cases, polluting them. In arid lands, wastewater is sometimes recycled, mainly for irrigation of crops or urban landscapes.

The hydrologic system of a city is therefore a composite of natural and engineered components. Governance, economics, lifestyle, and customs also affect the urban hydrologic cycle. Thus we must think of the stressor "drought" as not merely a physical phenomenon but as a socioecological phenomenon (Kallis 2008).

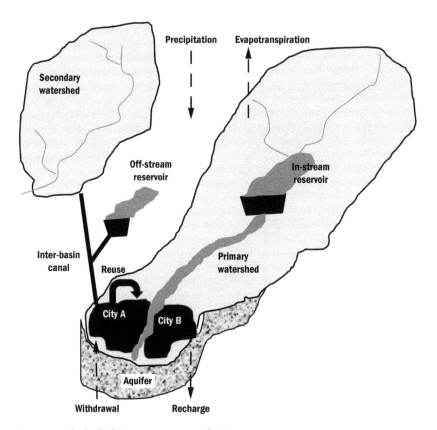

Figure 5.1. The hydrologic environment of cities.

The capacity to withstand a drought can be separated into two processes: resilience and robustness. *Robustness* is the capacity to maintain constancy during environmental stress, whereas *resilience* is the capacity of a system to recover from stress. Read (2005) provides this visualization: A solid tree (sycamore) that withstands increasing wind without bending but then snaps when a critical wind speed is reached is robust but not resilient. By contrast, the flexible palm, which bends further and further as the wind increases, but then returns to its vertical position when the wind abates, is resilient. Five scenarios in figure 5.2 illustrate the interrelationship between these terms. A city might be robust to drought over the short term if it withdraws water from both surface reservoirs and groundwater. Even with no water conservation, water can be supplied without citizens even noticing the drought, until both sources

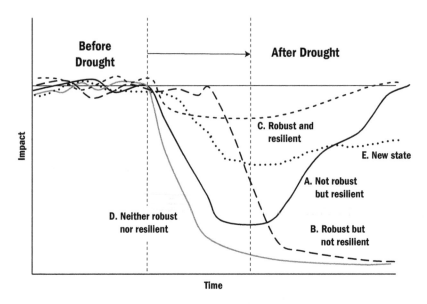

Figure 5.2. The relationship between resilience and robustness in relation to drought stress.

are exhausted. At this point, having taken no other measures, it will collapse (curve A). Another city might lack great robustness—perhaps it might be unable to afford the investment of large reservoirs—but be quite resilient. Economic diversity, strong governmental conservation programs, and laws requiring equitable distribution would typically confer resilience to drought. This city (curve B) might falter under water stress but would recover to its original functionality as the drought diminishes. A third city (curve C) is both robust and resilient. It might experience little social or economic impact from a drought. A fourth city might be utterly unprepared for a drought, lacking both robustness and resilience (curve D); such a city might undergo severe disruption and even collapse. Note that I am using the engineering definition of resilience, with the resilient city returning to its original state. One might also envision drought resilience in the ecological sense (Cadenasso and Pickett 2018), with the city returning to an *alternative state*. For example, a modern U.S. city with profligate water consumption might shift to an alternative state where water is conserved, greatly reducing per capita consumption (curve E).

Urban Droughts as a Destabilizing Stress

One reason for focusing on drought as an ecological stressor is that droughts have the capacity to severely disrupt the functioning of cities. The decline of the Akkadian Empire in Mesopotamia, ca. 2200 BCE (Cullen and deMenocal 2000); Mayan cities in the first millennium CE (Haug et al. 2003); Ankor, Cambodia, ca. 1200 CE (Buckley et al. 2010); and perhaps the Hohokum settlements in Arizona (Bayman 2001) have been attributed (with varying degrees of evidence) to increased aridity and increased climatic variability, often with droughts punctuated with flooding. In all of these cases, climate change alone was never the sole cause of decline of any city; instead, climate change may have simply accelerated incipient decline, a tipping point toward demise.

Droughts have remained an environmental hazard into the twenty-first century and may become a greater hazard in the future. The impact of droughts depends on the region of the globe affected. In Africa and Asia, hundreds of millions of people have been affected by drought since 1970, but far fewer in other continents. Droughts are deadliest in Africa, having killed nearly 700,000 since 1970 (see table 5.1, summarized from Kallis [2008]). In wealthier countries, droughts cause few deaths but greater economic damage, at least in absolute terms.

Understanding how droughts affect cities is becoming increasingly important because the impact of urban droughts is likely to grow throughout the next century. If predictions of regional climate patterns are correct, much of the world is likely to be hotter and drier, and hydrologic cycles are likely to become more variable (Intergovernmental Panel on Climate Change 2001). To exacerbate the problem, global cities are

TABLE 5.1. Impact of global droughts, 1970–2007. Summarized from Kallis (2008).

	Africa	Asia	South and Central America	North America	Europe
Number of disasters	222	226	87	12	36
Millions affected	310	1,493	61	0.03	14
Cost, million U.S. $	6	30	9	6,500	20
Deaths	672,647	5,381	0	2	60

growing rapidly and often haphazardly. From 2000 to 2030, the global urban population is projected to increase by 74 percent, from 2.9 billion to 5.0 billion (United Nations 2006). Nearly all of this urbanization is occurring in the Global South, much of it in poor, arid regions, which are most vulnerable to climate warming. Moreover, much of this urbanization is occurring in peri-urban "unorganized areas" with minimal municipal infrastructure, making their populations especially vulnerable to drought.

Finally, per capita wealth is increasing globally, and wealthier citizens use more water. A hierarchy of water needs, modeled after Maslow's hierarchy of needs (Maslow 1970) illustrates how increasing water availability satisfies human needs (fig. 5.3). At the base of the triangle, humans need only about 3–4 L/day for bare survival (L = liters). Gleick (1998) argued that the minimum water requirement for human subsistence is 50 L/day, sufficient for drinking, bathing, laundry, and cooking. Moving up the triangle, to get beyond the level of subsistence, paid work is needed, and much urban production—such as food processing, energy production, and manufacturing—requires water. Production provides taxes, allowing collection of sewage, and a paycheck may allow a family to buy a

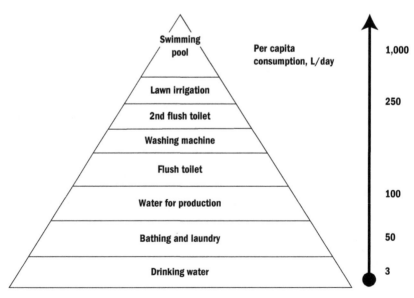

Figure 5.3. Hierarchy of water needs, modeled after Maslow (1970). L = liters.

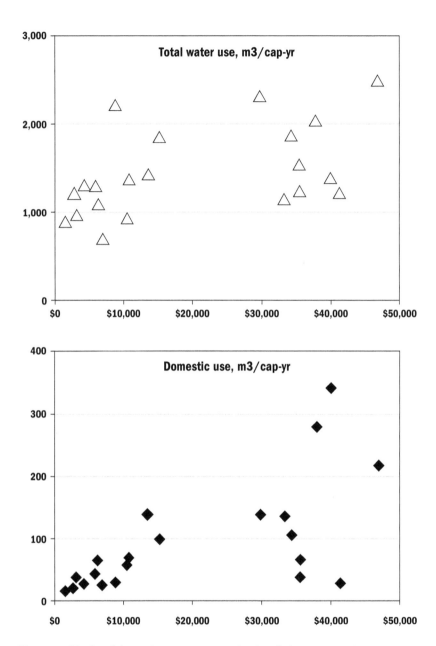

Figure 5.4. Total and domestic water consumption in relation to per capita income, (US $) for twenty-one countries. *Top*: Total per capita water use, with each country represented by an open triangle; *Bottom*: Domestic per capita water use, with each country represented by a solid diamond. Source: Water consumption data are from Hoekstra and Chapagain (2007); income data are from Central Intelligence Agency (2012).

toilet to connect to the sewer. With a bit more money, one can purchase a washing machine; a bit more allows a second bathroom. In wealthy countries, lawn irrigation modestly improves well-being and greatly increases water consumption. In arid cities of the United States, outside irrigation can account for two-thirds of municipal water use. Finally, at the peak of the triangle, floating in a swimming pool might allow one to achieve complete self-actualization, or at least to relax. In ascending the triangle, per capita water use increases from a few liters per day to roughly 1,000 L/day in some arid cities of the American Southwest (Mayer et al. 1999).

As one might expect, both total and domestic per capita water use increases with increasing per capita income among countries. Domestic consumption increases for the reasons discussed above. Total water consumption, which is generally dominated by the agricultural and energy sectors, also increases as wealthier countries increase their consumption of meat and use of energy. Hence, an increasingly wealthy world translates to an increasingly thirsty world, placing additional stress on water resources. The exceptions are a few countries in Europe (the Netherlands, Germany, United Kingdom, and France), which have domestic water consumption rates comparable with countries having far lower per capita income (see cluster at lower right in Figure 5.4).

In summary, urban droughts are more likely to occur and more likely to have severe impact on human well-being because of the conflation of three trends: (1) continued global warming, especially in the Global South; (2) growing urban populations, especially in poor countries; and (3) increasing per capita wealth, which increases water consumption.

Can We Predict the Resilience of Cities to Drought?

The central hypothesis of this chapter is that the resilience of cities to future droughts can be understood based on biophysical, economic, and social factors. A geography colleague of mine, Michael Goldman, once joked, "If you want to develop a water system, hire a sociologist." There is some wisdom in this statement, but as an engineer, my rejoinder would be, "You can't drink equity." Engineers are still needed, not only to build pipes and dams but also to harness the technology that can empower citizens to manage their hydrologic well-being (Baker 2013).

Finding ways to develop resilience to urban droughts requires transdisciplinary teams that include not only engineers and sociologists but also hydrologists, political scientists, and economists, among others.

Research to test this hypothesis would advance our theoretical understanding of urban ecosystems, but it would also have tremendous practical application, providing cities with the understanding to develop drought resilience. This chapter presents three specific hypotheses regarding resilience of urban systems to drought and a research program to test them. Because urban drought resilience is in part situated by wealth, I develop several contrasts between wealthy cities and poorer ones.

Condition of the Hydrologic Environment

A first hypothesis is that *the current condition of the hydrologic environment is a good predictor of a city's resilience to drought.* In other words, we can predict (in part) the resilience of a city to an incipient drought simply by looking at its current hydrologic (physical) environment, both the natural and engineered components.

Condition of Aquifers

One key predictor would be the condition of the aquifers that underlie a city and those located outside the city that are tapped to supply water to the city. Many cities withdraw more water from their aquifers than can be sustained by recharge, even under normal hydrologic conditions. This *overdraft* of urban aquifers, which lowers groundwater levels, is probably the rule rather than the exception. In the United States, urban regions that have severely depleted their aquifers include not only those in arid lands—like Phoenix, Tucson, and Las Vegas—but also those in temperate regions, including Chicago, Illinois; Memphis, Tennessee; Houston, Texas; and Baton Rouge, Louisiana (Bartolino and Cunningham 2003). Internationally, Mexico City (Romero-Lankao 2011), Damascus (Mahayni 2013), and Beijing (Qui 2010) are examples of cities that have severely depleted their aquifers. During a prolonged drought, when surface water supplies are limited, cities often increase their use of groundwater, accelerating aquifer depletion, sometimes lowering groundwater levels by hundreds of feet. A city might survive one drought by overdrafting its aquifer, but unless there is a very deliberate effort to recharge the depleted aquifer after a drought ends, resilience to a subsequent drought will be weakened.

Further weakening resilience, many aquifers are polluted, mainly with salt, nitrate, and bacteria. In many coastal cities, salt contamination occurs by seawater intrusion, which happens when seawater flows into aquifers that are pumped down. Examples include Miami, Florida, and the Gaza Strip. The addition of salts to municipal sewage by households (especially water softeners) and industries can elevate salt levels in wastewater to the point that it can no longer be used for crop irrigation, often a major use of recycled wastewater in arid regions (Miyamoto et al. 2001; Thompson et al. 2006). Salts in irrigation water are further concentrated by evaporation, sometimes increasing the salinity of the remaining water by 50–75 percent. If this water infiltrates through soils, it can contaminate groundwater. For inland cities in arid climates, salt can accumulate in both groundwater and soil; two-thirds of the salt entering the Phoenix, Arizona, urban region accumulates within the basin (Baker, Brazel, and Westerhoff 2004). Alternatively, salts that are not leached salinize soils, sometimes making them unsuitable for plant growth. Even in wealthy cities, removal of salt from source waters used for municipal water supply by reverse osmosis is expensive; for inland cities, the issue of disposing of concentrated brines is an unresolved problem.

Nitrate contamination of aquifers, often the result of heavy agricultural fertilization, becomes an urban problem when cities expand into areas that have been farmed (Xu, Baker, and Johnson 2007). Nitrate contamination of aquifers is also common in cities that use cesspools and latrines, a common situation in sub-Saharan Africa (Wakida and Lerner 2005). In these cases, the origin of the nitrate is human excretion, which leaches downward. Nitrate contamination in urban aquifers can easily reach levels that exceed the World Health Organization's health guideline of 50 mg NO_3/L (mg = milligram; World Health Organization 2017). Fecal bacteria also contaminate urban groundwater, allowing the spread of cholera, typhoid, and others gastrointestinal diseases. Bacterial contamination occurs mainly when there is a source at the surface (septic systems, latrines, etc.), the distance from the land surface to the groundwater is short, and soils are permeable.

Condition of Water Infrastructure

As noted earlier, cities often have vast water infrastructure, which may include considerable redundancies to reduce the impact of droughts. This may include multiple reservoirs, sometimes in watersheds that are located at some distance from each other and from the cities they serve. This may lessen the impact of a regional drought because water can be imported from more distant sources that may not be experiencing drought. Many urban regions have the capacity to use both surface water and ground water, allowing them to switch sources as needed. For cities located near one another, cross-connections between their water systems allow uninterrupted supply of water if either city's primary water source becomes unavailable.

On the negative side, poor infrastructure can reduce a city's resilience to drought. Globally, 95 percent of urban dwellers have access to improved drinking water, and 81 percent have access to improved sanitation, but these values fall to less than 50 percent for cities in many African countries (World Health Organization 2006). Many urban dwellers who have no access to clean water or limited access (e.g., community wells located at some distance from homes) have access to several other sources of water, including private wells, informal community wells, and tanker vendors (Collignon and Vézina 2000). These may confer some resilience advantage by providing alternative sources (even for those who normally have access to community water supply), but because these sources may be contaminated, using them may increase the spread of waterborne disease, which would diminish resilience.

The lack of efficient use of water may increase drought impacts. In many cities, water distribution systems leak; in a study of ten African cities, leakage from water pipes ranged from 13 percent to 50 percent (Collignon and Vézina 2000), a situation that contributes to water scarcity even without a hydrologic drought. The lack of capacity to meter and bill water properly also contributes to inefficient use of water. Finally, wastewater can be recycled, mainly for irrigation, thereby extending a city's water supply, but if wastewater is not properly treated, its use for crop irrigation can spread disease.

On the downstream side of cities, many cities discharge untreated, or minimally treated, sewage to rivers, lakes, and estuaries because they lack modern wastewater treatment facilities. The UN Development Program (2006) estimates that 80 percent of the sewage collected in developing countries is untreated. Even relatively wealthy cities like Buenos Aires and Mexico City treat less than 10 percent of their sewage (Romero-Lankao 2011). Discharge of untreated or minimally treated wastewater causes oxygen depletion in rivers below cities, sometimes severe enough to kill fish and aquatic life and cause economic harm to fisherman. This effect is intensified during droughts because decreased flows reduce the capacity of surface waters to assimilate organic pollution. Oxygen depletion in rivers can be entirely eliminated with modern wastewater treatment systems.

Understanding the hydrologic condition of a city with respect to drought resilience would be based on a dynamic water balance. Conceptually, this is simple, but implementation of a complete, dynamic water balance is complex and expensive, with some knowledge gaps. Even in the United States few cities have developed this level of knowledge of their water systems to accurately forecast conditions that would lead to water stress. We are, however, rapidly developing new ways to collect, store, and process hydrologic information, which may lead to a revolution in water management. For example, the Gravity Recovery and Climate Experiment (GRACE) satellites, launched in 2002, have enabled a first-time global assessment of groundwater resources (Famiglietti 2014).

Capacity of Water Governance

Water governance is nearly always fragmented across spatial scales ranging from municipalities to transnational watersheds of major rivers. In addition to traditional, hierarchical units of governance (municipalities, states, nations), specialized units of government are often developed for various aspects of water management. As with other types of *polycentric* governance, advantages may be conferred at multiple levels (Ostrom 2010). This observation leads to a second hypothesis: *Scaling of water governance to achieve drought resilience must correspond to physical (hydrologic) scales in time and space.* Some countries have hierarchical national water government systems, with national-level water resources agencies and regional authorities, whereas others have largely decentralized water governance. South Africa, one of the few countries whose constitution calls for "right to sufficient water," is an example of a country with a highly structured water governance system, with a well-defined hierarchy from the municipal level to the Ministry of Water and Forests (James 2003). In contrast, the United States is an example of a country with virtually no federal water governance to manage water allocation on non-federal lands; each state has its own laws regarding appropriation of ground and surface water, and the federal government intervenes only through the organization of interstate compacts among states, done on an ad hoc basis.

Water at the scale of urban regions is sometimes managed by general-purpose units of governance (e.g., municipalities) and sometimes managed by special units of governance designed particularly for governance of water or some aspect of water management. These water governance units may supply water, collect and treat sewage, or (less commonly) both. They may sometimes encompass multiple cities and/or operate reservoir and canal systems, and they often derive their funding from either taxes or fees. In many countries, special units of water governance also are formed to manage groundwater, surface water, or both. An example is Kenya, which has a well-developed hierarchy of water governance, with local water service boards in charge of water and sewage at the regional level (Osinde 2007). Others arise during periods of water crisis, like the active management areas in Arizona (developed by the 1980 Groundwater Act), which were formed to reverse the profound overdraft of groundwater that had been occurring (Holway 2009). Others may have more general functions (like those managing drinking water supply) that can adapt their mission to respond to a drought. One would predict that specialized structures for water governance would be more effective at managing water during a drought than conventional (general purpose) units of governance for several reasons: (1) They often transcend multiple conventional units of government, reducing fragmentation and aligning governance with hydrological units; (2) they provide value at each level of governance; (3) their function is often directly financed, often in sustainable ways (like fees for service); and (4) they are more likely to have specialized water expertise.

At a larger scale, 260 freshwater basins that cross national boundaries are governed in part by 157 treaties negotiated in the last half century (Wolf 2007; Program in Water Conflict Management and

Transformation 2012). Water allocation (along with infrastructure issues) is one of the main causes of international tensions surrounding international water conflicts, yet most treaties do not explicitly address drought (Giordano and Wolf 2003). McCaffrey (2003) discusses four mechanisms that international treaties could use to gain the flexibility needed to address hydrologic changes: (1) Develop flexible "framework" agreements; (2) use short, renewable treaty periods; (3) make explicit provisions for drought; and (4) develop a joint institutional mechanism to make adjustments. Refining these agreements to better address water allocation during drought may increase resilience to droughts, both by making allocations clearer and by reducing the potential for political tensions among countries.

Finally, non-governmental actors have a major influence on water management, especially in the Global South. Probably the most significant of these is the World Bank, which uses its capacity to provide funding as a mechanism for shaping water policies, including dam building and water privatization (Budds and McGranahan 2003), often with mixed or clearly negative effects (Budds and McGranahan 2003; Goldman 2005).

Capacity of Governance for Adaptation

Whatever the scaling of governance, there is varying capacity of governance units to manage urban water systems in ways that are resilient. This leads to the third hypothesis: *Drought resilience depends upon the capacity of governments to adapt to hydrologic change.* This can be broken down into two corollaries: (1) Governments may not have the administrative capacity to organize and provide feedback; and (2) they may not have the economic capacity to respond.

Capacity to Organize and Generate Feedback

One of the most important aspects of developing drought resilience would be the capacity to generate *feedback* so the condition of the hydrologic system is well understood by all parties involved (units of government, non-governmental organizations, local community organizations, and citizens). A key element of *participatory governance* is the provision of hydrologic feedback to stakeholders. This would include measurements of hydrologic parameters, such as river flows and groundwater pumping rates, water use by water consumption sectors, and surveys and other methods to determine the quality of water service to customers. The actual collection of data is probably the easiest part of a feedback system, except perhaps in the very poorest cities. A more challenging process is making this data *transparent*, so that it can be used for decision making by multiple entities. Transparency requires making data *accessible*—which is to say, comprehensible—to non-specialists. This is a problem even in the most modern cities. A second obstacle is political impediments. For various reasons, political leaders may not want hydrologic information to be widely available. In Israel, for example, some hydrologic data had been a state secret to avoid sharing it with Palestinians (Lonergan 1999).

Although the virtues of civic participation in governance have been debated, likely virtues with respect to drought resilience are that civic participation can increase trust and knowledge, allowing improved decision making (Botes and van Rensburg 2000; Innes and Booher 2004). Closely related is the development of a long-term drought resilience plan, ideally an articulation of a broad strategic vision for the urban region. For a city in the Global South, such a plan might, for example, consider the type of water distribution in peri-urban "unorganized areas," quantities of water to be delivered, the extent of centralization of sewage treatment, and a plan to secure water to accommodate population expansion. For many urban regions, overuse of water has resulted in "second-order scarcity" that threatens water supplies even in normal hydrologic periods. Few urban regions have well-articulated plans to provide for resilience to prolonged drought. In the Global South, multi-sector, community-level water planning may be more realistic that Western-style, top-down planning. Phadke (2002) presents an example of intensive collaboration among local farmers, two non-governmental organizations, and the Indian government that led to greatly improved decision making regarding a local dam, thereby alleviating the impact of long-term drought.

Finally, water allocation law would shape drought resilience—although not always in a positive way. As an example, the *prior appropriations* doctrine, codified in arid states within the United States, allocates water on the basis of "first in time, first in right." As a result, the allocation of water is tiered based on the time at which the allocation was made. Hence, a modest drought might have major impacts on those holding *junior* rights and virtually none for those holding *senior* rights. In Phoenix, Arizona, this type of water allocation would cause severe spatial inequities of water distribution during a drought (Boline, Seetharamb, and Pompeii 2010). Dinar, Rosegrant, and Meinzen-Dick (1997) reviewed various approaches to water allocation (marginal cost pricing, public, user-based, and market allocation), concluding that no one mechanism is appropriate for all circumstances.

Capacity to Respond

A city's water management could be designed to provide feedback but may still not be resilient because it does not have the economic capacity to prepare for a drought or to respond once it occurs. A poor city may not be able to extract water from a distant watershed, repair its water mains to prevent leakage, or collect and treat its wastewater to prepare it for reuse. An analysis by the World Bank (Banerjee and Morella 2011) showed that sub-Saharan African countries currently invest 1.2 percent of their gross domestic product in water and sanitation infrastructure, but they would have to invest 3.5 percent to meet the UN's Millennium Development Goals; low-income, non-fragile African nations invest 1.1 percent of their gross domestic product but would have to invest 7.1 percent to meet the Millennium Development Goals. This mismatch between needs and current investment suggests that external funding would be needed to fill this gap.

A Research Agenda to Understand Urban Drought Resilience

Despite rapid global urbanization, increasing per capita water consumption, and the growing threat of global warming—all factors that point toward greater vulnerability to urban drought—there has been remarkably little systematic research to understand resilience to urban drought. In part, this is because urban drought resilience is a "wicked problem" that would require an unprecedented level of transdisciplinary research to solve. Finding solutions would require a wide range of research approaches, a major integration effort, a long study period, and an unusually large research investment. This level of integration requires tools that transcend disciplinary knowledge—such as systems dynamics models (SDMs), which have the ability to represent complex systems as they change over time—with the capacity to include numerous subsystems and feedback among the subsystems, including non-linearities (Sterman 2001). Beyond integrating the work of research across disciplines into a modeling framework, SDM has also been used as a tool for public and stakeholder engagement for water resources planning (Stave 2002; Tidwell et al. 2004; Welling 2011). For example, one could use a SDM to ask the question, How many people are likely to get cholera if a specified percentage of the peri-urban population withdraws water from private wells when the community water supply fails? or, What happens to water supply if an international treaty is modified to change water allocation among countries? In practice, using an SDM would be somewhat akin to playing the popular *Sim City* video game of the mid-1990s.

Research at this scale would be slow and expensive but would generate a suite of tools that cities could use to develop resilience to drought. Among these would be the development of quantifiable metrics of resilience, including metrics of equity, following the approaches used by economists (Stiglitz, Sen, and Fitoussi 2009). The broader impact of this research could be prevention of much human misery that might otherwise accompany rapid urbanization of mostly poor cities in the regions of the globe most likely to experience extensive climate warming during the next century.

Conclusions

The resilience of cities to drought is weakened by global climate change, rapid urbanization, and growing per capita wealth and water consumption. These drivers are especially strong in cities of the Global South. Drought is not simply a hydrologic phenomenon but a socioecological phenomenon as well. The hydrologic status—the condition of aquifers and water infrastructure—is important, but governance is equally important in building resilience. Our capacity to acquire, store, and utilize hydrologic data has improved greatly in recent years, but this capacity has not yet been translated into the development of feedback loops to inform governance. Poor cities must also have the capacity to respond, which in some situations may require external infusions of money. Research focused on urban drought resilience has been largely lacking. Such research, which would require a transdisciplinary approach involving both biophysical and social scientists, could provide knowledge and guidance to cities that seek to develop resilient physical and social infrastructures to withstand urban droughts.

REFERENCES

Baker, L. 2006. Perils and pleasures of multidisciplinary research. *Urban Ecosystems* 9:45–47.

Baker, L. 2013. Hegemonic concepts and water governance from a scientific-engineering perspective. In *Critical Perspectives on Contemporary Water Governance: Scarcity, Privatization and Participation*, edited by L. Harris, J. Goldin, and C. Sneddon. New York: Routledge.

Baker, L., A. Brazel, and P. Westerhoff. 2004. Environmental consequences of rapid urbanization in warm, arid lands: Case study of Phoenix, Arizona (USA). In *The Sustainable City II*, edited by N. Marchettini, C. Brebbia, E. Tiezzi, and L. C. Wadhwa, 155–164. Advances in Architecture Series. Cambridge, MA: MIT Press.

Banerjee, S. G., and E. E. Morella. 2011. *Africa's Water and Sanitation Infrastructure: Access, Affordability, and Alternatives*. Africa Infrastructure Country Diagnostic series, V. Foster and C. Briceño-Garmendia, series editors. Washington, DC: World Bank.

Bartolino, J. R., and W. Cunningham. 2003. *Ground-Water Depletion across the United States*. Washington, DC: U.S. Geological Survey.

Bayman, J. M. 2001. The Hohokam of southwest North America. *Journal of World Prehistory* 15(3):257–311.

Boline, R., M. Seetharamb, and B. Pompeii. 2010. Water resources, climate change, and urban vulnerability: A case study of Phoenix, Arizona. *Local Environment* 15(3):261–279.

Botes, L., and D. van Rensburg. 2000. Community participation in development: Nine plagues and twelve commandments. *Community Development Journal* 35(1):41–58.

Buckley, B. M., K. J. Anchukaitis, D. Penny, R. Fletcher, E. R. Cook, M. Sano, N. Le Canh, A. Wichienkeeo, M. T. That, and H. T. Mai. 2010. Climate as a contributing factor in the demise of Angkor, Cambodia. *Proceedings of the National Academy of Sciences* 107(15):6748–6752.

Budds, J., and G. McGranahan. 2003. Are the debates on water privatization missing the point? Experiences from Africa, Asia and Latin America. *Environment and Urbanization* 15(2):87–114.

Cadenasso, M. L., and S. T. A. Pickett. 2018. Situating Sustainability from an Ecological Science Perspective: Ecosystem services, Resilience, and Environmental Justice. In this volume.

Central Intelligence Agency. 2012. *World Factbook*. www.cia.gov.

Clark, W. D. 2007. Sustainability science: A room of its own. *Proceedings of the National Academy of Sciences* 104(6):1137–1138.

Collignon, B., and M. Vézina. 2000. Independent water and sanitation providers in African cities: Full report of a ten-country study. New York: International Bank for Reconstruction and Development/World Bank.

Cullen, H., and P. deMenocal. 2000. Climate change and the collapse of the Akkadian empire: Evidence from the deep sea. *Geology* 28(4):379.

Dinar, A., M. Rosegrant, and R. Meinzen-Dick. 1997. Water allocation mechanisms: Principles and examples. Washington, DC: World Bank.

Famiglietti, J. S. 2014. The global groundwater crisis. *Nature Climate Change* 4:945–948.

Gibbons, M., C. Limoges, H. Nowotny, S. Schwartzman, P. Scott, and M. Trow. 1994. *The New Production of Knowledge.* New York: Sage Publishers.

Giordano, M. A., and A. T. Wolf. 2003. Sharing waters: Post-Rio international water management. *Natural Resources Forum* 27(2):163–171.

Gleick, P. 1998. The human right to water. *Water Policy* 1:487–503.

Goldman, M. 2005. *Imperial Nature: The World Bank and Struggles for Social Justice in the Age of Globalization.* Yale Agrarian Studies series, J. C. Scott, series editor. New Haven, CT: Yale University Press.

Harlan, S. L., A. J. Brazel, L. Prashad, W. Stefanov, and L. Larsen. 2006. Neighborhood microclimates and vulnerability to heat stress. *Social Science and Medicine* 63:2847–2863.

Haug, G., D. Gunther, L. Peterson, D. Sigman, K. Hughen, and B. Aeschlimann. 2003. Climate and the collapse of Maya civilization. *Science* 299:1731–1735.

Hoekstra, A., and A. Chapagain. 2007. Water footprints of nations: Water use by people as a function of their consumption pattern. *Water Resources Management* 21(1):35–48.

Holway, J. 2009. Adaptive water quantity management: Designing for sustainability and resiliency in water scarce regions. In *The Water Environment of Cities*, edited by L. Baker. Lowell, MA: Springer Science.

Hope, D., C. Gries, W. Zhu, W. F. Fagan, C. L. Redman, N. B. Grimm, A. L. Nelson, C. Martin, and A. Kinzig. 2003. Socioeconomics drive urban plant diversity. *Proceedings of the National Academy of Sciences* 100:8788–8792.

Innes, J. E., and D. E. Booher. 2004. Reframing public participation: Strategies for the 21st century. *Planning Theory and Practice* 5(4):419–436.

Intergovernmental Panel on Climate Change. 2001. *Climate Change 2001: Impacts, Adaptation, and Vulnerability.* Geneva: Intergovernmental Panel on Climate Change.

James, A. J. 2003. Institutional challenges for water resources management: India and South Africa. Water, Households and Rural Livelihood (WhiRL) Working Paper no. 7 (draft). The Hague: IRC (WASH).

Kallis, G. 2008. Droughts. *Annual Review of Environment and Resources* 33(1):85–118.

Lonergan, S. C. 1999. Environment and society in the Middle East: Conflicts over water. In *The Handbook of Environmental Sociology*, edited by M. Redclift and G. Woodgate. New York: Oxford University Press.

Mahayni, B. 2013. Tensions in narratives and lived realities or water crisis in Damascus. In *Contemporary Water Governance in the Global South: Scarcity, Marketization and Participation*, edited by L. Harris, J. Goldin, and C. Sneddon, 45–60. New York: Routledge.

Maslow, A. B. 1970. *Motivation and Personality*. 2nd ed. New York: Harper & Row.

Mayer, P. W., W. B. DeOreo, E. M. Optiz, J. C. Kiefer, W. Y. Davis, B. Dziegielewski, and J. O. Nelson. 1999. Residential end use of water. Final report. Denver: American Water Works Association.

McCaffrey, S. C. 2003. The need for flexibility in freshwater treaty regimes. *Natural Resources Forum* 27(2):156–162.

Miyamoto, S., J. White, R. Bader, and D. Ornelas. 2001. El Paso guidelines for landscape uses of reclaimed water with elevated salinity. El Paso: El Paso Public Utilities Board, Water Services.

Osinde, R. N. 2007. *Improving water governance in Kenya through the human rights approach*. Nairobi: UN Development Program and the Kenya-UNDP Water Governance Facility.

Ostrom, E. 2010. Polycentric systems for coping with collective action and global environmental change. *Global Environmental Change* 20:550–557.

Phadke, R. 2002. Assessing water scarcity and watershed development in Maharashtra, India: A case study of the Baliraja Memorial Dam. *Science, Technology, and Human Values* 27(2):236–261.

Qui, J. 2010. China faces groundwater crisis. *Nature* 466:308.

Program in Water Conflict Management and Transformation. 2012. *The Program in Water Conflict Management and Transformation (PWCMT)*. Corvallis: Oregon State University. www.transboundarywaters.orst.edu.

Read, D. 2005. Some observations on resilience and robustness in human systems. *Cybernetics and Systems: An International Journal* 36:773–802.

Romero-Lankao, P. 2011. Missing the multiple dimensions of water? Neoliberal modernization in Mexico City and Buenos Aires. *Policy and Society* 30:267–283.

Stave, K. 2002. Using system dynamics to improve public participation in environmental decisions. *System Dynamics Review* 18(2):139–167.

Sterman, J. D. 2001. System dynamics modeling: Tools for learning in a complex world. *California Management Review* 43(1):8–25.

Stiglitz, J., A. Sen, and J.-P. Fitoussi. 2009. The measurement of economic performance and social progress revisited: reflections and overview. Working paper. Paris: Centre de recherche en Économie (OFCE), Sciences Po/Paris Institute of Political Studies.

Tansley, A. G. 1935. The use and abuse of vegetational concepts and terms. *Ecology* 16 (3):284–307.

Thompson, K., W. Christofferson, D. Robinette, J. Curl, L. Baker, J. Brereton, and K. Reich. 2006. *Characterizing and Managing Salinity Loadings in Reclaimed Water Systems*. Denver: American Water Works Research Foundation.

Tidwell, V. C., H. D. Passell, S. H. Conrad, and R. P. Thomas. 2004. System dynamics modeling for community-based water planning: Application to the Middle Rio Grande. *Aquatic Sciences* 66:357–372.

TWCMT. 2012. *The program in water conflict management and transformation (PWCMT)* Oregon State University 2012]. Available from www.transboundarywaters.orst.edu.

UN Development Program. 2006. *Human Development Report, 2006: Beyond Scarcity: Power, Poverty and the Global Water Crisis.* New York: UN Development Program.

United Nations. 2006. *World Urbanization Prospects: The 2005 Revision.* New York: UN Department of Economic and Social Affairs, Population Division.

Wakida, F. T., and D. N. Lerner. 2005. Non-agricultural sources of groundwater nitrate: A review and case study. *Water Research* 39:33–16.

Welling, K. N. 2011. Modeling the water consumption of Singapore using system dynamics. Master's thesis, Massachusetts Institute of Technology, Boston.

Wolf, A. T. 2007. Shared waters: Conflict and cooperation. *Annual Review of Environment and Resources* 32:241–269.

World Health Organization. 2006. Meeting the MDG drinking water and sanitation target: The urban and rural challenge of the decade. Geneva: World Health Organization and UNICEF.

World Health Organization. 2017. Guidelines for Drinking-Water Quality. 4th ed., incorporating the first addendum. Geneva: World Health Organization, 2017. Licence: CC BY-NC-SA 3.0 IGO.

Xu, Y., L. Baker, and P. Johnson. 2007. Effect of land use changes on temporal trends in groundwater nitrate concentrations in and around Phoenix, Arizona. *Ground Water* 27(2):49–56.

PART II

Positionality, Power, and Situated Sustainabilities

6

Indigenous Lessons about Sustainability Are Not Just for "All Humanity"

KYLE WHYTE, CHRIS CALDWELL, AND MARIE SCHAEFER

Legend of Spirit Rock

One night long ago a Menominee Indian dreamed that Manabush, grandson of Ko-Ko-Mas-Say-Sa-Now (the Earth) and part founder of the Mitawin or Medicine Society, invited him to visit the god. With seven of his friends the Indian called on Manabush who granted their request to make them successful hunters. One of the band, however, angered the god by asking for eternal life. Manabush, seizing the warrior by the shoulders, thrust him into the ground and said, "You shall be a stone, and thus you will be everlasting." The Menominee say that at night kindly spirits come to lay offerings of tobacco at the rock and that if one looks closely he can see their white veils among the trees. The legend is that when the rock finally crumbles away the race will be extinct.[1]

Story of Menominee Relationship to Wild Rice

The Menomini came into possession of wild rice at the very inception of their tribal organization. Mi'nibush . . . created the bear [and] determined to make an Indian of the bear. . . . He called the Indian "Shekatcheke'nau." . . . Then taking the Indian to the river he showed it to him and gave it into his hands, with all its fish, its great beds of wild rice, and many sugar trees along its banks. He said, "I give these things to you, and you shall always have them—the river, the fish, the wild rice, and the sugar trees." When Weskineu the Thunderer came from Lake Winnebago to the Menominee River, the Bear clan turned everything, including the river and the wild rice, over to the Thunderer. But the Thunderer always brought rain and storms, so the rice harvest was ruined. Weskineu then returned the rice to Sekat-sokemau. So after that when rice harvest came Shekatcheke'nau called all his people together, and they made a feast, and smoked, and asked the Great Spirit to give them fair weather during the harvest. Since then there has always been a fine, stormless harvest season.[2]

Introduction

The first legend, displayed in a sign on Menominee lands, demonstrates some concepts of the Menominee for planning for the future. While the above depiction of the story is a simplified version of the actual telling, we can glimpse several concepts. People or communities that boast about certain visions of the future may not understand that for which they wish. We have to pay respect to the uncertainty that at any time our lives could change so drastically that our very existence is threatened. The second story, about wild rice, emphasizes the importance of human responsibility within ecosystems.[3] Human motivation to be responsible is energized through cultural activities, from feasts to ceremonies. Humans must always honor the power of ecosystems. The history of the Menominee Nation bears witness to many of these concepts—concepts that serve as lessons about sustainability.

The Menominee refer to themselves as "Mamaceqtawak" (the ancient ones). Since time immemorial, the Menominee have lived in close relation to the plants, animals, and ecosystems of the area now known by most as the Upper Midwestern United States and Great Lakes Region.[4] The Menominee ancestral territories are around ten million acres in the states of Wisconsin and Michigan (the Upper Peninsula part). Menominee governance systems involved highly mobile seasonal rounds in which the societal institutions shifted structure and geographic location systematically throughout the year to take advantage of the best times to access certain plants and animals. We use "seasonal rounds" in the plural to suggest that, among even one group, such as the Menominee, it was likely that different families, clans, and communities had their versions of seasonal rounds that were more tailored to the particular areas they tended to inhabit most each year.

The name of and activities associated with each month in the Menominee calendar generally correspond with an important plant that should be harvested in that month. Menominee seasonal rounds include complex regimes of monitoring, harvesting, and storing foods and medicines from hundreds of plants and animals in the region, including berries in the summer, wild rice in the fall, and maple sugar and sturgeon in the spring. In light of the seasonal rounds, "Menominee"—a name given them by other Indigenous peoples—means "wild rice people," indicating the importance of wild rice harvesting for Menominee society as part of the seasonal rounds. It was often said that, wherever the Menominee go, there is wild rice. As one historian states, "Menominee tradition says that when the Bear invited the Thunderer to become his brother, the Bear brought wild rice and the Thunderer brought corn and fire to the new family. This family consisted of distant band units comprising from several dozen to over one hundred members."[5]

The Menominee wild rice camps usually began to form in early to mid-September. The Moose Clan was charged with the responsibility of protecting the wild rice beds and the harvest, and they ensured an equal distribution of the wild rice for the members.[6] Once the rice was ripe, the guards would tell the leaders, who would then inform all Tribal members that it was harvest time.[7] Just as with their Anishinaabe neighbors, people with the gender identity approximating *women* in the culture of U.S. settler society tended to lead the harvesting and processing of wild rice, including threshing, dancing, winnowing and cleaning of the rice.[8]

During the nineteenth century, the Menominee started to learn lessons about how drastically their ways of life could change. European invasion through the fur trade and eventually U.S. settler colonialism imposed violence and disruption on the Menominee people. In the Treaty of 1854, the United States pressured the Menominee onto a 354-square-mile reservation that is a fraction of the territory they had been accustomed to using. The subsequent Treaty of 1856 carved out land for the Stockbridge-Munsee Band of Mohican Indians, a Tribe that had been forcibly relocated from the East Coast, further diminishing Menominee lands. Overall, Menominee land cessions occurred across ten different treaties from 1817 to 1856 and transformed the once ten-million-acre range to roughly 226,000 acres.

As the Menominee range decreased, the population decreased, too, owing to the turmoil of the fur trade and U.S. settlement, poverty, and disease. An 1834 smallpox outbreak and an 1849 cholera epidemic drastically reduced the Menominee population to 3,900 members (from a much larger population).[9] Since time immemorial, the Menominee had developed a governance system centered on seasonal rounds and a certain type of mobility in a large territory. In a fairly short amount of time in the nineteenth century, the Menominee were faced with a much smaller population and a more fixed location of inhabitation.

Despite these changes and hardships, the Menominee adapted creatively under very uncertain conditions where their mobility had changed drastically. They designed a sustainable timber supply enterprise in 1856 upon establishment of the reservation.[10] Although it is not generally discussed in the history of North American environmental stewardship, the birth of sustainable forestry can be traced back to the Menominee when the first federal laws mandating sustainable forest harvesting in the United States were enacted on the Menominee Indian Reservation.[11] Today, Menominee Tribal Enterprises, an institution authorized under the Constitution & Bylaws of the Menominee Indian Tribe of Wisconsin, oversees forest management and sawmill operations through a board of directors of elected Menominee Tribal members on behalf of the Tribe. The Menominee sustained yield forest is approximately 220,000 acres of forestland broken into 9,000 distinct timber stands according to various attributes, such as tree species composition, tree size, soil type, and topographical or geologic features interspersed with streams and lakes. This combination of physical and biological elements provides an abundant and diverse array of plant and animal communities.

Different from monocrop commercial forests, Menominee Tribal Enterprises seeks to pay respect to the agency of the forest itself as a living ecosystem that has cultural and spiritual significance for the Menominee people. Management efforts of the Menominee have resulted in an old-growth forest that supports a wealth of species and natural communities that are unique in northeastern Wisconsin. For example, the white pine forests within the Menominee Reservation are unlike any other stands within the Great Lakes states owing to their having specific ecological niches that are documented.[12] Menominee forestry continues to be world renowned for producing high-quality timber and economic resources for the community while maintaining and enhancing the health of the forest ecosystems.[13]

Many Menominee persons have close spiritual and cultural connections to the forest, using the forest as a place for ceremonies, family recreation, and planting and harvesting. The idea to have these connections certainly arises from the Menominee's interpretation of their own history, where cultural and spiritual practices have served to motivate human responsibility within ecosystems. The forest is also a point of pride that Tribal members enjoy showing to respectful and appreciative visitors. Members feel this way because the forest reflects the community's unique history, creativity, and culture, expressing at once honor for Menominee ancestors and the future continuance for generations of Menominee people to come.

The planning it took to establish the forest contributes to the Menominee's continuance despite the fact that U.S. settler colonialism sought to eliminate and erase Menominee peoples from their own homelands. "Continuance" here refers to Indigenous survival and flourishing in the face of change, including change stemming from oppression. By the mid-twentieth century, the United States terminated its sovereign-to-sovereign relationship with the Menominee Nation even though the Menominee ran a successful forestry business and hospital. Post termination, the Menominee closed the hospital and created a business with Menominee persons as shareholders—Menominee Enterprises, Inc.—to generate financial support for the expenses of the newly designated Menominee County. One solution involved a collaboration between MEI and a development corporation that flooded several lakes on the former reservation to increase the shoreline for thousands of recreation properties to be sold to settler Americans, which came to be known as Legend Lake.

The lots were widely advertised by settler Americans as a chance to buy land that was "never before owned" and "The Last Untouched Lake Forest Area in the U.S."[14] In response to issues such as Legend Lake, some Menominee formed DRUMS (Determination of Rights and Unity for Menominee Stockholders). One of DRUMS's expressions was that the land loss would make the Legend of Spirit Rock (found at the beginning of this chapter) a reality.[15] Through DRUMS and other political activism, a generation of prominent Menominee leaders emerged, including Ada Deer, who worked to push the United States to recognize Menominee sovereignty again. Restoration of Menominee sovereignty occurred in 1973. The Menominee continue to fight with other Indigenous peoples in the region against environmental injustices involving lands and waters that matter to them, including the now shut-down Crandon mine project and, more recently, the Back 40 mining project.

Given this history, it is not surprising that the Menominee created the Sustainable Development Institute (SDI). The institute's goal is to reflect on what lessons can be learned from the Menominee's stories of continuance and to share with and learn from others. The institute, housed at the College of Menominee Nation (CMN), was founded in 1993 at the same time the college was founded. The Sustainable Development Institute is one of the first Indigenous-run research institutions. In collaboration with CMN, SDI has provided one of the first Indigenous-run higher education programs in sustainability. The goals of SDI are to reflect on and interpret lessons about sustainability from the Menominee's transition from a seasonal round society to a primarily forestry dependent society and lessons about sustainability that arise from the Menominee experience regarding all areas of community life. The heart of SDI is critical reflection that is situated *in place*.

The authors of this chapter are Potawatomi (Whyte), Menominee (Caldwell), and Odawa (Schaefer). Caldwell is the current director of the Sustainable Development Institute. Schaefer spent several years working for the institute, and Whyte is a frequent collaborator at the institute. While, as members of Indigenous communities, we are often asked about whether our cultures have lessons about how humans and human societies can live sustainably or resiliently, we rarely have the chance to share the histories and processes of how our communities and nations have continued despite settler colonial oppression. Thinking about the Menominee case, "Indigenous planning" refers to how we as Indigenous peoples endeavor to sustain, revitalize, and continue our social, cultural, and ecological integrity under conditions of settler colonial oppression.

Indigenous Planning and Settler Colonialism

"Indigenous peoples" refer to the nearly 400 million people across the world whose communities, polities, and nations exercised self-determination according to their own social, cultural, and ecological systems—that is, governance systems—prior to periods in which other human groups dominated them through various combinations of imperial invasion, colonial exploitation and occupation, and settlement of their territories. Many Indigenous peoples continue to exercise self-determination today even though the nation-states formed by the descendants of initial settlers, imperialists, and allies of invaders are recognized by the majority of people in the world as the primary self-determining political sovereigns in those territories, such as the United States or New Zealand.[16]

While Indigenous peoples are distinct from one another, they often see themselves in mutual solidarity because they have overlapping political aspirations to continue their own self-determining governance systems in the face of colonial oppression. Planning is an important way in which to exercise collective self-determination. Broadly, we define "planning" as practical activities whereby a collective, such as a society or community or nation, envisions different futures that are more or less desirable for itself and its members, determines what capacities and strategies must be developed today to be prepared for different future scenarios, and revisits and revises its current capacities for preparedness to adjust to current and expected challenges.[17]

Many Indigenous persons in North America, such as ourselves, seek to play a role in Indigenous planning in our everyday lives as community members and in our professional careers, whether as Indigenous professionals and academics or community and cultural leaders or as Indigenous government officials and staff. Collectives can range from neighborhoods to nations and have many vague boundaries and hybrid members. For example, many Indigenous persons in North America are not only citizens of an Indigenous Nation but also citizens of the United States or Canadian nation-states. Or some persons may be Indigenous but, for various reasons, are not enrolled formally in a Tribe. Indigenous communities today feature many religions and walks of life. Indigenous and settler collectives overlap, have borderlands, and hybrid social formations that have different expectations of the terms of negotiation and diplomacy. The Menominee, for example, include both Menominee living on or nearby the Menominee reservation and those living in Green Bay, Chicago, and other areas. Native American and Indigenous studies scholars, such as Mishuana Goeman, have challenged understandings of Indigenous collectives that hold strict reservation/urban divides.[18]

For many Indigenous peoples, collectives are not anthropocentric. That is, they do not exclude animals, plants, and ecosystems as members with the responsibilities of active agents in the world. In many cases, plants, animals, and ecosystems are agents bound up in moral relationships of reciprocal responsibilities with humans and other nonhumans. Humans often identify themselves according to clans that are named for animals that those humans have a close connection to, such as cranes, wolves, bears, and martens. Or in some cases humans see their own origins as arising from these particular clan species. Animals, plants, and entities, such as water, are often considered as bearers of knowledge in their own right. Humans must exercise respect in their requesting counsel from these knowledge bearers.[19]

Within Indigenous collectives, planning processes include diverse activities. That is, they can involve many slices of life. They involve ceremonies that express hope and emotional interpretations of the future. They involve researching knowledge archives. "Archives" may refer to the oral tradition or to actual formations in ecosystems, such as formations in the landscape created by plant and animal ancestors that can be used to reconstruct lessons from their time about how to live well.[20] Of course, knowledge archives also include old books and reports found in most Tribal offices or libraries. Planning processes involve ceremonial, narrative, and analytical techniques for forecasting future scenarios, such as quantitative risk analysis used by elected Tribal officials or ceremonial protocols for building and expressing guiding visions for the future, or community storytelling.[21] They involve educational and ceremonial institutions for cultivating certain future-oriented attitudes and behaviors in younger generations, such as summer science education programs or traditional lodges.[22]

Even though planning processes are processes of collectives—or collective processes—they are not always democratic or inclusive, and hence they can be quite problematic. As we can imagine, collective planning processes could be dominated by one person or a small committee of elite members or by members privileged by a form of oppression (e.g., patriarchy). Planning can be externally compelled by outsiders, as we have seen in North America when the United States imposed its own educational institutions, patriarchal gender systems, and governmental structures on many Indigenous peoples.

In these ways, as a general concept, "planning" can refer to a number of types of more or less democratic, inclusive, or exploitative processes. For this reason, collective planning processes have enormous moral implications. In addition, what planners in one collective decide to do can affect many other collectives. The recent Indigenous resistance to the Dakota Access Pipeline is an example of this, as the United States, the pipeline company, and the investors (by implication) can be said to have engaged in a planning process that, among other things, led to the pipeline's route being moved away from Bismarck, North Dakota, and closer to the Standing Rock Sioux Tribe.[23]

"Indigenous planning" does not refer necessarily to all planning processes in which every Indigenous people engages. Rather, for us here, it is more narrowly understood as planning concerned with the challenges of issues with which many Indigenous peoples identify, settler colonial oppression being a major one. Ted Jojola summarizes these shared issues well by claiming that Indigenous planning is an approach to "community planning" and an "ideological movement."[24] He writes that the "key to the process is the acknowledgment of an indigenous world-view. . . . A world-view is rooted in distinct community traditions that have evolved over a successive history of shared experiences."[25]

We take Jojola to mean that Indigenous planning is related to Indigenous governance systems that have roots prior to the incursion and establishment of North American settler societies and states. That is, Indigenous peoples have planning processes to draw on that are not part of the planning processes of settler states. Hirini Matunga refers to this as "classical" Indigenous planning, in which planners rely on "traditional knowledge, worldviews and values" and "traditional approaches, processes, and institutional arrangements to implement decisions."[26] These classic planning processes can be useful for many reasons, depending on the context. They may use structures of leadership and decision-making processes that are more trustworthy to Tribal members. They may be based on values and knowledges of the ecosystem that have greater local precision and relevance. They may rely on symbolism, storytelling, and cultural practices that are intrinsically valuable to Tribal members as part of their identities and family, clan, and band lives. They may require processes of research and recovery to restore traditions (in cases where traditions are no longer practiced or remembered widely) that serve to bring community participants together, thereby building better relationships through engagement in the processes of research and recovery.

We see Jojola as referencing "shared experiences" to *also* indicate the histories of Indigenous peoples having to adapt to settler colonialism. Indigenous peoples have learned many things from these experiences about what it means to achieve continuance under severe conditions of oppression and powerlessness. These points are why we discuss Indigenous planning as how we as Indigenous peoples endeavor to sustain, revitalize, and continue our social, cultural, and ecological integrity under conditions of settler colonial oppression.

Indigenous Futurity

The United States and Canada continue to practice multiple forms of colonialism, including global imperialism, colonial occupation (e.g., U.S. territories), and neocolonialism.[27] They also perpetrate *settler colonialism*, which is one focus of our discussion here. Settler colonialism is a form of oppression in which settlers *permanently* and *ecologically* inscribe homelands of their own onto Indigenous homelands. Settlers do not, as in imperial or metropolitan forms of colonialism, seek fundamentally to extract wealth and harness Indigenous labor for the sake benefiting peoples in central homelands located somewhere else.[28] Some argue that settler colonialism is one condition for strengthening U.S. imperialism abroad because it establishes the needed land base for U.S. food security, manufacturing, military development, and metropolitanism (i.e., being a global intellectual and cultural hub).[29]

For the Menominee, U.S. settlement has contained them on a small reservation to open up land for settlers to engage in the terraforming and hydraulic engineering needed to build and validate settler cultures and economies. Settlers quickly laid claim to lands in what became known as the United States and then, specifically here, the lands in what is now known as the state of Wisconsin. They developed social identities and attachments to the land in relation to settler agricultural, industrial, cultural, and recreational activities in the region. Settlers ignored and erased Menominee and other peoples' social identities and attachments to the land, removing the footprints on the land that mark Indigenous histories and Indigenous cultural and economic activities (e.g., the seasonal rounds). For a territory to emerge as a meaningful homeland for settlers, the origin, religious, and cultural narratives, ways of life, and political and economic systems (e.g., property) must be engraved and embedded into the waters, soils, air, and other environmental dimensions of the territory. That is, settler *ecologies* have to be inscribed so settlers can exercise their own governance systems.[30] So it was no accident that U.S. settlers created the idea of Legend Lake as "unowned" and "untouched"—*such an ideal spot for (settler) recreation!*

"Ecologies" are systematic arrangements of humans, nonhuman beings (animals, plants, etc.) and entities (spiritual, inanimate, etc.), and landscapes (climate regions, boreal zones, etc.) that are conceptualized and operate purposefully to facilitate a society's capacity to survive and flourish in a particular landscape and watershed. Waves of settlement seek to incise their own ecologies required for their societies to survive and flourish in the landscapes they seek to occupy permanently. In settlement, the territories were already inscribed with Indigenous ecologies that result from Indigenous practices of survival and flourishing.[31]

The Indigenous ecologies *physically manifest* Indigenous governance systems through origin, religious, and cultural narratives, ways of life, political structures, and economies. The Menominee seasonal rounds described earlier serve as an example of Menominee ecology. The physical manifestation of the Menominee ecology featured extensive ricing lakes whose hydrology and biodiversity reflected Menominee stewardship. The rice ecology embodies environmentally the Menominee origin and other cultural stories that feature rice so prominently. The rice ecology, as it is inscribed in the land, bears witness to the Menominee people's exercise of responsibilities to rice. The physical manifestations affirm the importance of, and motivation for, protecting ricing traditions for the sake of future generations.

For settlers, the presence of Indigenous ecologies—from the human activities themselves to their physical manifestations as particular ecosystems and ecological flows—delegitimizes settlers' claims to have honorable and credible religious "missions," universal property rights, and exclusive political and cultural sovereignty. To remove all markers or physical manifestations that challenge their moral legitimacy, power, and self-determination, settlers systematically seek to erase the ecologies required for Indigenous governance systems, such as Indigenous seasonal rounds.[32] Although the "-ology" in "ecology" may sound like a peculiar usage, we use it to denote human agency within ecosystems, whether that agency is the Indigenous knowledge of seasonal rounds that shaped the lands and waters of the Menominee ancestral territories or the settler desires to shape the same lands and waters to reflect and support their aspirations.

Shawano Lake was formerly a major Menominee wild rice bed and area for fishing, hunting, and berry cultivation through systematic burning. Wisconsin settlers terraformed and hydrologically engineered the lake area into a recreational lake. The lake area no longer supports Menominee ricing or harvest and is now dominated by settler homes and recreational businesses. The lake is, according to settler law, "off-reservation"; hence settlers believe they are not on Menominee lands or waters. In a short time, the ecology of the lake has been terraformed into a settler ecology, with few physical manifestations of Menominee ecologies remaining.[33] We seek to pause during this part of the essay to go into further detail about why settler processes, such as the terraforming and hydraulic engineering of Shawano Lake, are harmful to Indigenous peoples.

One society's erasure of the ecologies of other societies is harmful because, among other reasons, doing so undermines *qualities of relationships* of the colonized societies that have developed over many years. These qualities of relationships bolster continuance, as in the case of Menominee rice ecologies and the clan and gendered responsibilities to rice and rice's support of Menominee self-determination. Qualities of relationships are properties of relationships that make it possible for a relationship to have wide societal impact. Qualities of relationships motivate the discharge of responsibilities among the parties or relatives within relationships. *Quality* is different from *type* of a relationship. A type of relationship is simply the description of the relationship itself, for example, the human nutritional or religious connection to wild rice (e.g., "humans eat wild rice; humans use wild rice in ceremonies").

The qualities of a relationship are the actual properties of that relationship that motivate humans to care for rice and to gain and protect knowledge of rice. The motivation makes it possible for humans to have an emotional disposition to take responsibility for rice. As we discuss shortly, the more humans take responsibility, the more the other parties or relatives reciprocate (e.g., flourishing rice harvests) if the appropriate causal relationships are also in place (such as causal relationships known via Indigenous knowledge systems about the impact of certain human practices on the growth of rice and the impact of certain ceremonies and educational practices on motivating and training humans to engage in stewardship practices skillfully). This reciprocity further secures and strengthens human motivation as the benefits of taking responsibility are physically manifest. We review just two qualities of relationships here.

Trust refers to a quality of relationships among people in the community in which each party or relative, human and nonhuman, takes to heart the best interests of the other party or relative. People trust one another when they feel confident and at ease that the trustor takes the trustees' best interest to heart.[34] Trust facilitates collective well-being and collective planning when people can be trusted to discharge particular responsibilities, leaving others to take up the many other responsibilities in the society. Trust is emotional and takes time to develop among different parties or relatives in a relationship.

Clan systems are based on trust. Specific clans are often charged with different responsibilities. Members of those clans, through exercising protocols and ceremonies and furnishing results, reaffirmed their identifies as trustors having those responsibilities. For example, the Menominee's Moose Clan has the responsibility of protecting the wild rice until it is ripe, overseeing the harvest, and ensuring an equitable and communal distribution. Clans provide leadership and expertise in multiple forms, from the political and diplomatic responsibilities of the Bear Clan to the knowledge of the Crane Clan in building products from naturally available materials. Clan members have particular knowledges and skills that are trusted by everyone else to contribute to seasonal rounds on the whole.[35]

Gender is also closely related to trust. As discussed earlier, women of Menominee and related groups had special leadership and expert positions in relation to activities such as those involving wild rice. Gender difference, then, was not associated with oppression but with responsibilities entrusted within a society. This is why the connection between patriarchy and settler colonialism creates distrust between men, women, and two-spirit persons in many Indigenous peoples, as trust is replaced with oppressive gender relations. This oppressive connection has played a role in what are now many morally problematic, male-dominated Tribal governments and agencies today and the heightened risks of sexual violence and murder that Indigenous women and two-spirit persons face. And even the most clearly recorded articulations of some Indigenous traditions, including perhaps the stories at the beginning of this chapter, are now told in a masculinist way.[36]

Redundancy is a quality that refers to states of affairs that have multiple options for adaptation when changes occur and that are able to guarantee sufficient opportunities for education and mentorship for community members. For example, in the case of wild rice harvesting, a society with high redundancy is one that can harvest from multiple ricing lakes in the event that some lakes stop producing rice for some period of time, whether naturally or through destruction or occupation by settlers. As described earlier, the Menominee seasonal rounds ranged over a large region that included many rice lakes and other sources of food and medicine. Redundancy is a quality of relationship because it refers to more than just the fact of there being a commodity or religious relationship to rice in some society. Redundancy means that there are many options for maintaining the type of relationship. It is sustained by human motivation toward performing stewardship, mentorship, and ceremonial, educational, monitoring, training, harvesting, and disposal practices with relatives of the nonhuman world. Analogous to language fluency, people are more motivated to learn and will learn better if all generations in a society speak (and prefer to speak) a particular language. Having many fluent speakers can, by analogy, be compared to having many rice lakes. In literatures on sustainability, concepts such as *buffering* may also be compared to redundancy.[37]

It is very important to note the ecological dimensions of these qualities of relationships. Redundancy and trust figure within the dynamics of ecosystems. Redundancy requires deep connections to lands and waters that allow people to monitor for change and maintain, as best as possible, the amount and diversity of habitats. Having a lot of habitats ensures that there are also sufficient opportunities to mentor youth and to foster the independence of particular families and other groupings through their being able to have easier access within their seasonal rounds to harvesting opportunities. For trust, in order to maintain a wild rice habitat as part of a rice ecology, precipitation, water levels, and integrity of the shoreline and those plants and animals that interact with rice must be monitored by people, such as clan members. Trust is often rooted in knowledge that certain members or groups of a society have in-depth knowledge of certain aspects of the ecosystem and that there are processes in place in a society to adequately vet and train knowledge bearers (including nonhuman knowledge bearers).

Importantly, qualities of relationships support the ongoing futurity or future continuance of Indigenous societies. "Futurity" refers to the idea that members of a society ought to be able to experience that their own efforts and contributions to their society play a part in making it so that a vibrant future is possible for the coming generations and in the perceptual experiences of young people living today. Futurity has been shown to be significant for Indigenous peoples, for one way of understanding settler colonialism is as a form of oppression that destroys Indigenous futurity.[38] Settler colonialism, in relation to planning, attacks our capacities to assert or stage our own futurities.[39] To believe that we and our societies have futures, we need to witness a sufficient degree of our relationships and histories in the physical manifestations of ecologies. The physical manifestations furnish credence in our efforts' and contributions' potential to move forward or move cyclically into the next generation.

In other words, we need to witness that there is sufficient territory, with particular habitats, to sustain seasonal round activities. We need to witness landscapes that are referenced in stories. We need to be able to experience that what younger and older generations do in relation to one another affects the capacity of each generation to live well into the future. We need to be immersed in the presence of the markers of our ancestors in the lands and waters. Redundancy supports futurity because it allows us to witness the capacity of an ecology to support an Indigenous people throughout time. Trust is a basis for futurity because we see that people in positions of political or epistemic authority take our best interest to heart and that it is worthwhile in our lives to put in the efforts required to cultivate ourselves as trusted members of our societies. In this way, the replacement of Indigenous ecologies with settler ecologies can inflict rapid changes. These changes, such as the destruction of rice ecology, undermine the plant and related species whose physical manifestations in ecosystems foster qualities of relationships (trust, redundancy, and others) that are important for our continuance.

Connecting Planning to Indigenous Studies and Institution Building

In planning, Indigenous peoples imagine themselves strategically in ways that are not reliant on settler and other oppressive desires, discourses, and needs. Planning involves imagining futures in which qualities of relationships, such as trust and redundancy (but others too), flourish. We see these insights and principles reflected in the Menominee's planning through the Tribe's forestry and other programs. The Menominee forest establishes and protects multiple relationships of redundancy and trust across humans and nonhumans of the Menominee collective. The forest relies on Menominee history, culture, and knowledge in resistance to settler colonial oppression. Indigenous scholars and Indigenous persons working for Indigenous institutions offer lessons through their studies and work that are certainly in dialogue with what we have discussed already. We share some of these lessons here.

Mishuana Goeman and Jennifer Denetdate write that "the structures of our lives as Native women and men are shaped by racism, sexism, and discrimination. We strive to recover our former selves and push toward creating better future selves by reclaiming Native values, which have seen us through multiple traumas, including land dispossession and the loss of our freedoms."[40] Leanne Simpson claims that "resurgence happens *within* Indigenous bodies and through the connections we make to each other and our land. That's how we strengthen ourselves within *Nishnaabeg* intelligence."[41] Gerald Vizenor's concept of survivance refers to "an active sense of presence, the continuance of native stories, not a mere reaction, or a survivable name. Native survivance stories are renunciations of dominance, tragedy, and victimry."[42] One commentator interprets survivance as "renewal and continuity into the future rather than memorializing the past."[43] Audra Simpson's politics of refusal arises from *Kahnawà: ke* actions, words and stances. Describing them, she writes that they "used every opportunity to remind non-Native people that this is not their land, that there are other political orders and possibilities." She sees that "it is just this sort of cognizance of differing social and historical facts that make for the posture of refusal."[44]

Dian Million draws on the concept of *naw'qinwixw* from Jeanette Armstrong. On Million's interpretation, it is a concept of inclusivity in which "Indigenous people of many genders, ages, and abilities perform radical acts of determination around, above, and outside of nation-states' heteronormative, homophobic, misogynist, regulatory Indian policies. In [Million's] reading, "*naw'qinwixw* informs first practices, effectively performed ethical acts of interrelationship that involve all in any sustained effort to live in a place, with one another, generatively with life, rather than as that which seeks control."⁴⁵ Million's philosophy of "healing" looks to Indigenous women as "[offering] a specific vision of polity that encompasses diverse alliances, one that is informed by practices of *naw'qinwixw* in political struggles for land, food, and environmental justice."⁴⁶

Māori scholar Te Kipa Kepa Brian Morgan in Aoteoroa/New Zealand has created a model for environmental assessment based on their concept of Mauri. The concept is "central to Tangata Whenua belief regarding the environment. Mauri is the binding force between the physical and the spiritual aspects. When the mauri is totally extinguished, this is associated with death. . . . Mauri is considered to be the essence or life force that provides life to all living things. Water also has mauri."⁴⁷ As an ecology, "Mauri also establishes the inter-relatedness of all living things. The linkages between all living things within the ecosystem are based on the whakapapa or genealogies of creation. This establishes the basis for the holistic view of the environment and our ecosystem held by the Tangata Whenua."⁴⁸ This concept has been used to design a metric for evaluating the environmental actions of the New Zealand settler state in terms of whether particular actions increase or decrease Mauri, instead of relying on settler notions of economic costs and health impacts.⁴⁹

In the St. Lawrence River/Great Lakes Region, the Akwesasne Mohawk Nation's Environmental Department, whose key lead contributors include Angela Benedict, Mary Arquette, and numerous community members,⁵⁰ created a climate change plan based on their own knowledge of what we are calling "ecologies" instead of relying heavily on the scientific concepts of a U.S. federal agency or on non-Mohawk adaptation planning organization. For example, the department's plan is organized according to the ecology of the Mohawk Thanksgiving Address, which includes, as categories through which to understand climate change, "The People, Mother Earth, The Waters, The Fish, Small Plants and Grasses, The Berries, Three Sisters, Medicine Herbs, Animals, Trees, The Birds, The Four Winds, The Thunderers, Grand Mother Moon, The Sun, The Stars, the Four Beings and the Creator." Each of these categories involves intricately woven human and nonhuman relationships and responsibilities. In terms of community engagement, and quoting from the plan itself, it calls for the Tribe to hold "a number of Adaptation

Planning classes to teach community members how to prepare for climate change now, and uphold the traditional culture of the Tribe under the changed climatic conditions of the future."[51]

The Diné Policy Institute of the Navajo Nation also uses its own ecology to create a food sovereignty plan, using the principle of *Hozho*, or holistic well-being (a Navajo word that is hard to translate into English). The plan, whose lead author is Dana Eldridge, seeks to "foster greater self-sufficiency, health, and sustainability for Diné people . . . by reconnecting them with traditional foods and revitalizing knowledge and practices around foods." According the plan, "restoring *Hozho* will have positive impacts on the health of the people, relationships of the people as well as our interconnectedness with the land, while also leading to greater self-sufficiency for the Diné people and the Navajo Nation." The plan recommends "rebuilding of a self-sufficient food system for the Diné people." The plan carefully documents how settler colonialism has been enacted to create a disconnect between Indigenous people and their land, food, and health, hence *Hozho* refers, among many things, to processes that can refuse and resurge against oppression.[52]

The Sustainable Development Institute of the College of Menominee Nation

The Menominee Nation's planning process for sustainability expresses many of the themes and ideas discussed earlier, especially through the work represented in its Sustainable Development Institute, founded by Tribal leadership in 1993 through the Tribe's college.[53] The College of Menominee Nation is one of thirty-seven Tribal Colleges and Universities (TCUs) in the United States.[54] Tribes founded TCUs starting in the late 1960s to provide culturally and socially supportive environments for American Indian students, to support local Tribal communities, and to produce indigenous research and scholarship.[55] The College of Menominee Nation was chartered by the Menominee Tribal Legislature in 1993 and reaffirmed by a vote from the general membership of the Menominee Tribe in 1996.

The mission of the College of Menominee Nation is "to provide opportunities in higher education to its students. As an institution of higher learning chartered by the Menominee People, the College infuses this education with American Indian culture, preparing students for leadership, careers and advanced studies in a multicultural world."[56] From CMN's founding, there has been a strong connection and commitment to sustainability. Interim President Dr. Diana Morris describes the deep connection between sustainability, education, and what we have described already as Indigenous planning. In an open letter, she affirms that, "for our College and the Menominee People who chartered CMN, sustainable development has roots in the moral code, governance structure, and sustainable forestry practices that evolved within the tribe over many centuries."[57]

Founding president Dr. Verna Fowler has discussed how the curriculum was built around "respect for the land, water, and air; partnership with other creatures of earth; and a way of living and working that achieves a balance between use and replenishment of all resources."[58] A commitment to sustainability is part of Menominee life. This commitment was specifically expressed by Menominee Nation leadership through the initiation of the Sustainable Development Institute (SDI). The institute's 1994 mission statement is "to continuously expand knowledge, understanding and resources related to Menominee Nation Sustainable Development for the purpose of ensuring ongoing protection, control and productivity of the Menominee culture, environment, economy, technology, and community."[59]

Initially, a board of directors made up of Menominee leaders and experts worked to create a theoretical model of sustainable development "to understand the success of Menominee forest management, to share the sustainability successes with others, and to begin to address sustainability issues in other aspects of Tribal life."[60] The initial framework articulated sustainability as interrelated aspects of community, technology, culture, governance, interconnectedness, economy, and Tribal control. A new Sustainable Development Advisory Council (launched in 1995) brought together Menominee leaders and Tribal experts with external partners and experts to further the theoretical model as a guide to research, education, and outreach. The College of Menominee Nation, the Sustainable Development Institute, and the Advisory Council arranged diverse meetings and conversations among their own members and staff, Menominee Tribal leaders, academics, and community members.

The goal of these discussions and conversations was to understand the Menominee sustainable development experience as a way of building the theoretical model.[61]

The model, introduced in the mid-1990s, "defines sustainability as comprising six discrete but highly interrelated dimensions: (1) land and sovereignty, (2) natural environment (which includes human beings), (3) institutions, (4) technology, (5) economics, and (6) human perception, activity, and behavior." The model can be used for a range of processes, including planning, research and evaluation.[62]

Land and sovereignty have specific legal and cultural meanings for the Menominee and other Indigenous peoples that preexist the creation of United States. They continue to use these conceptions of land and sovereignty as part of their contemporary exercise of self-determination.[63] This dimension expresses the idea of redundancy, discussed earlier, which is important to the Menominee because they have fought to retain their land and sovereignty for centuries.[64] The Menominee view this long struggle to have a terrestrial basis for (what we call) redundancy as one of the reasons they have been able to "maintain a reservation within their ancestral territory, maintain the ecological diversity and spiritual and cultural value of their forestland through time, develop a world-renowned forest management system, and establish the College of Menominee Nation."[65]

The natural environment dimension includes "people, human communities, plants, animals, rocks, water, and air. The natural environment dimension incorporates Menominee understanding that everything is connected and related."[66] It also incorporates the importance of building relationships based on trust, among other qualities of relationships, across these different living and nonliving beings and entities. The natural environment dimension is compatible with Western/U.S. science-based research methodologies, assuming that intercultural engagement occurs on fair terms. The institutional dimensions refers to "structures that develop and enforce rules of behavior and social interactions (which can include interactions among humans, plants, animals, and the environment). For the Menominee, institutions include the Menominee clan system, the contemporary Tribal government, and the College of Menominee Nation," where trust plays an important role in ensuring good relations among members of the community.[67]

The technology dimension is diverse, including "Menominee technology for building birch-bark canoes, processing wild rice, producing high-quality saw timber in a sawmill, and using geographic information systems to implement sustainable forestry management activities." Dockry et al. emphasize the idea that technology concerns the ways in which people get things done.[68] The economic dimension includes a range of scales, households, Tribes, regions, nations and the entire globe. For the Menominee, a key economic issue is the "coexistence of individuals engaged in subsistence harvesting and commercial timber harvesting for sale on the international market."[69] Key to both the technology and economic dimensions are the roles these systems play in collectives by providing trustworthy services that prioritize community well-being and establish and protect redundancy.

Human perception, activity, and behavior is a dimension that concerns diverse individual and community scales relating to sustainability. The dimension includes, on one end of the spectrum, "individual perceptions, activities, and behaviors" and, on the other end, "community understandings, values, and collective pursuits."[70] Dockry et al. discuss how "this dimension incorporates everything from Menominee cultural beliefs and practices to the creation of forestry management plans that limit timber harvesting to sustainable levels."[71] This dimension can be used to cover the importance for peoples' motivation and commitment to be able to live in ecologies that bear witness to Indigenous histories, cultures, economies, and futurities. The dimension can pertain to how growing trustworthy relationships, for example, is a deeply emotional process requiring time to establish. It can also take into consideration a difference of perspectives between different tribal member groups within the community, while considering the differing perceptions between the Tribe as a collective and external communities.

Dockry et al. describe succinctly how the model operates:

According to the SDI model, sustainable development is defined as the process of maintaining balance and reconciling the tensions within and among the six dimensions of sustainability. This does not mean to imply that there is a functional equilibrium or a "natural" balance; change is an explicit feature of the model. Each SDI model dimension is dynamic, both in respect to its internal organization and in relationship to each of the other five dimensions of the model. Change within one dimension will affect other dimensions in an ever-unfolding diffusion of responses to change. Change can be externally driven or inherent to the dynamic nature of any of the six dimensions. The SDI model recognizes that there will always be tensions within and among model dimensions. Tensions can be illustrated by placing SDI model dimensions adjacent to one another. Furthermore, as tensions among model dimensions are relieved, new tensions will arise. Because new tensions will always arise, sustainable development is defined as a continual, and sometimes iterative, process. The model is intergenerational in its framework.[72]

The Sustainable Development Institute is a case of Indigenous planning through its processes of reflection on how the Menominee and other Indigenous peoples have adapted to settler colonial oppression. The reflection concerns both lessons learned and how to apply them in planning processes to other areas of community life. It is all part of the sustainable forestry story that continues to have physical and ecological credence today in the presence of the forest itself as a living agent. The model is a planning tool that can be used to examine the tensions of human-environmental relationships within (what we call) ecologies. The model, if changed, should be changed in the manner in which it was created. The model is dynamic; it can change, and it should change.

The Sustainable Development Institute is significant as an Indigenous research institution within the Tribal college framework. Tribal colleges typically focus on Tribal needs in a culturally relevant setting. The Sustainable Development Institute seeks to empower students to delve deep into their own Tribal histories, experiences, and insights and explore the physical/ecological manifestations of Indigenous governance that express futurity, such as the Menominee sustainable forest. This is why SDI conceives of itself as based on the idea of reflection on insights and lessons about sustainability in place. The institute is a place for students to delve deeper into programs guided by Indigenous peoples. Additionally, SDI is able to create opportunities for TCU students and other Tribal students to explore their own stories across the boundaries of Tribal college settings and mainstream academic institutions.

The Sustainable Development Institute on Climate Change

Consistent with SDI's core mission to share insights within the Menominee community and beyond, it has embarked on a number of projects, with climate change emerging as a larger thematic area for exploring Indigenous ecologies and human-environmental relations more broadly. Climate change poses a threat to the traditional livelihoods and the sustainably managed forestlands of the Menominee Nation. However, climate change also presents an opportunity—a chance to apply Indigenous knowledge to adapt and sustain Native communities and, for the Menominee Nation especially, to share its understandings with others seeking to address this global issue. The experience and ability of SDI to work within and across the worldviews of both Indigenous knowledge and "Western science" allows for opportunities to address a complex issue like climate change from multiple perspectives. The Sustainable Development Institute is a case of an institution that uses an overall process that seeks to understand, through multiple projects, how Menominee and other Indigenous peoples can sustain the continuance of our own societies despite the oppressive conditions we face.

The SDI model itself, a summary of Menominee indigenous planning expertise, provides a framework, or representation of an ecology, for addressing climate change outside of the mainstream thinking in a more integrative and holistic manner, taking into consideration—rather than separation from—spiritual aspects related to resilience and adaptation and the inclusion of elder and youth voices with the scientific voices. This focus on different perspectives and voices is just part of the overall picture of Menominee's lessons on the meaning of place-based sustainability. The resulting climate change projects include those operating at regional, national, and global climate scales. In all of these projects, SDI has served as a boundary organization that facilitates processes of Indigenous planning for climate change in the context of interactions with settler institutions, especially U.S. federal agencies.

For the last few years, the SDI has held a "Shifting Seasons Summit" to respond to the growing local, national, and global need to monitor and respond to climate change. The most recent summit was funded largely by the U.S. Department of Interior's Bureau of Indian Affairs and Northeast Climate Science Center. The conferences were organized dialogically, with Indigenous persons, nations, and organizations as the lead planners and major speakers, instructors, and attendees. Participants had the opportunity to spend time directly on the Menominee land—for example, visiting the Menominee Forest, culturally significant areas, and specific communities. Participants also sat in circles or in other communicative arrangements, at different points in the conference, to discuss the importance of talking about topics not typically discussed in relation to climate change, which ranged from collaboration across cultural difference to colonialism to gender and patriarchy.

Measuring the Pulse of the Forest was a three-year project funded through a U.S. Department of Agriculture National Institute of Food and Agriculture Tribal College Research Grant Program. Project partners included the Center for First Americans Forestlands (part of SDI), the Smithsonian Institution, and Michigan State University's Native American Institute. The integrated resource approach of this project not only identified predicted climate change impacts on the Menominee forest but also how that would influence the Menominee peoples' relationships with the forest and affected species. The study included the installation of three one-hectare climate change monitoring plots and the development and use of semi-structured interviews to assess community members' relationships and Indigenous knowledge with the forest in the past, present, and future. This project was a direct example of Indigenous planning through the use of a framework based on Indigenous knowledge and the utilization of Western science to help illustrate these relationships from another perspective. In this instance, the work is controlled by a Tribal entity (College of Menominee Nation) with an Indigenous community as the main beneficiary.

Through a project funded by the U.S. Department of Interior's Northeast Climate Science Center, SDI has worked to collaborate with Indigenous nations throughout the Northeast region to find planning solutions to climate change impacts that can be pursued by individual Tribes or through cooperative solutions. Initial development for this project grew from an earlier project between the Center for First Americans Forestlands (at CMN), the U.S. Forest Service, and the Great Lakes Integrated Sciences + Assessments Center (U.S. National Oceanic and Atmospheric Administration) to develop Indigenous methods of strategic foresight for adaptation planning. The project focuses on how Indigenous peoples can develop, specific to their locations, culturally guided and community-based climate change programs, often inspired by seasonal rounds and other governance systems coming from the Indigenous communities. Some of the key developments have been the creation and refinement of nation- or community-specific public engagement strategies, a methodology of Indigenous scenario planning and culturally rooted educational programs on climate change for youth.

The Sustainable Development Institute seeks to expand its work to better understand how to evaluate Indigenous partnerships with scientists and to offer more educational opportunities for Indigenous students that will prepare them for future work on climate change planning. The Sustainable Development Institute and Michigan State University recently received funding from the National Science Foundation to evaluate ethical training for scientists in climate science organizations, and the SDI worked with Carla Dhillon to evaluate the 2015 meeting of "Rising Voices: Collaborative Science for Climate Solutions" at the National Center for Atmospheric Research.[73] In both projects, SDI is developing Indigenous frameworks for evaluation that can measure or gauge relationship issues such as trustworthiness—expressed through Indigenous concepts such as family relatedness—that matter to many Indigenous persons in their interactions with scientists.

In 2015, SDI hosted its first Indigenous Planning Summer Institute for SDI summer interns at the College of Menominee Nation. In 2016 and 2017, the Indigenous Planning Summer Institute invited Indigenous students along with SDI summer interns and instructors from the Indigenous Design and Planning Institute at the University of New Mexico and expanded its curriculum to include three Indigenous planning concepts from the institute's work that engender credence in Indigenous futurities: Seven-generation planning and Indigenous knowledges and cultures are already powerful resources for planning, and the history of oppression in Indigenous communities needs to be understood and learned from. The institutes developed with support through the DOI Northeast Climate Science Center have also provided a means for securing additional funding and support over the years.

These concepts were shown in practice through place-based and activity-based curricula conducted by and occurring at the Menominee Nation, Oneida Nation, and the Stockbridge-Munsee Community.

The curriculum was developed in collaboration with Ted Jojola and Michaela Shirley of the Indigenous Design and Planning Institute at the University of New Mexico. In this way, the Indigenous students had the opportunity to learn from other Indigenous peoples about planning. The planning institute seeks to provide Indigenous-based, experiential training for the next generation of Indigenous scientists, leaders, activists, and professionals. The institute seeks to motivate students' creativity and provide what is unfortunately a rare but powerful opportunity for Indigenous persons to engage in intercultural exchange across different Indigenous peoples.

Conclusion

The Sustainable Development Institute focuses on what can best be described as reflective planning processes of Indigenous sustainability. The processes are rooted in what we can understand and recover from our experiences prior to and during recent settler colonialism and how our own interpretations can be used to support the continuance of Indigenous peoples. A huge part of what SDI does is not so much centered on Indigenous lessons on sustainability for all humanity. Rather, SDI's work considers what processes support Indigenous peoples' sustainability in the face of the challenges of settler colonialism, starting from the Menominee experience and then branching out to others when mutual benefits are possible. This reflection on sustainability arises from concern about how Indigenous peoples can put planning processes into practice. It is an active effort that expresses our gratitude to those before us and shows our responsibility to those who will come after us. This line of sustainability is maintained by sharing cultural values that have been passed down from generation to generation to show how we can act on the potential futurities of our peoples.

This is different from how some non-Indigenous communities seek to understand our lessons of sustainability for the purpose of saving themselves or humankind. Instead, Indigenous planning, as a way of reflecting on Indigenous sustainability, is about figuring out the planning processes arising from the contexts that we actually live in today, in which our societies are greatly limited and threatened by settler colonialism and other forms of oppression. Reflecting on sustainability in this way—whether regarding climate change, biodiversity conservation, or food sovereignty—keeps us aware of how oppression endures as one of the largest threats to Indigenous peoples and many other groups. Whether settler and other privileged populations ultimately can achieve sustainability in the near- or long-term planning horizons is not so much our concern. Regardless of what happens with them, the odds are that Indigenous peoples will continue to face different forms of colonial oppression and must innovate strategies for protecting our continuance no matter what non-Indigenous populations end up doing.

NOTES

1 Wisconsin State historical marker on the Menominee Nation reservation.
2 David Beck, *Siege and Survival: History of the Menominee Indians, 1634–1856* (Lincoln: University of Nebraska, 2002): 8; also quoting Albert Ernest Jenks, *The Wild Rice Gatherers of the Upper Lakes: A Study in American Primitive Economics*, Extract from the Nineteenth Annual Report of the Bureau of American Ethnology (Washington, DC: Government Printing Office, 1901).
3 In both stories, spellings vary owing to source.
4 David Grignon et al., "Menominee Indian Reservation Historical Review—Commemorating the Reservation Sesquicentennial, 1854–2004," ed. Menominee Historic Preservation Department (Keshena: Menominee Tribe of Indians of Wisconsin, 2004).
5 Beck, *Seige and Survival*, 7.
6 University of Wisconsin–Stevens Point, *The Menominee Clans Story*, n.d., www.uwsp.edu.
7 Beck, *Seige and Survival*, 16.
8 Ibid.; and Brenda Child, *Holding Our World Together: Ojibwe Women and the Survival of Community* (New York: Penguin, 2012).
9 Felix Keesing, *The Menomini Indians of Wisconsin: A Study of Three Centuries of Cultural Contact and Change* (Madison: University of Wisconsin Press, 1939), 102.
10 David Beck, *The Struggle for Self-Determination: History of the Menominee Indians since 1854* (Lincoln: University of Nebraska Press, 2005); Brian Hosmer, *American Indians in the Marketplace: Persistence and Innovation among the Menominees and Metlakatlans, 1870–1920* (Lawrence: University Press of Kansas, 1999); and Marshall Pecore, "Menominee Sustained-Yield Management: A Successful Land Ethic in Practice," *Journal of Forestry* 90, no. 7 (1992): 12–16.
11 Beck, *The Struggle for Self-Determination*; and Michael J. Dockry, "Indigenous Forestry in the Americas: Comparative Environmental Histories in Bolivia and Wisconsin" (PhD diss., University of Wisconsin–Madison, 2012).
12 Menominee Tribal Enterprises, *Menominee Forest Management Plan* (Keshena, WI: Menominee Tribal Enterprises, 2012).

13 Pecore, "Menominee Sustained-Yield Management."

14 Advertisement in the *Appleton (WI) Post Crescent*, May 16, 1969; credit to Michael Dockry for this research.

15 *DRUMS Newsletter*, July 1, 1972; credit to Michael Dockry for this research.

16 James Anaya, *Indigenous Peoples in International Law* (New York: Oxford University Press, 2004); and Douglas Sanders, *The Formation of the World Council of Indigenous Peoples* (Copenhagen: International Secretariat of the International Work Group for Indigenous Affairs, 1977).

17 Ted Jojola, "Indigenous Planning—An Emerging Context," in "Canadian Planning and Policy/Aménagement et politique au Canada," supplement, *Canadian Journal of Urban Research* 17, no. 1 (2008): 37–47; and Ryan Walker, Ted Jojola, and David Natcher, eds., *Reclaiming Indigenous Planning*, McGill-Queen's Native and Northern Series, no. 70 (Montreal: McGill-Queen's University Press, 2013). See also S. Yvonne Prusak, Ryan Walker, and Robert Innes, "Toward Indigenous Planning? First Nation Community Planning in Saskatchewan, Canada," *Journal of Planning Education and Research* 36, no. 4 (2016): 440–450.

18 Mishuana Goeman, *Mark My Words: Native Women Mapping Our Nations* (Minneapolis: University of Minnesota Press, 2013).

19 Robin Kimmerer, *Braiding Sweetgrass: Indigenous Wisdom, Scientific Knowledge and the Teachings of Plants* (Minneapolis: Milkweed Editions, 2013).

20 John Borrows, *Recovering Canada: The Resurgence of Indigenous Law* (Toronto: University of Toronto Press, 2002); and Val Napoleon, *Thinking about Indigenous Legal Orders* (Dordrecht: Springer, 2013).

21 Treaty Indian Tribes in Western Washington, "Treaty Rights at Risk: Ongoing Habitat Loss, the Decline of the Salmon Resource, and Recommendations for Change" (Olympia, WA: Northwest Indian Fisheries Commission, July 14, 2011), www.nwifc.org.

22 Kate McCoy, Eve Tuck, and Marcia McKenzie, eds., *Land Education: Rethinking Pedagogies of Place from Indigenous, Postcolonial, and Decolonizing Perspectives* (London: Routledge, 2016); and Andrejs Kulnieks, Dan Roronhiakewen Longboat, and Kelly Young, eds., *Contemporary Studies in Environmental and Indigenous Pedagogies: A Curricula of Stories and Place* (Rotterdam: Sense Publishers, 2013).

23 Kyle P. Whyte, "The Dakota Access Pipeline, Environmental Injustice and U.S. Colonialism," *Red Ink—An International Journal of Indigenous Literature, Arts and Humanities* 19, no. 1 (2017): 154–169.

24 Jojola, "Indigenous Planning," 42.

25 Ibid.

26 Hirini Matunga, "Theorizing Indigenous Planning," in Walker, Jojola, and Natcher, *Reclaiming Indigenous Planning*, 11.

27 Alyosha Goldstein, *Formations of United States Colonialism* (Durham, NC: Duke University Press, 2014); and Adam Barker, "The Contemporary Reality of Canadian Imperialism Settler Colonialism and the Hybrid Colonial State," *American Indian Quarterly* 33, no. 3 (2009): 325–351.

28 Tate LeFevre introduces the literature on settler colonialism that appreciates the
    diverse contributions, especially Indigenous feminism and gender studies. See
    Tate LeFevre, "Settler Colonialism," in *Oxford Bibliographies in Anthropology*, ed.
    John Jackson (Oxford: Oxford University Press, 2015), 1–26. Lorenzo Veracini
    points out, though, that settlers certainly engage in the other forms of colonialism
    during processes of settlement. See Lorenzo Veracini, *Settler Colonialism* (New
    York: Palgrave Macmillan, 2010). See also Eve Tuck and K. Wayne Yang, "Decolo-
    nization Is Not a Metaphor," *Decolonization: Indigeneity, Education and Society* 1,
    no. 1 (2012): 1–40.

29 Goldstein, *Formations of United States Colonialism*.

30 Kyle P. Whyte, "Indigenous Food Systems, Environmental Justice, and Settler-
    Industrial States," in *Global Food, Global Justice: Essays on Eating under Globaliza-
    tion*, ed. Mary C. Rawlinson and Caleb Ward (Newcastle upon Tyne: Cambridge
    Scholars Publishing, 2015), 143–166.

31 Ibid.

32 Ibid.

33 We learned of this history through teachings at the Indigenous Planning Summer
    Institute in 2017, hosted by the Sustainable Development Institute of the College
    of Menominee Nation in Shawano, WI. Although see also the Menominee testi-
    monies about rice in Jenks, *The Wild Rice Gatherers*.

34 Annette Baier, "Trust and Anti-trust," *Ethics* 96 (1986): 231–260.

35 For a philosophical account of trust and knowledge related to the claims here, see
    Naomi Scheman, "Toward a Sustainable Epistemology," *Social Epistemology* 26,
    nos. 3–4 (2012): 471–489.

36 Mishuana Goeman and Jennifer Denetdale, "Native Feminisms: Legacies, Inter-
    ventions, and Indigenous Sovereignties," *Wicazo Sa Review* 24, no. 2 (2009): 9–13;
    Joyce Green, ed., *Making Space for Indigenous Feminism* (London: Zed Books,
    2007); and Sarah Deer, *The Beginning and End of Rape* (Minneapolis: University
    of Minnesota Press, 2015).

37 Ronald Trosper, "Northwest Coast Indigenous Institutions That Supported Resil-
    ience and Sustainability," *Ecological Economics* 41, no. 2 (2012): 329–344.

38 Eve Tuck & Rubén Gaztambide-Fernández, "Curriculum, Replacement, and Set-
    tler Futurity," *Journal of Curriculum Theorizing* 29, no. 1 (2013): 72–89.

39 Ibid.

40 Goeman and Denetdale, "Native Feminisms," 9–10.

41 Leanne Simpson and Glen Coulthard, interviewed by Eric Ritskes, *Decoloniza-
    tion: Indigeneity, Education and Society* (journal blog), November 26, 2014, https://
    decolonization.wordpress.com.

42 Gerald Vizenor, *Manifest Manners: Narratives on Postindian Survivance* (Lincoln:
    University of Nebraska Press, 1994), vii.

43 Karl Kroeber, "Why It's a Good Thing Gerald Vizenor Is Not an Indian," in
    Survivance: Narratives of Native Presence, ed. G. Vizenor (Lincoln: University of
    Nebraska Press, 2008), 25.

44 Audra Simpson, "Consent's Revenge," *Cultural Anthropology* 31, no. 3 (2016): 326–333.

45 Dian Million, *Therapeutic Nations: Healing in an Age of Indigenous Human Rights* (Tucson: University of Arizona Press, 2013), 28.

46 Ibid., 32.

47 Te Kipa Kepa Brian Morgan, "A Tangata Whenua Perspective on Sustainability using the Mauri Model: Towards Decision Making Balance with Regard to our Social, Economic, Environmental and Cultural Well-Being," paper presented at the International Conference on Sustainability Engineering and Science, July 7–9, 2004, Auckland, New Zealand, [5], Sustainability Society, www.thesustainability society.org.nz.

48 Ibid.

49 Te Kipa Kepa Brian Morgan, "The Value of a Hapū Perspective to Municipal Water Management Practice: Mauri and Potential Contribution to Sustainability Decision Making in Aotearoa New Zealand" (PhD diss., University of Auckland, 2008), "Waiora and Cultural Identity Water Quality Assessment Using the Mauri Model," *AlterNative: An International Journal of Indigenous Peoples* 3, no. 1 (2006): 42–67, and *Mauriometer*, www.mauriometer.com, accessed 2016.

50 Mary Arquette, "Tribal Adaptation Case Study," presentation at the Shifting Seasons Summit: Building Capacity for Tribal Climate Change Adaptation, 2014, College of Menominee Nation, Keshena, WI.

51 St. Regis Mohawk Tribe, Environment Division, "Climate Change Adaptation Plan for Akwesasne" (Akwesasne: St. Regis Mohawk Tribe, August 30, 2013), www.srmtenv.org.

52 Diné Policy Institute, "Diné Food Sovereignty" (Tsaile, AZ: Diné Policy Institute, April 2014), www.dinecollege.edu.

53 This section draws significantly from the rigorous historical account of the development of the Sustainable Development Institute and the theoretical model of sustainability in Michael J. Dockry, Katherine Hall, William Van Lopik, and Christopher M. Caldwell, "Sustainable Development Education, Practice, and Research: An Indigenous Model of Sustainable Development at the College of Menominee Nation, Keshena, WI, USA," *Sustainability Science* 11, no. 1 (2016): 127–138.

54 See the American Indian Higher Education Consortium at www.aihec.org for information about tribal colleges and universities.

55 Paul Boyer, "First Survey of Tribal College Students Reveals Attitudes," *Tribal College* 9, no. 2 (1997): 36.

56 College of Menominee Nation, President position description and college mission statement (Keshena, WI: College of Menominee Nation, January 30, 2017), www .menominee.edu.

57 Diana Morris, "Letter from the President" (Keshena, WI: College of Menominee Nation, n.d.), www.menominee.edu., accessed December 19, 2017.

58 Verna Fowler, quoted in Clifton Conrad and Marybeth Gasman, *Educating a Diverse Nation: Lessons from Minority-Serving Institutions* (Cambridge, MA: Harvard University Press, 2015), 74.
59 Dockry et al., "Sustainable Development Education, Practice, and Research," 129.
60 Ibid., 129.
61 Ibid.
62 Ibid.
63 See Vine Deloria and Clifford Lytle, *The Nations Within: The Past and Future of American Indian Sovereignty* (New York: Pantheon Books, 1984).
64 Beck, *Seige and Survival,* and *The Struggle for Self-Determination*; Grignon et al., "Menominee Indian Reservation Historical Review"; and Nicholas Peroff, *Menominee Drums: Tribal Termination and Restoration, 1954–1974* (Norman: University of Oklahoma, 2006).
65 Dockry et al., "Sustainable Development Education, Practice, and Research," 130.
66 Ibid.
67 Ibid.
68 Ibid.
69 Ibid.
70 Ibid.
71 Ibid.
72 Ibid., 131.
73 Julie Maldonado et al., "The Story of Rising Voices: Facilitating Collaboration between Indigenous and Western Ways of Knowing," in *Responses to Disasters and Climate Change: Understanding Vulnerability and Fostering Resilience,* ed. Michèle Companion and Miriam S. Chaiken, 15–26 (New York: CRC Press, 2016).

7

Situating Sustainability in the Luxury City

Toward a Critical Urban Research Agenda

MIRIAM GREENBERG

On November 3, 2013, a new monument to sustainability was inaugu
rated with much fanfare on the eastern edge of San Francisco's Golden
Gate Park, abutting the famed hippie haven of Haight Ashbury. Dubbed
the "Golden Gate Park CommUNITY Garden," the site included sixty-
seven gardening plots, a greenhouse, an orchard, a tool-lending shed,
and outdoor classrooms in which free courses in "Pollinators of San
Francisco" and "Vermicomposting" were to be offered.[1] The project
seemed the ultimate expression of contemporary planners' and policy
makers' embrace of eco-consciousness, now driven by a new generation's demand for sustainable and locally grown food. As the Recreation
and Parks Department press release announced, the garden was built
"to meet the need for more community garden plots" citywide—with a
waiting list five hundred long for these plots cited—as well as to advance
former mayor Gavin Newsom's "Executive Directive 09-03: Healthy
and Sustainable Food for San Francisco," which called for a historic
increase in space allocated for urban agriculture through rezoning and
land reclamation (Newsom 2009; San Francisco Recreation and Parks
2013). Meanwhile, the semiotically lettered CommUNITY Garden was
presented as not just another Recreation and Parks Department community garden, of which there were already thirty-six citywide. Rather,
it was elevated as a "demonstration" of cutting edge urban agricultural
design and practice, as well as the power of popular participation in such
efforts.

Yet, at the same time, the launch of this new garden revealed quite
starkly the degree to which contemporary urban sustainability projects do not simply respond to popular demand or reflect a policy and

planning objective that furthers clear social and ecological ends. Rather, the high-profile demonstration value of the CommUNITY Garden had a number of lower-profile, if quite powerful, backers and beneficiaries. Upon closer inspection one finds that the "community" the garden served was largely that of real estate and business interests at the local and city scale as well as new and prospective upper-income residents on the Haight's nearby, rapidly gentrifying streets.

One sign of this was the garden's sponsorship and branding. Private donors included Levi Strauss & Co., the global communications firm YP (formerly the Yellow Pages), and CBS EcoMedia, with all helping to cut the ribbon at the opening ceremony, posting extensive coverage of the event through their social media feeds, and inserting their brands through signage in key spots around the garden's grounds. Thus the demonstration value of the project advanced best practices in garden design as well as the companies' own green branding and marketing efforts. As EcoMedia and San Francisco Recreation and Parks announced, Levi Strauss's gift funded the innovative "permeable paving" that "contributes to the environmentally friendly nature of the garden by allowing rainwater to flow through the earth and recharge the city's groundwater." YP's gift "funded the construction of the community garden's vibrant vertical gardening space, which demonstrates the possibility of having a garden even in small spaces and dense urban environments where residents may not have a yard." Janine Lappin, general manager of sales in San Francisco for YP, added: "Our mission is to help local businesses and communities grow—and we're committed to doing this daily by partnering with our valued customers and through projects like this. . . . Our brand mantra is to 'help get things done' and this project is a great opportunity to help get something great done for the San Francisco community" (San Francisco Recreation and Parks 2013). Here "sustainability" was understood as much in terms of community and ecological "growth" as in the growth of brand equity for the sponsoring companies and their clients who were now associated with this cutting-edge green space.

Yet another indication of the CommUNITY Garden's market-oriented approach, if harder to spot, was in the very different kind of sustainability project it was replacing—and, indeed, actively displacing. The very site on which this demonstration garden was being erected was the former home of the Haight Ashbury Neighborhood Council

Recycling Center (HANC RC). The HANC RC had been the inhabitant of this space for forty years until being forcibly evicted in January 2013, after two years of entrenched opposition by longtime community members, in order to put the CommUNITY Garden in its place.[2] These community members included the low-income and often homeless recyclers for whom the recycling center was a vital source of livelihood. And it included the recycling activists and advocates who had created and maintained it, together with a distributed network throughout the city, for decades. Indeed, HANC RC had been a leader in the "green guerrilla" movement that led to the passage of the original "bottle bills" in California and across the United States in the 1970s. The displacement of this neighborhood fixture revealed much about a shift in understandings of "what we mean by green" and what was to be sustained by sustainability projects in this increasingly affluent and unequal city.

The city's battle to replace the recycling center with a high-end garden played out over the course of two years, as HANC's defenders built a new garden of their own, with some ultimately locking themselves to fences in an attempt to block demolition. The battle played out on the front pages of rival newspapers, where opposition to HANC often served as shorthand for growing animus against a more visible homeless population arising amid San Francisco's tech gentrification and housing shortage. This battle went unmentioned at the ribbon cutting for the celebrated, state-of-the-art, corporate-sponsored garden. Yet HANC, the community it served, and the community that had fought to defend it, haunted the ceremonies—as did the alternative, non-market oriented, and apparently obsolete approach to sustainability it represented.

Understood politically, the battle of the HANC RC versus the CommUNITY Garden represented a clash between rival forms of sustainability, one "grey" and one "green" (Angelo 2017), one less real estate and business friendly, one more so. To put this emerging approach to sustainability in class terms, as recent scholarship has begun to do, it also signaled a shift from "popular" to "luxury" ecologies and a struggle for dominance between these (Cohen 2017).[3] Such struggles between rival and unequal approaches to sustainability are far from isolated. Indeed, I would argue, they have become a constitutive part of the broader struggle to advance urban sustainability in an era of widening wealth gaps, neoliberal governance, and luxury city development.

In this chapter, and in line with the goals of this volume, I argue that we need to "situate sustainability" within particular epistemological fields and communities in order to understand this growing contentiousness between rival versions of the concept. Further, it helps to see how these epistemological formations are themselves quite literally situated geographically, shaped by, and shaping of, the places, communities, social relations, and political ecologies in which they emerge. As investments into greening are increasingly designed to serve economic aims for powerful actors in aspiring global cities and regions, prevailing historically and culturally rooted understandings of sustainability are often reframed and redefined, if not replaced, in favor of a more instrumentalist, market-oriented interpretation. The latter is based on competitive—as opposed to cooperative—approaches to the local economy, on the exchange versus use value of urban space, and on the interests and aesthetics of those groups—understood in class as well as racialized terms—in a position to develop that space. In this sense market-oriented approaches frequently come into conflict with the "equity" and "ecology" orientation we commonly assume underlies classic understandings of the "3 E's" of sustainability, as laid out in the Brundtland Report (World Commission on Environment and Development 1987). They also pose fundamental questions about how environmental justice politics are to be practiced today. As I argue here, a more critical approach to sustainability that takes seriously the role of power, place, and history in shaping our use of the term will be necessary for any such politics, and scholarship, moving forward.

Market-Oriented Sustainability in the Luxury City

The closure of the HANC RC due to local pressures and preferences was not an isolated case. It came in the midst of a wave of recycling center closures concentrated in the northern, most rapidly gentrifying parts of the city—with some recycling activists arguing that the fall of HANC sparked a "domino effect" that accelerated this ongoing process (Dunn 2013; Sabatini 2014). One of the striking, ironic aspects of these closures was that they came at a time when San Francisco was winning awards as one of the greenest cities on the planet due in large part to its "Zero Waste" campaign, run by private waste hauler Recology and focused on curbside recycling. The metrics of the city's advance toward "zero" were dubious, not least because the materials that once went to local recycling centers were now largely diverted into waste transfer stations and landfills in poorer, non-white, southern areas of the city and beyond the city's borders.[4] Yet they earned the city plaudits and symbolic capital in the world of urban sustainability rankings.

These changes speak to the degree to which market-oriented, eco-branded urban sustainability solutions are not only directed at driving local land exchange values—values depressed by proximity to messy grey ecologies like recycling centers—but also at positioning cities themselves within a growing global system of place-based competition. In part this development is a continuation of decades of interurban and interregional competition. But the rise of sustainability rankings as coin of the realm also speaks to the ascension of urban sustainability policy, planning, and metrics within the broader global sustainability movement of the last twenty years. In effect, cities are increasingly held up as both the leading culprit in, and solution for, the planet's mounting climate-related environmental problems.[5]

We can identify a number of reasons for this focus. The first is an objective one, namely that, in a period of "urban revolution" (Lefebvre [1968] 2003) popularly termed "the urban age," as urban environments and infrastructures have extended their reach over the surface of the globe, awareness of the role of cities in climate change is now common knowledge and common sense. Another reason cited by the United Nations as well as by urban policy networks is a pragmatic one: Cities and other sub-national units operating as networked actors can be more agile and effective in responding to climate threats than politically hamstrung national governments and international governing bodies (Gordon 2016).

Finally, while environmental justice groups have long recognized the role of urban ecology for public and planetary health, the popularity of urban sustainability in policy and planning discourse is increasingly spread via the advocacy and self-promotion of entrepreneurial cities, as well as that of the corporations, real estate developers, design firms, and financial interests based in, or working with, these cities. Many have formed or benefited from influential global alliances and think tanks—like C40 Fund for Cities, the 100 Resilient Cities initiative of the Rockefeller Foundation—to support "best practices" in urban sustainability policy and planning through awards, networking, and publicity. Gaining a "sustainability edge" over competitor cities, as well as over corporations, has become de rigueur in broader economic development efforts (Greenberg 2015). Cities and urban regions now race to win green credentials, in part as a tool to attract affluent residents and achieve global city status. In the process, sustainability in design, building, and amenities has become increasingly associated with high-end, luxury development and a necessary component of the "luxury city."[6]

One might argue, not inaccurately, that this highly competitive approach to urban sustainability has been an effective way to popularize the "3 E's" and to sell sustainability by demonstrating its return on investment. In the long tradition of technocratic and modernist notions of ecology, the argument that sustainability can be a profit-generating "win-win" option—good for the environment and good for capitalism—is now widely endorsed.[7] Yet, as critical scholars of eco-modernism have themselves long argued, the contradictions of this approach are less frequently acknowledged (Hajer 1995; Smith 2008; McKendry 2013). Namely, market-oriented urban sustainability has arisen alongside of—and helped drive—escalating rents and inequality, displacement, and sprawl, as well as increased consumption and greenhouse gas emissions. In the United States researchers have found a correlation between inequality and unaffordability of metro regions and their "progressivism," including emphasis on sustainable policy and projects (Thompson 2014). Meanwhile, scholars of "just sustainabilities" have written of a widespread "equity deficit" in mainstream urban sustainability policy and planning (Agyeman 2013). With their emphasis on environmental upgrades that lead to gentrification (Chapple 2009; Checker 2011)—and without attention to mitigating displacement by protecting affordable housing, cultural institutions, and small business—many of the most successful urban greening projects today, and many of the "greenest" cities, are also associated with excluding and disadvantaging the low income and, disproportionately, people of color.

Clearly there is much to learn from studying these perverse urban sustainability success stories. They beg the questions: Whose "sustainability" are we talking about? How are we to make sense of the competing and contradictory uses of the term in sites like the Golden Gate Park CommUNITY Garden, and so many other cases? And what are the new environmental politics inherent in these struggles? In the rest of this chapter, I introduce a research agenda called *critical sustainabilities*, which I think can be helpful in addressing these questions.

Critical Sustainabilities

We may begin by stating the problem: Dominant forms of urban sustainability today, beyond simply *not addressing* issues of equity sufficiently, play a significant role in *contributing to inequity*. In common parlance we associate sustainability with the balance between human and non-human systems and among the "3 E's" of economy, ecology, and equity (World Commission on Environment and Development 1987). Further, with the 1992 Rio Convention and its landmark Agenda 21 initiative, these goals have been extended and embraced most fervently at the local, urban scale. Yet in many contemporary urban contexts since the neoliberal shift of the 1970s, in which austerity undercuts social programs and "economy" is understood primarily in free market terms, potential market impact plays an outsized role in determining which sustainability projects get funding. Such market orientation can fuel out-of-balance development that reduces both social equity and ecosystem health. Further, given the complex metabolic interrelationships between urban and natural systems in cities and regions (Gandy 2004), we also see how these impacts can create unintended consequences, both social and ecological, at multiple geographic scales.

As a result, we must address the contradictions in our core conception and practice of sustainability and become more critical in our use of the term. Here I would reference an approach to the study of sustainability that I, together with a group of scholars across universities in Northern California, developed, called *Critical Sustainabilities: Competing Discourses of Urban Sustainability in California* (Greenberg 2013).[8] Across academic and professional domains, we found multiple and divergent uses and forms of "sustainability" and sought to take a critical approach to its study, in hopes this might inform future sustainability scholarship, practice, planning, and policy. As a first step, we recognized the importance of "situating sustainability" both spatially and epistemologically, to understand the emergence of and relationality between these multiple forms.

Spatially, we situated our study in our own famously green North-ern California region—including the San Francisco and Monterey Bay areas, in which our campuses are located. Epistemologically, we sought to trace the production of sustainability knowledge and practice rooted historically in this region. Drawing on the work of Donna Haraway that animates this volume, we came to recognize that the distinct sustain-abilities circulating in our region must be understood as always situated in "particular communities," and further, their particular rationalities must be seen as a product of "ongoing critical interpretation among 'fields' of interpreters and decoders" (Haraway 1991, 196). These fields can themselves be situated spatially and historically within particular regions, and thus they bear lessons for broader analysis of how distinct fields emerge elsewhere.

Northern California happens to be a particularly renowned space of urban sustainability practice. From San Francisco to Silicon Valley to Santa Cruz, its cities and urban regions are considered by many—not the least their own boosters—as meccas for sustainability policy, plan-ning, and experimentation going back (at least) to the 1970s. In this sense it has been at the forefront of numerous movements—cultural, scientific, and political—associated with advancing urban sustainabil-ity, with the green guerrillas behind the California Bottle Bill just one example (e.g., Walker 2009). It is also a space of tech and design in-novation tied to counterculture green movements, home of "eco-city" builders, "locavore" cuisine, *Whole Earth Catalogue*–inspired lifestyles, and a generation of seekers inspired by "ecotopian" fantasies in science fiction literature and film (Kirk 2007; Callenbach 2015; Sadler 2015a, 2015b).

Yet the region is also home to some of the greatest urban and en-vironmental inequality in the United States, with San Francisco itself the most unequal city in the nation. (Berube 2014; Berube and Holmes 2015; National Low Income Housing Coalition 2015). Not unrelatedly, it has become ground zero for some of the most entrenched battles over many of its most celebrated sustainability projects. Increas-ingly in the last decade, these projects have been found to exacer-bate place-based inequality and waves of displacement—not only of lower-income people but also of rival forms of sustainability, and with these, of socionatural urban ecologies. The participants in the *Critical*

Sustainabilities project explore the tensions, impacts, and struggles emerging out of this contradiction in numerous sites throughout the region. These include the threat posed by "Google Buses" to embattled public transit networks (Miller 2015) and the devastating impact of the reclamation of wetlands and construction of a luxury eco-city in Bayview Hunters Point on the last majority African American neighborhood in San Francisco (Dillon 2014; Brahinsky 2015), as well as the impact on livelihoods and rents posed by the eviction of HANC RC to build the Golden Gate Park CommUNITY Garden (Pudup 2015).

The *Critical Sustainabilities* project shows that even in famously sustainable Northern California—perhaps *especially there*—differences in and conflicts over the uses of sustainability abound, are central to the broader politics of urban change, and require our critical analysis and engagement. In what follows, I explore some of the epistemologies we traced through this regional research, in hopes this might inform analysis beyond the borders of California.

Multiple and Competing Sustainabilities

Where are we to begin in a critical analysis of "sustainability" practice? One must acknowledge that we are operating in a world in which multiple sustainabilities circulate, some more powerfully than others, and with often confusing and contradictory effects. These differently situated sustainabilities are not mutually exclusive, and they frequently operate in tandem and find common cause. But by distinguishing among them we can see how they emerge from distinct epistemological roots, privilege different values and "environments" to be sustained, and entail different technologies, practices, aesthetics, and modes of governance in bringing about their visions of a sustainable future.

One of these sustainabilities, discussed above in the case of the CommUNITY Garden, may be called *market oriented*. Here there is an overriding effort to sustain the "environment for capital" and with it the quality of life required for a corporate-friendly metropolis, as well as the technologies that enable this quality of life. From hybrid tech buses to vertical gardens, these solutions are both gray and green, advancing modernist infrastructural plans and romantic notions of nature. What unites them is their instrumentality and, as such, the degree to which they are distinct from—if often seeking to incorporate—a range of other, alternative, non-market sustainabilities.

One of these alternative approaches might be called the *vernacular sustainabilities* that privilege everyday, popular, low-cost, and culturally rooted ways of living and working with nature. Examples include recycling, biking, carpooling, community gardens, and communal and affordable housing (see, e.g., Lugo 2015). These are often taken-for-granted, if not unrecognized, forms of sustainability, and as Daniel Aldana Cohen argues, their practitioners are not counted among the "low-carbon protagonists" in battles for the climate friendly city (Cohen 2017). In the midst of these high-profile approaches, Northern California has been home to generations of vernacular sustainability practices rooted in the region's diverse low-income, immigrant, and indigenous communities, both urban and rural.

Other non-market approaches include the *eco-oriented sustainabilities* that privilege science-based approaches to living within ecosystem limits. Here the "environment" is understood largely, though not exclusively, in non-human terms, and emphasis is placed on recognition of how complex ecosystems and metabolisms are entangled with, but also separate from, human systems. The rise of the science of ecology itself, and with it ecologically holistic approaches to architecture and design, may be seen as a leading example of this (Sadler 2015c).

Another prevalent approach is that of *justice-oriented sustainability*. Here the human tends to be emphasized over the non-human, with a focus on questions of social equity, access, and diversity in relation to the environment, rather than analysis of the materiality of the bionatural environment. This approach, as many contributors to this volume and the *Critical Sustainabilities* project explore, reaches across green/gray boundaries into questions of food, transportation, and climate justice (Gray-O'Connor 2015; Guthman 2015).

A New Politics of Sustainability

Close analysis of these competing approaches to sustainability—both market and non-market—reveals that politics matters with regard to the ultimate form of sustainable policy and planning that is pursued. Greening and sustainability are now playing a crucial role in the uneven production of space under capitalism. Meanwhile, the capitalist production of space is playing a crucial role in reshaping how we understand "greening" and "sustainability" and where and how we see it occurring. Much attention has focused, and rightly so, on "ecological" or "environmental gentrification" to help analyze the political economy and political ecology of this form of urbanization, and in particular the extent to which displacement and sociospatial inequality can result from sustainability projects (Quastel 2009; Checker 2011; Gould and Lewis 2016). A critical sustainabilities framework builds on such analyses to also make sense of those forms of sustainability that are displaced in this process and the politics surrounding this displacement. In a process I call *uneven sustainable development*, a critical perspective also examines those spaces of devalorization and environmental sacrifice outside the frame of environmental gentrification in the urban core. There, in cities' poorest neighborhoods and their expanding peripheries, we find unsustainable forms of urbanization—from the relocation of toxins, waste, and industry to sprawl, deforestation, and habitat loss (Greenberg, n.d.).

These contradictory politics of sustainability are inextricably tied to the normative cultural and ideological role played by "nature" and the "urban" in our society (Williams 1973; Angelo and Jerolmack 2012; Angelo 2017). Sustainable urban development may be seen as a "good thing" because it makes cities more natural or beneficial to nature and, as a correlative, because it counters what are imagined to be innately negative features of cities and urban life. In this sense, urban development that is "sustainable" and "green" can be more difficult to oppose or contest than that which is not and can have a depoliticizing, or "postpolitical," effect in the context of struggles over urban development and the "right to the city" more broadly (Swyngedouw 2009).

Yet this (de)politicization is itself contingent. As we can see in the case of the multiple alternative approaches to sustainability, whether oriented primarily toward vernacular practice, ecology, or social justice, these may or may not be subsumed by market-oriented and elite-serving agendas. From community gardens to recycling, these projects can take wildly distinct forms depending on their context and situated-ness, spatially, epistemologically, and politically. Indeed, emerging struggles in defense of vernacular, ecological, and justice-oriented approaches to sustainability, and against the environmentally degrading and socially displacing impacts of market-oriented ones, point to a new politics of environmental justice. Environmental justice movements increasingly recognize the need to situate themselves within these broader debates, both over the meaning of sustainability and the right to the city and region.

Conclusion

To "situate" our studies of sustainability, we must dig deeper into the urban social relations and urban political ecologies that provide the soil for particular sustainability projects to grow and flourish or to die on the vine. When we do this digging, we find out how rooted many of the leading sustainability projects are in the market-oriented political economy and ecology of contemporary cities. From these roots, we find urban sustainability taking the form of luxury eco-development and growing alongside of, and helping to drive, increasing unaffordability and displacement. We also can trace the ramifying impact that such heavily marketed projects have in mobilizing prevailing understandings of, and approaches to, urban greening and sustainability nationally and globally. In essence, these high-profile projects help to define urban greening and sustainability as an elite practice, as well as one that is integral to market-oriented urban development.

Yet as revealed by so many urban sustainability success stories today—with San Francisco and the city regions of Northern California—it is impossible to disaggregate the contradictory impacts of approaches to sustainability linked primarily to market-oriented growth. Limited understandings of the "E" of economy attract investment and increase property values and rents, benefiting elite urban actors over others by not providing shared benefits—whether those might be jobs, or affordable housing, or the taxing and redistribution of corporate profits. As a result, in too many sustainability plans, the "E" of equity is watered down, excluding people and practices that are pushed or priced out. Significant, too, is the impact on ecology within this unbalanced approach, as evidenced by the limits to achieving San Francisco's "zero-waste" goal once it means sharing valuable real estate with recycling centers and their users, as well as by the impact on greenhouse gas emissions as low-income people are increasingly displaced to, and forced to commute from, the periphery.

Clearly the case must be made that we need to rethink the balance of the 3 E's, as well as a simple celebration of the inherent capacity of cities to bring about our dream of a sustainable future. To conceive of and realize this vital dream will require a much broader reimagining of how cities are governed, by whom, and according to whose vision of sustainability. Crucial in this reimagining will be a situated and critical approach to sustainability in our policy, planning, scholarship, and political practice.

NOTES

1 San Francisco Recreation and Parks (2013).

2 The geographer and garden scholar Mary Beth Pudup was the first to document the battle over the HANC RC and its implications for sustainability. See Pudup (2015, and forthcoming).

3 Battles over the visibility of garbage and recycling have figured large, particularly in class- and race-inflected debates over urban sustainability. See Pellow (2002) and Greenberg (n.d.).

4 On the politics of waste diversion metrics, and Recology in particular, see Mac-Bride (2011, 2013).

5 For scholars who lay out these arguments, see the overview in Portney (2003). For the United Nations account, see UN Habitat (2009).

6 The idea of the "luxury city"—one that competes with other cities on the basis of providing a high-value and high-cost product—was advanced in 2003 via a behind-the-scenes economic development campaign carried out by New York's "CEO-mayor" Michael Bloomberg. See Greenberg (2008); and Brash (2011). It should be added that Bloomberg, who trumpeted sustainability through his citywide, urban sustainability blueprint PlaNYC 2030 and as co-founder of the C40 Fund for Cities, a market-oriented, global network of sustainable cities, was instrumental in showing the usefulness of urban sustainability for the luxury city approach (Greenberg 2015).

7 The UN embrace of "sustainable development" in the late 1980s may be seen as an effort to find a kinder, more regulated form of capitalism at the end of the Cold War. In this sense, the effort was initially alligned with slow-growth environmentalist movements. See the introduction to Isenhour, McDonough, and Checker (2014).

8 See the *Critical Sustainabilities* website at https://critical-sustainabilities.ucsc.edu. The *Critical Sustainabilities* project originated in 2012–2013 as a series of workshops attended by students and faculty at the University of California, Santa Cruz; the University of California, Berkeley; the University of California, Davis; and the University of San Francisco, and it was supported by the University of California Humanities Research Institute. It continues today, in expanded form, through this website.

BIBLIOGRAPHY

Agyeman, Julian 2013. *Introducing Just Sustainabilities: Policy, Planning, and Practice.* London: Zed Books.

Angelo, Hillary. 2017. "From the City Lens toward Urbanisation as a Way of Seeing: Country/City Binaries on an Urbanising Planet." *Urban Studies* 54, no. 1: 158–178. DOI: 0042098016629312.

Angelo, Hillary, and Colin Jerolmack. 2012. "Nature's Looking Glass." *Contexts* 11, no. 1 (Winter): 24–29.

Berube, Alan. 2014. "All Cities Not Created Unequal." Report, February 20. Washington, DC: Brookings Institution. www.brookings.edu.

Berube, Alan, and Nathalie Holmes. 2015. "Some cities are still more unequal than others—an update." Report, March 17. Washington, DC: Brookings Institution. www.brookings.edu.

Brahinsky, Rachel. 2014. "The Death of the City?" *Boom: A Journal of California* 4, no. 2 (Summer): 43–54.

Brahinsky, Rachel. 2015. "Bayview Hunters Point." *Critical Sustainabilities: Competing Discourses of Urban Sustainability in California*, June 1. www.ucsc.edu.

Brash, Julian. 2011. *Bloomberg's New York: Class and Governance in the Luxury City.* Athens: University of Georgia Press.

Callenbach, Ernest. 2015. *Ecotopia.* 40th anniversary ed. San Francisco: Heydey.

Chapple, Karen. 2009. "Mapping Susceptibility to Gentrification: The Early Warning Toolkit." Report, August. Berkeley: Center for Community Innovation.

Checker, Melissa. 2011. "Wiped out by the Green Wave: Environmental Gentrification and the Paradoxical Politics of Urban Sustainability." *City and Community* 23, no. 2:201–229.

Checker, Melissa. 2015. "Green Is the New Brown: 'Old School Toxics' and Environmental Gentrification on a New York City Waterfront." In *Sustainability in the Global City: Myth and Practice*, edited by Cynthia Isenhour, Gary McDonough, and Melissa Checker, 157–179. Cambridge: Cambridge University Press.

Cohen, Daniel Aldana. 2017. "The Other Low-Carbon Protagonists: Poor People's Movements and Climate Politics in a Global City." In *The City Is the Factory: New Solidarities and Spatial Strategies in an Urban Age*, edited by Miriam Greenberg and Penny Lewis, 140–157. Ithaca, NY: ILR Press, 2017.

Dillon, Lindsey. 2014. "Race, Waste, and Space: Brownfield Redevelopment and Environmental Justice at the Hunters Point Shipyard." *Antipode* 46, no. 5 (November): 1–17.

Dunn, Ed. 2013. "Domino Theory Proven: Wave of Recycling Center Closures." Haight Ashbury Neighborhood Council, October 2. www.hanc-sf.org.

Gandy, Matthew. 2004. "Rethinking Urban Metabolism: Water, Space and the Modern City." *City* 8, no. 3 (December): 363–379.

Gordon, David J. 2016. "The Politics of Accountability in Networked Urban Climate Governance" *Global Environmental Politics* 16, no. 2 (May): 82–100.

Gould, Kenneth A., and Tammy L. Lewis. 2016. *Green Gentrification: Urban Sustainability and the Struggle for Environmental Justice*. New York: Routledge.

Gray-O'Connor, Jen. 2015. "Transit Oriented Development." *Critical Sustainabilities: Competing Discourses of Urban Sustainability in California*, June 1. www.ucsc.edu.

Greenberg, Miriam. 2008. *Branding New York: How a City in Crisis Was Sold to the World*. New York: Routledge.

Greenberg, Miriam. 2013. "What on Earth Is Sustainable?" *Boom: A Journal of California* 3, no. 4 (Winter): 54–66.

Greenberg, Miriam. 2015. "'The Sustainability Edge': Crisis, Competition, and the Rise of Green City Branding." In *Sustainability in the Global City: Myth and Practice*, edited by Cynthia Isenhour, Gary McDonough, and Melissa Checker, 105–130. Cambridge: Cambridge University Press.

Greenberg, Miriam. n.d. "Whose Ecotopia?: Displacement and Uneven Sustainable Development in the Green City." Unpublished manuscript.

Guthman, Julie. 2015. "Food Justice." *Critical Sustainabilities: Competing Discourses of Urban Sustainability in California*, June 1. www.ucsc.edu.

Hajer, Maarten A. 1995. *The Politics of Environmental Discourse: Ecological Modernization and the Policy Process*. New York: Oxford University Press.

Haraway, Donna. 1991. *Simians, Cyborgs, and Women: The Reinvention of Nature*. New York: Routledge.

Isenhour, Cynthia, Gary McDonough, and Melissa Checker, eds. 2015. *Sustainability in the Global City: Myth and Practice*. Cambridge: Cambridge University Press.

Kirk, Andrew. 2007. *Counterculture Green: The Whole Earth Catalog and American Environmentalism*. Lawrence: University Press of Kansas.

Lefebvre, Henri. [1968] 2003. *The Urban Revolution*. Minneapolis: University of Minnesota Press.

Lugo, Adonia. 2015. "Bicycling." *Critical Sustainabilities: Competing Discourses of Urban Sustainability in California*, June 1. www.ucsc.edu.

MacBride, Samantha. 2011. *Recycling Reconsidered: The Present Failure and Future Promise of Environmental Action in the United States*. Cambridge: MIT Press.

MacBride, Samantha. 2013. "San Francisco's Famous 80% Waste Diversion Rate: Anatomy of an Exemplar." *Discard Studies*, December 6, 2013. https://discardstudies.com.

McKendry, Corina. 2013. "Environmental Discourse and Economic Growth in the Greening of Postindustrial Cities." In *The Economy of Green Cities: A World Compendium on the Green Urban Economy*, edited by Richard Simpson and Monika Zimmerman, 23–32. New York: Springer.

Miller, Kristin. 2015. "Google Bus." *Critical Sustainabilities: Competing Discourses of Urban Sustainability in California*, June 1. www.ucsc.edu.

National Low Income Housing Coalition. 2015. "Out of Reach 2015," May 19. Washington, DC: National Low Income Housing Coalition. www.nlihc.org.

Newsom, Gavin. 2009. "Executive Directive 09-03: Healthy and Sustainable Food for San Francisco," July 9. San Francisco: Office of the Mayor, City and County of San Francisco.

Pellow, David Naguib. 2002. *Garbage Wars: The Struggle for Environmental Justice in Chicago*. Cambridge, MA: MIT Press.

Portney, Kent. 2003. *Taking Urban Sustainability Seriously: Economic Development, the Environment, and Quality of Life in American Cities*. Cambridge, MA: MIT Press.

Pudup, Mary Beth. 2008. "It Takes a Garden: Cultivating Citizen-Subjects in Organized Garden Projects." *Geoforum* 39, no. 3 (May): 1228–1240.

Pudup, Mary Beth. 2015. "HANC Recycling Center." *Critical Sustainabilities: Competing Discourses of Urban Sustainability in California*. www.ucsc.edu.

Pudup, Mary Beth. Forthcoming. "The (New) Soul of San Francisco." In *The Garden in the City*, chapter 5.

Quastel, Noah. 2009. "Political Ecologies of Gentrification." *Urban Geography* 30, no. 7:694–725.

Sabatini, Joshua. 2014. "Debate Heats up over SF's Dwindling Recycling Centers." *San Francisco Examiner*, July 8.

Sadler, Simon. 2015a. "Mandalas or Raised Fists? Hippie Holism, Panther Totality, and Another Modernism." In *Hippie Modernism: The Struggle for Utopia*, edited by Andrew Blauvelt, Greg Castillo, and Esther Choi, 114–125. Minneapolis: Walker Art Center.

Sadler, Simon. 2015b. "Ecological Design." *Critical Sustainabilities: Competing Discourses of Urban Sustainability in California*, June 1. www.ucsc.edu.

Sadler, Simon. 2015c. "Whole Earth Catalogue." *Critical Sustainabilities: Competing Discourses of Urban Sustainability in California*, June 1. www.ucsc.edu.

San Francisco Recreation and Parks. 2013. "Golden Gate Park CommUNITY Garden Opens: SF Rec and Park and Local Community Celebrate the Opening of a New Place to Grow." Press release, November 5. http://sfrecpark.org.

Smith, Neil. 2008. *Uneven Development: Nature, Capital, and the Production of Space*. Athens: University of Georgia Press.

Swyngedouw, Erik. 2009. "The Antinomies of the Postpolitical City: In Search of a Democratic Politics of Environmental Production." *International Journal of Urban and Regional Research* 33, no. 3 (September): 601–620.

Thompson, Derek. 2014. "Why Middle Class Americans Can't Afford to Live in Liberal Cities." *Atlantic*, October 29.

UN Habitat. 2009. "Cities and Climate Change Initiative: Launch and Conference Report." March 17. Oslo: UN Habitat.

Walker, Richard. 2009. *The Country in the City: The Greening of the San Francisco Bay Area*. Seattle: University of Washington Press.

Williams, Raymond. 1973. *The Country and the City*. London: Chatto & Windus.

World Commission on Environment and Development. 1987. *Our Common Future*. The Brundtland Report. Oxford: Oxford University Press.

8

Man Destroys Nature?

Gender, History, and the Feminist Praxis of Situating Sustainability

TRACI BRYNNE VOYLES

The historian can interpret the world while trying to change it.
—Joan Wallach Scott, *Gender and the Politics of History*, 1999

Hope, possibility, alternative, tradition, history, and creativity
can be remarkably powerful in the face of danger and absurdity.
—Christine Cuomo, *Feminism and Ecological Communities*, 1998

Every year on Earth Day, our social media accounts are flooded with
memes and cartoons that deliver particular kinds of messages about the
environment and environmentalism. In one, a doctor with a clipboard
informs the earth, perched on an exam table, "The bad news is you've
got advance-stage humans. The good news is they've just about run
their course and you should be on the mend soon." Similarly, one cartoon features Saturn sidling up to Earth to whisper, "Psst, if you want to
survive . . . never, *never* become infested with humans!" Another quips,
rather darkly, "I wonder if the next planet we destroy will also get its
own holiday." Or my personal favorite: Earth wears a T-shirt that reads,
"I'm with stupid," over an arrow pointing to a man with a shirt labeled
"mankind."

I could go on.

These memes all send a message that is familiar to most of us.
They are not new but rather draw from old themes in environmental
thought—reincarnations of, say, the popular cartoon character Pogo in
his dejected Earth Day message in 1971, as he gazed across a woodsy
scene cluttered with litter: "We have met the enemy," Pogo conceded
sadly, "and he is us."

In short, human-nature relationships are figured in a particular way that can be summed up with a basic equation: *Man destroys nature; subject verb object.* Human life itself, the equation implies, is inherently unsustainable. This is perhaps the simplest way to shorthand an important hegemonic environmental narrative that undergirds contemporary environmental politics. Environmental studies scholars have a term for this narrative: "environmental declensionism," or the notion that human-nature relations will always end in environmental decline and devastation.[1] This narrative has been central to mainstream stories about sustainability and particularly to the notion emerging from deep ecology that nature will be most self-sustaining, most resilient, and most itself if left entirely untouched by the hand of Man. This declensionism has even bled into—or, in some cases, become constitutive of—the field of environmental history, which often has the reputation (rightly or wrongly) of producing narratives of "just one damn decline after another."[2] As a result, students of environmental studies and environmental history, like the creators and sharers of dejected Earth Day messages, often report feeling distinctly pessimistic about possibilities for environmentalist change, having garnered the impression "that the American environment had gone from good to bad in an unrelentingly depressing story that left little or no hope for the future."[3]

The declensionist narrative—*Man destroys nature*—is unhelpful, even counterproductive, for a critical examination of human-nature relationships for more reasons than the need for college students to leave their classes feeling hopeful. Its limitations as a narrative framework are far more problematic than that. Positing "nature" as the victim of "mankind" is just too simple: It reduces all humans to "Man," the universal subject of Western philosophy and history; reduces all human-nature interactions to destruction; posits humans and nature as opposed poles of a dichotomy—pure and uncompromised by overlap or hybridity; and inheres Man with agency and nature with none, making nature exclusively an object to be acted upon. This, in short, is a totalizing, universalizing framework that flattens the diversity of human relationships to the nonhuman world. Situated sustainability, like the feminist science studies theorist Donna Haraway's concept of situated knowledges, "require[s] that the object of knowledge"—in this case, nature—"be pictured as an actor or agent, not seen as a screen or a ground or a resource."[4] Because the declensionist narrative places "nature" as victim and "Man" as victimizer, it runs the risk of obscuring the power dynamics involved in the basic narrative equation that undergirds it: *Man destroys nature; subject verb object.* By the mere fact of being the acted-upon object, with no agency of its own, nature is backgrounded, turned into a hapless resource for "Man's" own subjectivity and history.

This chapter asserts that the project of "join[ing] up" sustainability with gender, class, and racial justice requires a close analysis of what we mean by "sustainability."[5] Discourses of sustainability are steeped in the history of environmentalism. In fact, the very division of sustainability from social justice—cleaved in many academic and popular understandings of those spheres—reflects a Enlightenment-derived discursive cleavage of "Man" from "nature." Bringing together sustainability and justice, as the essays in this volume seek to do, requires nothing short of unmapping those deeply rooted (Western) ontological binaries. This essay takes up one particular iteration of sustainability discourse, rooted in the American environmentalist tradition: seeing "Man," writ large, as an undifferentiated and usually malevolent force affecting "nature." While this is but one strand of environmental thought, it is important (and, clearly, enduring). Here, I use this *Man destroys nature* framework as a foil for this particular strand of environmental thought. As Julie Sze et al. point out in the introduction to this volume, "how people *talk about* . . . environmental crises is important." That we often talk about environmental decline as a one-way street, from Man to nature, reflects larger problems in how sustainability and justice are imagined.

When it comes to producing critical, situated sustainabilities that hold promise for more justice-oriented environmental and social futures, the oversimplified formulation *Man destroys nature* will not do. Our environmental narratives, rather, must be grounded historically and pay heed to "situating sustainability" both historically and culturally; they must take an intersectional feminist approach to understanding who is doing the destroying, who is not, and what kinds of historical, interpersonal, and indeed *natural* contingencies produce those interactions.

This chapter explores the ways in which feminist environmental theories (such as, but not limited to, ecofeminism), environmental history, and environmental justice studies give us the tools to destabilize the declensionist environmental narrative, thinking more critically about "Man," "nature," and "destruction" alike.[6] I outline key themes and contributions in these fields that offer new insights into how we can understand the complex milieu of our human relationships to the nonhuman world. I argue that what these fields suggest to us is that sustainabilities, like feminist epistemology, must be situated in contingent and intersectional environmental knowledge and experience. This chapter's subtitle refers to the *praxis* of situating sustainabilities because I am interested in precisely that—the unity and simultaneity of thinking and doing. How do we *conceptualize* the need to situate our knowledge about sustainability, and how have activists and scholars gone about the work of *doing* it? And, given that, in Ariel Salleh's estimation, "ecological feminists are both street fighters and philosophers," how are many of us already engaged in this praxis?[7]

Subject Verb Object: Intersectional Feminist Theory on "Man," "Woman," "Power," and "Nature"

As some readers may already have guessed, I borrow my opening framework—*Man destroys nature*—from the feminist theorist Catharine MacKinnon, who wrote in 1982 on the theme of sexual objectification that "sexual objectification is the primary process of the subjection of women. It unites act with word, construction with expression, perception with enforcement, myth with reality. *Man fucks woman; subject verb object*."[8] In patriarchy, according to MacKinnon, "Women have been the nature, the matter, the acted upon, to be subdued by the acting subject seeking to embody himself in the social world."[9]

Similar to MacKinnon's argument about patriarchy and sexual objectification, I argue that this central formulation of human-nature relations—*Man destroys nature*—has both represented our environmental imaginaries and been imbricated in hegemonic material relationships to the nonhuman world; nature has been "the matter, the acted upon, to be subdued by the acting subject seeking to embody himself." As this might suggest, I set much store by the ecofeminist argument that patriarchy and environmental degradation are related power structures:[10] they share material and epistemological common ground, not least of which is the fact that both forms of power tend to operate by a mutual constitution—the feminization of nature and animals and the naturalization (and animalization) of women, people of color, and other Others.[11]

However, feminist theory has covered significant terrain since MacKinnon's formulation (in 1982) reduced women in general to the universal signifier "woman" and men to "man." Most importantly, feminists of color have revolutionized feminist theory by insisting on intersectional frameworks of patriarchy, sexism, and gender constructions, noting the ways in which the category of "woman" must always be understood as a subject position and an embodiment that is multiply and simultaneously produced through the social rubrics of race, class, gender, and sexuality. Put simply, there is no universal "woman"-hood—and, for that matter, no universal "man." As Christine Cuomo points out, false universalizations about women tend to be "based on the experiences and interests of women with privilege and power" and thus foreclose or erase the experiences and interests of women *without* privilege and power.[12] Nor are all women simply or equally acted upon—fucked—by patriarchy (nor are patriarchal actors always men). Intersectional feminist theory, rather, must account for difference, inequality, and privilege in the articulation of gender difference and gender justice.

With this in mind, I focus in the sections below on the need for intersectional, gendered, and historically contingent approaches to environmentalism and sustainability. To unpack the limitations of the declensionist narrative—*Man destroys nature*, full stop—is to unpack hegemonic environmental discourses, and particularly those that universalize sustainability and sustainable solutions to our current environmental problems. The solution to nature's affliction is not, as one Earth Day meme suggests, "for all of us to die"—or for a planet to never have been "infested" with humans in the first place (a metaphor, notably, that articulates its disapproval of humans by animalizing them)—but rather for particular kinds of relationships to nature to be disassembled, transformed, and reimagined in ways that are historically, socially, and geographically situated.

Gender, History, and the Feminist Praxis of Situating Sustainability

The declensionist narrative—*Man destroys nature*—is gendered in multiple ways that prevent a feminist approach to environmental sustainability. First, and most obviously, it explicitly reduces all people to "man" or "mankind," implicating all humans (women included) in a system of environmental destruction that, in reality, is perpetuated by certain kinds of people engaged in certain kinds of political, economic, and cultural practices. These practices and people are historically grounded, and their relationships to the environment are both *particular* and *contingent*, a point well demonstrated in many works in environmental studies and environmental history. In short, environmental destruction is situated, both in quality and in scale, as are other kinds of human relationships to the nonhuman world.

Second, the declensionist narrative thinly veils the gendered nature of what the literary critic Annette Kolodny deems "probably America's oldest and most cherished fantasy": that nature "is essentially feminine," not just a Mother (Earth), but "the total female principle of gratification"— mother, yes, but also virgin, wife, temptress, whore.[13] The land in this fantasy is in "repose," a passive receiver of human agency and human action. In this way, "nature" as passive receiver of "man's" destruction inheres patriarchal representations of women's roles as passive receivers of *men's* agency and action. This critique resonates with ecofeminist theory on the Western epistemological habit of thinking of the world in binary terms. Modern binaries cleave men from women, humans from nature, and self from other in ways that render the latter term (what Eve Sedgwick calls "Term B") subordinate, dependent, and part of the background—an object or resource for the former term's ("Term A's") agency and self-articulation.[14] These binaries share three central characteristics: they are treated as *universal* or *natural* ways of seeing the world; they are *hierarchical*, placing Term A in a position of dominance over Term B; and they are *relational* and *oppositional*—one constitutes the other, and knowledge about one implies knowledge about the other by inverse (if women are weak, men are strong; if Natives are primitive, whites are civilized; if nature is the object, humans are the subject; and so on). As ecofeminists would have it, this creates an alliance among those enclosed as Term B—women, nonwhites, nature, and other Others—not because of a mystical connection between, say, women and nature or Natives and nature (or a category Stacy Alaimo sums up as "woman-native-animal-other")[15] but because of a shared experience of oppression by power structures that are "intimately connected and mutually reinforcing."[16] Patriarchy and environmental destruction, according to ecofeminists and feminist environmentalists, are co-constituted and authorized by similar forms of power and domination. The relationship between women and nature, and people of color and nature, is thus neither mystical nor mere metaphor—it is, rather, one of humans and nonhumans subjected to co-constituted systems of domination.[17]

The third way that the declensionist narrative is gendered is germane to the first. Whereas environmental destruction cannot be said to be the responsibility of *all* humans universally, men and women in turn experience environmental decline differently, as a result of their different socially constructed roles and responsibilities—as do whites and people of color. Environmental destruction is, in important ways, a feminist issue because environmental decline is often experienced more acutely by women—and particularly women of color, indigenous women, and poor women—even as women are often the most excluded members of a community in regard to making the environmental decisions that affect their lives. Women are also, not coincidentally, at the forefront of many environmentalist and most environmental justice social movements, with many environmental justice organizations made up almost entirely of women activists.[18]

I take these points one at a time, exploring how different scholarly fields (environmental and feminist history, ecofeminism and feminist environmentalism, and environmental justice studies) have developed helpful frameworks for thinking in more complex ways about how to go about doing the work of situating sustainabilities in ways that might be liberating for women, people of color, nonhuman animals, and nature alike.

I'm Not with Stupid: What We Mean When We Say "Man" and "Nature"

The idea that *Man destroys nature* and that this is the beginning and end of our environmental relationships, is both relatively new and very, very old. The declensionist narrative is based on both the American wilderness ethic, which some historians consider a uniquely American notion of nature, and a long-standing trend of Romantic anti-modernism in Western thought.[19] Long before U.S. environmentalists idealized the fiction of the untouched wilderness, European romantics idealized the "wilderness condition," and the primitivists among them fantasized about the purifying effect of uncultivated nature on civilized men and "noble savages" alike.[20]

Although long-standing, the declensionist narrative was intensified—crystallized, even—in the latter half of the twentieth-century by what the environmental historian William Cronon calls the "postmodernist assault on narrative," in which the world wars, and their aftereffects, transformed the self-congratulatory bent in the study of human history and in many (if not all) traditional academic disciplines.[21] In this postwar period, women's and gender studies, ethnic studies, postcolonial studies, and, yes, postmodernism offered multi-faceted critiques of the ways in which academia had long been complicit in the production of narratives and epistemological models that propped up heteropatriarchy, racism, colonialism, settler colonialism, and environmental degradation.

One reaction (out of many) to this "postmodernist assault on narrative" and attendant justice-based interdisciplinary interventions was to upend the traditional understandings of protagonists and antagonists: that is, good guys became bad; bad guys, good. In studies of the U.S. West and its environments, "winning" the West became "conquering" the West; managing resources became decimating them to colonial ends (much to the consternation of many a traditional historian, who had made a living from the more self-congratulatory brand of history).[22] In environmental history, as one might imagine, declensionist narratives of environmental destruction reigned, elbowing out previous tendencies toward progressive narratives "in which the plot line gradually ascends toward an ending that is somehow more positive—happier, richer, freer, better," for man if not so much for nature.[23]

These kinds of narrative inversions, with familiar-looking anti-heroes, rather than heroes, and lots of imperialist nostalgia, turned out not to be always entirely helpful (or particularly postmodern).[24] Indeed, the environmental declensionist narrative—*Man destroys nature*—should remind us in its binary construction of man versus nature inhered in the old "morality play of westward expansion," in which "wilderness was the villain, and the pioneer, the hero, relished its destruction."[25] Take out the relishing, and reverse the villain role, and you have the declensionist narrative presented whole and unchanged, in which the idea that *Man destroys nature* is not sad—it is righteous. The sentiment is different, but the narrative infrastructure is not. Europeans, even before arriving in the Americas and witnessing firsthand what they took to be "wilderness," "instinctively understood [wilderness] as something alien to man—an insecure and uncomfortable environment against which civilization had waged an unceasing struggle."[26]

As a result of this long-standing commitment to particular kinds of narratives about "man" and "nature," whether progressive or declensionist, environmental history and environmentalism in general have what Virginia Scharff calls a "buried" "sex secret": environmental history, Scharff argues, "remains at present not a story of people and other things but is instead a story of man and nature."[27] "Nature," in turn, is written about "as if it were singular, a term parallel and comparable to the singular term *man*."[28] According to Scharff, women's diverse epistemological standpoints on their environments, and the diversity, agency, and instability of "nature," simply do not fit into the narrative equation. More to the point, standard environmental history leaves readers with a sense that the "'epic ecological events'" chronicled therein, involving the "heroic rendezvous between man and nature," are more important than "women's actions, desires and choices" and how they have "shaped the world."[29]

In answering Scharff's call to unbury this "sex secret" (the "submergence of women's experiences in many environmental history books"),[30] feminist historians have played an important role in destabilizing—or, for that matter, disassembling—rather than merely inverting the declensionist narrative and the human-nature binary on which it is constituted. These scholars have done work, in other words, that interrupts our tendency to produce narratives of "just one damn decline after another" in ways that universalize "man" and "nature" alike as pure categories.[31] These scholars offer us a commitment to complexity and contingency that staid narratives, whether progressive or declensionist, tend to smother.

In particular, feminist environmental studies scholars, environmental historians among them, have done crucial work to understand how men and women have made meaning out of the "wilderness" in ways that reflected their social, cultural, and emotional worlds.[32] Men and women bring their own epistemological models to their interactions with the environment, and their gendered (and racialized, sexualized, and classed) experiences shape the meaning they make out of the human and nonhuman world around them. Perhaps most famously, the feminist literary critic Annette Kolodny did this in her set of texts, *The Lay of the Land* and *The Land before Her*.[33] In the wryly titled *The Lay of the Land*, Kolodny traces the ways in which men settlers in the West understood and figured the land as feminine. The environmental historian Susan Schrepfer builds on this work, writing in her book *Nature's Altars* that

> nineteenth- and twentieth-century men looked to terrains that they visualized as both threatening and metaphorically feminine in order to cultivate the "primordial" impulses they variously wished to refine, thwart, or sublimate. They sought arenas in which to exercise control over the external world and their own bodies. In wild areas, they exercised strong emotions—anger, fear, hate, and love—in the ambivalent agenda of escaping from, yet succeeding in, everyday life.[34]

Studies of (white, settler) women's experiences with "wild areas" provides a crucial counterpoint to the rather more well documented studies of (white, settler) men's experiences; in *The Land before Her*, Kolodny explores the very distinct ways in which women settlers understood and even experienced the land—in a kind of double vision, these women perceived the landscape both through their masculine counterparts' sexualized frontier fantasies *and* through their own more domestic desires to cultivate gardens and thereby "tame" wild and unfamiliar terrain. Changes wrought by settlers on the environment were thus deeply gendered: women planted gardens and introduced rose cuttings and cuts from fruit trees; men hunted big game, cleared big swathes of land, and laid claim to big properties. This is not to excuse women settlers from culpability in the environmental (and, for that matter, racial) violence of conquest but, rather, to point to the significant, and significantly gendered, difference in women's versus men's environmental impact. In environmental politics generally, women gravitated toward observational recreation of, for example, birds, whereas men were focused on grand landscapes and large animals.[35] If women were drawn to botany, men preferred geology. And so on.[36] As Giovanna Di Chiro points out, this gendered approach to environmental history complicates "the relationships between humans and their environments by starting from the marginalized, ecoepistemological standpoints of the lives of women"—in other words, women's own situated approaches to environmental sustainability.[37]

These studies, while offering profound insights into differently gendered "ecoepistemologies," focus largely on white (and often middle- or upper-class) men and women. Others have produced work that accounts for the ways in which people of color understand the environment in different ways than do whites, pointing to different epistemological standpoints produced by different social and class locations—and, certainly, by experiences of racial oppression and settler colonialism.[38] Kimberly Ruffin, for example, notes that, even while African Americans have historically "had no entitlement to speak for or about nature" and have in fact been placed under extreme "ecological burden" through environmental racism and forced labor, black environmental epistemologies have provided a rich and complex counterpoint to white (and capitalist) exploitation of both nature and people.[39] The environmental justice scholar Robert Bullard points out that environmental degradation in the United States was in fact enabled by the exploitation of "free" land—dispossessed from indigenous nations and Mexicans (and, in the twentieth century, from Asian immigrant landowners through the combination of racially exclusive naturalization laws and Alien Land Acts)[40]—and the exploitation of "free" or radically undercompensated labor—performed by black slaves and sharecroppers, Braceros, and im/migrant laborers of all kinds.[41]

As this range of contributions illustrates, studies of gendered and raced environmental epistemologies have added significantly to our understanding of how environmental knowledge and experience are richer and more complex than simple reductions to "man" and "nature." There is a need, however, for more intersectional applications of this scholarship, looking to the ways in which gender, race, sexuality, and class *together* have formed our relationships to the nonhuman world. This is precisely because "the processes of environmental degradation and appropriation of natural resources by a few have specific class-gender as well as locational implications. . . . 'Women' therefore cannot be posited . . . as a unitary category, even within a country."[42] Studies from a range of disciplines offer windows into the promise of this approach, but more work remains to be done, particularly, as Merchant points out, with regard to Latina/o, Asian immigrant, and Asian American environmental experiences.[43]

I offer a final point about the promises of environmental scholarship in producing a more nuanced (and more accurate) picture of situated sustainabilities that disrupts (or disassembles) the nature-as-victim approach. The wilderness ideal that produced the declensionist narrative in the first place requires that nature be an object to be acted upon; in the *Man destroys nature* narrative equation, man is the subject (the doer) and nature the object (the done-to). Environmental historians are perhaps uniquely positioned to set fire to this fiction—even if they sometimes hesitate to do so—precisely because this field has been founded in large part on the recognition that, even as humans shape and influence (and, yes, destroy) nature, *nature also shapes human history* in profound and diverse ways. In addition, nature has a history of its own that environmental historians are just now coming to recognize and understand, a history of "growth, maturation and decline," but also replete with what Aldo Leopold called nature's own "hidden meaning."[44]

If a poststructuralist, gendered approach to history allows us to see, as Joan Wallach Scott puts it, the "remarkable absence or subordination of women in the narratives of the 'rise of civilization'" that have traditionally provided the infrastructure of both history and philosophy, then the combination of gender history, ethnic history, and environmental history allows us to see the similar (and related) subordination of *nature* in the narratives of the "rise of civilization."[45] Nature, like women, can, in this epistemological viewpoint, become a "historical subject"—acting, active, and endowed with agency and history of its own—rather than merely a subordinated object.[46] As a general rule, an "adversarial stance towards nature as a fearsome"—or, for that matter, pitied—"Other" limits our abilities to know it in all of its subjectivity, differentness, and complexity.[47]

The Total Female Principle of Gratification? Nature, Women, Animals, and Others

Clearly, "nature" is not destroyed by "man" writ large—in fact, it is often the naturalization, animalization, or simply marginalization of women and people of color, in effect grouping them into the category of "exploitable," that enables white, patriarchal, capitalist, and colonial forms of environmental degradation. This is built into the very fabric of Western philosophies of environment, property, and labor. No less a canonical Western thinker than John Locke grouped animals, nature, and servants together as necessary components of his formulation that nature plus labor equals private property. As Locke wrote in the *Second Treatise*,

> The grass my horse has bit; the turfs my servant has cut; and the ore I have digged in any place, where I have a right to them in common with others, become my property, without the assignation or consent of any body. *The labour that was mine*, removing them out of that common state they were in, *hath fixed my property in them.*[48]

The labor of horse and servant, for Locke, are equivalent to his own labor in the process of turning nature into a set of privately owned commodity resources. To this list, Locke might as well have added "the food my wife has prepared and the children she has raised," as women's bodies and labor in Western societies, like the bodies and labor of horse and servant (and "nature" itself) was subsumed as the property of her husband.

Val Plumwood begins her influential 1993 text, *Feminism and the Mastery of Nature*, by making precisely this point: that the domination of women, animals, and the environment has been such a constitutive feature of Western thought as to be overdetermined. It is almost too easy to illustrate this point. Plumwood achieves it with admirable concision, citing major thinkers in the Western philosophical tradition: Edmund Burke ("A woman is but an animal and an animal not of the highest order"), Jonathan Swift ("I cannot conceive of [women] to be human creatures, but a sort of species hardly a degree above a monkey"), Sigmund Freud ("Women represent the interests of the family and sexual life; the work of civilisation has become more and more men's business"), Georg Wilhelm Friedrich Hegel ("Women are certainly capable of learning, but they are not made for the higher forms of science, such as philosophy and certain types of creative activity; these require a universal ingredient"), and Thomas Aquinas ("A necessary object, woman, who is needed to preserve the species or to provide food and drink").[49]

"Nature," in this kind of binary formation, "includes everything that reason excludes": women, people of color, slaves and servants, and animals, to say nothing of mountains, rivers, deserts, and plants.[50] "Reason," in contrast, becomes a stand-in for the universalized figure of the "the paradigmatic Knower, Thinker, Politician and Party to the Contract"—in a word, Man.[51] Ecofeminist theory and feminist environmentalism begin from this premise, drawing from a long tradition of feminist thought about the patriarchal association between women and nature.[52] Simone de Beauvoir, for example, wrote of "Mother Earth" as the symbolic "maternal darkness" against which men struggled, "aspir[ing] to the sky, to light, to sunny heights"—nature-based metaphors for Enlightenment, all.[53] The "maternal darkness," in all its femininity, signified everything Other to Enlightenment and reason. To "aspire to the sky" was to aspire to progress, scientific knowledge, and civilization against the background of the womanly "maternal darkness."

The notion of progress has been a mediator of the binary relationship between man and woman, culture and nature, white and nonwhite. The core characteristics of the modern binary (universality, hierarchy, and relationality) all turn on the notion of progress. For de Beauvoir, this progress is that of educated men away from the "maternal darkness" toward "sunny heights." For others, progress "demands conquest of the wilderness" and those humans associated with wilderness ("Indians") and with animality generally (almost all people of color).[54] For no less a wilderness lover than John Muir, the binary between humans and nature, in which idealized nature was a resource for "man's" spiritual progress, "Indians" were not just animal-like—they were a *lower form* of animals, "unclean" and undeserving of the Edenic mountain landscapes Muir so loved.[55] In U.S. history, economic and political progress has been predicated on land dispossession and the genocide of "wild savages," the military conquest and differential inclusion of Mexicans ("no better than the Indians," according to the lauded Texan Sam Houston),[56] and the system of chattel slavery for wide-scale—and environmentally devastating—agriculturalism.

In general, "the march of civilization and progress" entailed rampant violence "over racially inferior peoples" who were marked as racially inferior because of their associations with animals and nature.[57]

Ecofeminists and others have likewise explored these connections between race, nature, and (nonhuman) animality, although this work remains problematically undertheorized—and haunted by the specter of essentialism.[58] In particular, animal rights ecofeminists and anti-speciesists point to the resonances between chattel slavery, and other forms of forced labor, and the enslavement of animal bodies in factory farming (to say nothing of the explicit animalization of bodies of color in racial pseudoscience and eugenics).[59] This critique is long-standing; as Henry Salt argued in 1897, the emancipation of slaves and animals are connected, and one cannot be achieved without the other, as both are victims of capitalism run amok.[60] Frederick Douglass made a more nuanced critique that addressed the mobility of power relations between humans and nonhuman animals in a speech in 1873: in the slave system, "The master blamed the overseer, the overseer the slave, and the slave the horses, oxen and mules, and violence fell upon the animals as a consequence."[61] Here Douglass goes beyond seeing slaves and animals as objects-in-affinity, a perspective fraught with essentializing traps in which ecofeminists and anti-speciesists tend to be caught, to put forward an analysis of the relationality and entanglement of multiple forms of power in the slave system: those of class, race, status, and species.

The animalization and naturalization of women and people of color point to the ways in which hegemonic environmental narratives, with *man* on one side and *nature* on the other, falsely universalize "man" as a stand-in for all humans. In fact, the domination of "nonmale, nonwhite, nonowning, and otherwise nonprivileged people, and nonhuman beings" has been built into the very structures of patriarchy, racism, and capitalism.[62] In this framework, "women, people of color, workers, ecosystems and cows" become "wives and mothers, slaves, exotics, foreigners and lower classes, Nature and meat"—utterly stripped of their own subjectivity and worth in favor of their iterations as resource commodities: private property and the raw material of total (feminized) patriarchal and capitalist gratification.[63] *Man destroys nature* erases this complex phenomenon at best; at worst it erases women and people of color entirely, re-creating the world as an oversimplified (although tragically destructive) dynamic between nature and man.

I'm Definitely Not with Stupid: Experiencing (and Embodying) Destruction

The understanding of nature as an isolated and separate sphere, against which the universal "man" does violence (in short: *Man destroys nature*) undergirds hegemonic environmental politics—particularly what environmental justice activists and scholars refer to as "mainstream environmentalism." Mainstream environmentalism has been critiqued by the environmental justice movement for being racist, exclusionary, and disruptive to communities of color and colonized peoples in its membership, politics, and ideas about the environment.[64] The reduction of environmental politics to the protection of nonhuman nature from the destructive tendencies of "man," for example, ignores and elides the ways in which people of color and poor people tend to experience environmental degradation—as industrial waste, pollution, and poor health where they live, work, play, and pray, in short, as "group-differentiated vulnerability to premature death."[65] One environmental justice activist tried to communicate this in a language familiar to mainstream environmentalists who tended to see their work as protecting a nonhuman "nature" separate from human communities: "Our communities and our peoples," she said, "are endangered species, too."[66]

This tension between environmental justice and environmentalism over how the environment is *imagined*—as nonhuman nature or as locales wherever humans live, work, play, and pray—shows the limits of the declensionist narrative. According to the environmental justice perspective, it is not "man" that destroys nature, but certain kinds of *people* with certain kinds of power and environmental privilege and a set of *systems* in which we are all coerced to participate, "based on the commodification of everything, including women" and workers.[67] Mainstream environmentalism's reliance on the human/nature binary and the declensionist narrative contributed greatly to the fact that, according to Bunyan Bryant, organizations like the Sierra Club simply cannot understand racism or its relationship to environmentalism.[68] The problem, in short, was and is an epistemological one.

Women of color and indigenous women working within environmental justice frameworks have made powerful statements about the ways in which women's particular gendered, racialized, sexualized, and classed experiences shape their relationships to the environment in ways that are distinct from that of mainstream environmentalism. To borrow Donna Haraway's framework of situated knowledges, with which she proposes that women have diverse and particular worldviews that help shape their knowledge of power and the world around them, women from diverse nonwhite communities have situated *environmental* knowledges (Di Chiro's "ecoepistemological standpoints") and thus situated perspectives on what "sustainability" means. Haraway's situated knowledge framework is appropriate, too, because it functions specifically to undermine the Western fiction of objective knowledge, coming from the universal "man's" experiences and observations of objects and Others—what she famously termed the "God trick of seeing everything from nowhere."[69] The universalization of "man's" actions on nature are just such a God trick, as are attempts to universalize ideas about what constitutes "good" environmentalism or approaches to sustainability. Quite simply, diverse women's work in environmental justice points out that top-down notions of sustainability are rarely useful for them in living—and saving—their lives.

Women, because of their socially constructed roles doing care work and domestic labor, are often most attuned to environmental problems in their communities: they have a situated knowledge about water quality, community health, food scarcity, desertification, and so on. This situated environmental knowledge is a key reason that women make up the majority of environmental justice and anti-toxics organizing; women, quite simply, are often the first members of a community to experience and understand the effects, including latent effects and combined effects, of toxins in their environments. They are also the community members who must mobilize when their husbands and fathers succumb to toxic exposure in male-dominated workplaces such as mines or factories or when children are born or become sick.

This was true for Lakota and Diné (Navajo) women subjected to the unendingly destructive uranium industry in the 1970s and the 1980s— dubbed the "uranium widows," the wives of miners who died of lung cancer were at the forefront of struggles for justice. It was also true for Lois Gibbs, the famed leader of the struggle against toxic waste in Love Canal, New York, and later the founder of the Center for Health,

Environment, and Justice.[70] Katsi Cook, a Mohawk midwife and environmentalist, likewise came into her activism from witnessing firsthand the effects of environmental pollution on the Akwesasne Mohawk Nation, particularly the reproductive health impacts for women. Teresa Leal co-founded the organization Comadres to support women workers in the maquila industry in the borderlands of her hometown, Nogales, Arizona.[71] Perhaps most famously, Hazel Johnson, the "Mother of Environmental Justice," came to her lifetime of engaged activism after losing her husband to lung cancer and subsequently surveying her community's exposure to air and water pollution and their attendant environmental health problems.[72] The fact that women make up the majority of environmental justice activists reflects the reality that

> women . . . often dealing themselves with debilitating illnesses, assume a considerable share of the burden of caring for their community writ large, which includes their immediate and extended families, their friends, their neighbors, their neighbors' children, the workers in the factory next door, and the health of the water, air, and land that sustains them.[73]

Women also live at the intersections of heteropatriarchy, racism, colonialism and settler colonialism, capitalism, and neoliberalism and thus experience intersectional impacts of environmental degradation. When indigenous activists, for example, assert that there can be "No Climate Justice without Gender Justice," they are pointing to the complex rubric of challenges women face in the context of climate change: women bear the responsibility for gleaning food and water from dwindling sources; women are the majority of small agriculturalists in places experiencing desertification; and women are subject to heightened rates of sexual and domestic violence in the upheavals that attend catastrophic storms, deadly epidemics, and intensifying poverty—as well as in mining communities, where fossil fuels are wrenched and dredged from the earth in ever-more-frenzied extraction schemes.[74] Women migrate to makeshift communities surrounding electronic waste dumps, factories, mines, and assembly plants, seeking desperately needed jobs and income when their "subsistence economies" at home are devalued and destroyed, but they find themselves in places with no infrastructure, no job security, and no social services.[75] In Mexico's Ciudad Juarez, where maquiladoras

caused a rapid boom in the border city's population with no corresponding boom in infrastructure and social services, women are subject to
nightmarish assaults escalating to what has been termed a "femicide"
involving the torture and murder of hundreds of women.[76] All of these
represent ways in which women's experiences of environmentally destructive industries are informed and shaped by the intersections of
multiple manifestations of power.

Women's environmental justice activism since the 1980s has transformed environmental and social justice politics in the United States
and globally; women have struggled, often in alliance with men, to
address urgent concerns in their communities while at the same time
providing frameworks for radical change that unearth the relationships
between intersecting forms of social domination and the destruction
of the nonhuman world. The organization Mothers of East Los Angeles (MELA), for example, formed from the work of roughly four hundred Chicana women organizing simultaneously against the siting of a
state prison, an oil pipeline, and a toxic waste incinerator in their community.[77] Demonstrating the flexibility of the environmental justice
framework to include concerns of mainstream environmentalists and
social justice organizations, MELA "view[ed] ecological issues through
a community lens," focusing their energy on issues that ranged from
more mainstream environmental causes, such as wetland preservation,
to farmworker struggles against pesticides, to prisons, to overcrowded
schools.[78] This pattern of women's environmental justice activism has
been repeated in a wide range of organizations, in the United States and
globally.[79]

These are situated approaches to sustainability at their best, demonstrations of how and why we need more complex understandings of
different peoples' diverse experiences of the world around them. It is
crucial, too, because, just as environmental justice is not (only) focused
on more mainstream environmental concerns like species extinction
and habitat loss, environmental degradation does not always *look* like
mainstream environmental pictures of destruction. Sometimes it looks
like lead paint in inner city homes. Sometimes it looks like a worker in
a microchip assembly plant. Sometimes it looks like persistent organic
pollutants, grasshoppering their way from production facilities to the
Arctic. Sometimes it looks exactly like our ideals of "pure" nature—wild

fish with unseen body burdens of pesticides or idyllic rivers polluted with dioxin. Just as environmental degradation is flexible, changeable, and particular, so too must be our approaches to environmentalism and how we situate our approaches to sustainability.

Conclusion

As I have argued throughout, hegemonic understandings of sustainability, built around the idea that nature is something separate from and requiring protection from humans—in short, that nature is most sustainable when unpolluted with humans or the human world—are problematic. Feminists have pointed to the ways in which this perspective on sustainability is troublingly limited and limiting, preventing us from branching out into more complex, historically and ecologically grounded knowledge of both the human and nonhuman worlds.

Our notions of sustainability beg particularity and context. Feminist situatedness, as it relates to sustainability, does not just help us *think* our way out of universalizing tendencies in hegemonic environmental logic. It also lends itself to situated environmental *praxis* by allowing for different kinds of relationships between the human and nonhuman worlds: thinking and working beyond destruction.

Acknowledgments

I thank Julie Sze for her editorial expertise and Mary E. Mendoza, Rebecca Kinney, and Sarah Jaquette Ray for their insights as I prepared this essay.

NOTES

1 Christine Cuomo, *Feminism and Ecological Communities: An Ethic of Flourishing* (New York: Routledge, 1998), 21.

2 J. R. McNeill, "Observations on the Nature and Culture of Environmental History," in "Environment and History," theme issue no. 42, *History and Theory* 42, no. 4 (December 2003): 35.

3 William Cronon, "The Uses of Environmental History," *Environmental History Review* 17, no. 3 (Autumn 1993): 1.

4 Donna Haraway, "Situated Knowledges: The Science Question in Feminism and the Privilege of Partial Perspective," *Feminist Studies* 14, no. 3 (1988): 592.

5 See Julie Sze, introduction in this volume, quoting Julian Agyeman, Robert Doyle
   Bullard, and Bob Evans, eds., *Just Sustainabilities: Development in an Unequal
   World* (Cambridge, MA: MIT Press, 2003).

6 "Ecofeminism" is a fraught and contested term and has subsequently fallen out of
   fashion since its heyday in the 1980s and 1990s. See Val Plumwood, *Feminism and
   the Mastery of Nature* (New York: Routledge, 1993), 19–22; and Greta Gaard, "Ecofeminism Revisited: Rejecting Essentialism and Re-placing Species in a Material
   Feminist Environmentalism," *Feminist Formations* 23, no. 2 (Summer): 26–53.
   The nature of the debate over ecofeminism involves whether or not ecofeminist
   texts resurrect or valorize the connections, made in Western patriarchy, between
   women and nature. Texts that have been accused, rightly or wrongly, of taking
   this position include Susan Griflin, *Woman and Nature: The Roaring inside Her*
   (New York: Harper Colophon Books, 1978); Joyce Contrucci, *Rape of the Wild:
   Man's Violence against Animals* (Bloomington: Indiana University Press, 1989);
   Judith Plant, ed., *Healing the Wounds: The Promise of Ecofeminism* (Philadelphia:
   New Society Publishers, 1989); Irene Diamond and Gloria Feman Orenstein,
   eds., *Reweaving the World: The Emergence of Ecofeminism* (San Francisco: Sierra
   Club Books, 1990); and Leonie Caldecotte and Stephanie Leland, eds., *Reclaim
   the Earth: Women Speak Out for Life on Earth* (London: Women's Press, 1983).
   Nonacademic texts branded as "ecofeminist" but taking this essentializing—
   even mystical—approach to women and nature have compounded the problem
   (preeminent among them, Starhawk's *The Fifth Sacred Thing* [New York: Bantam,
   1993]). Others focus instead on the affinities between environmental degradation
   and patriarchy as related, co-constituted, and intersectional forms of power; see
   Plumwood, *Feminism and the Mastery of Nature*; and Maria Mies and Vandana
   Shiva, *Ecofeminism* (1993; reprint, New York: Zed Books, 2014). Feminists have
   chosen to reject the term "ecofeminism" or have translated or qualified it to avoid
   such problematic associations—Christine Cuomo, for example, prefers "ecological feminism" (see Cuomo, *Feminism and Ecological Communities*, 6), as does
   Karen Warren (see Karen Warren and Jim Cheney, "Ecological Feminism and
   Ecosystem Ecology," *Hypatia* 6, no. 1 [1991]: 179–197). Bina Agarwal, "The Gender
   and Environment Debate: Lessons from India," *Feminist Studies* 18, no. 1 (1992):
   119–159; and Joni Seager, *Earth Follies: Coming to Feminist Terms with the Global
   Environmental Crisis* (New York: Routledge, 1993), use "feminist environmentalism." Val Plumwood writes of "feminist eco-socialism" in *Environmental Culture:
   The Ecological Crisis of Reason* (New York: Routledge, 2002). Despite these different names, these scholars are often making strongly related critiques that could
   easily be framed under "ecofeminism" (see Gaard, "Ecofeminism Revisited").
   Stacy Alaimo and Donna Haraway, in contrast, reject "ecofeminism" outright;
   see Stacy Alaimo, "Cyborg and Ecofeminist Interventions: Challenges for an Environmental Feminism," *Feminist Studies* 20, no. 1 (Spring 1994): 149; and Donna
   Haraway, *Primate Visions: Gender, Race, and Nature in the World of Modern
   Science* (New York: Routledge, 1989). In this essay, I make reference to "feminist

environmentalism" and "ecofeminism," understanding "ecofeminism" as the latter trend of scholarship (focusing on the related, co-constituted, and intersectional nature of anti-environmental and misogynist forms of power, rather than "women" and "nature" as knowable objects-in-affinity, which "forms the basis for a critical ecological feminism in which women consciously position themselves *with* nature" [Plumwood, *Feminism* and the Mastery of Nature, 21]).

7 Ariel Salleh, "Foreword," in Mies and Shiva, *Ecofeminism*, ix.

8 Emphasis added. See Catherine MacKinnon, "Feminism, Marxism, Method, and the State: An Agenda for Theory" *Signs* 7, no. 3 (Spring 1982): 541.

9 Ibid., 542.

10 See note 6 above.

11 See Plumwood, *Feminism and the Mastery of Nature* and *Environmental Culture*; and Warren and Chaney, "Ecological Feminism and Ecosystem Ecology."

12 Cuomo, *Feminism and Ecological Communities*, 6.

13 Annette Kolodny, *The Lay of the Land: Metaphor as Experience and History in American Life and Letters* (Chapel Hill: University of North Carolina Press, 1975), 4.

14 Eve Kosofsky Sedgwick, *Epistemology of the Closet* (Berkeley: University of California Press, 1990), 10.

15 Alaimo, "Cyborg and Ecofeminist Interventions," 149.

16 Ynestra King, "The Ecology of Feminism and the Feminism of Ecology," in Plant, *Healing the Wounds*, 18.

17 See Warren and Chaney, "Ecological Feminism and Ecosystem Ecology"; Plumwood, *Feminism and the Mastery of Nature* and *Environmental Culture*; and Alaimo, "Cyborg and Ecofeminist Interventions," for dissent and critique.

18 Rachel Stein, ed., *New Perspectives on Environmental Justice: Gender, Sexuality, and Activism* (New Brunswick, NJ: Rutgers University Press, 2004), 2.

19 Paul Sutter, for example, regards non-U.S. environmental histories as less invested in the "wilderness ideal," and William Cronon famously charted out the co-evolution of the wilderness ideal and Frederick Jackson Turner's frontier thesis. See Paul Sutter, "Reflections: What Can US Environmental Historians Learn from Non-US Environmental Historiography?" *Environmental History* 8, no. 1 (January 2003): 109–129; and William Cronon, "The Trouble with Wilderness; or, Getting Back to the Wrong Nature," in *Uncommon Ground: Rethinking the Human Place in Nature*, ed. William Cronon (New York: Norton), 69–90. However, Carolyn Merchant, among others, accounts for the ways in which the human/nature binary, of which the U.S. wilderness ideal is a manifestation, is actually constitutional to Enlightenment modernity as a whole (see Carolyn Merchant, *The Death of Nature: Women, Ecology, and the Scientific Revolution* [New York: Harper Collins, 1990]). Bruno Latour makes a related argument in *We Have Never Been Modern* (Cambridge, MA: Harvard University Press, 1993).

20 Roderick Frazier Nash, *Wilderness and the American Mind* (New Haven, CT: Yale University Press, 1967), 48–49, 50–52.

21 William Cronon, "A Place for Stories: Nature, History, and Narrative," *Journal of American History* 78, no. 4 (March 1992): 1349; and Alfred Crosby, *Ecological Imperialism: The Biological Expansion of Europe, 900–1900* (1986; reprint, New York: Cambridge University Press, 2004), xvi.

22 Cronon, "A Place for Stories"; and Patricia Nelson Limerick, "What on Earth Is the New Western History?," in *Trails: Toward a New Western History*, ed. Patricia Nelson Limerick, Clyde A. Milner II, and Charles E. Rankin (Lawrence: University Press of Kansas, 1991), 81–88.

23 Cronon, "A Place for Stories," 1352.

24 Walter Hixson calls this the "Indian-as-victim" narrative, which excised any sense of indigenous agency or complex personhood in its zeal to represent whites as murderous anti-heroes (although no less fully realized as humans). This narrative was later upended by studies that focused on indigenous agency and the complex milieu of power relations in colonial borderlands. See Walter Hixson, *American Settler Colonialism: A History* (Basingstoke: Palgrave Macmillan, 2013), 13.

25 Nash, *Wilderness and the American Mind*, 24.

26 Ibid., 8.

27 Virginia J. Scharff, "Man and Nature! Sex Secrets of Environmental History," in *Seeing Nature through Gender*, ed. Virginia J. Scharff (Lawrence: University Press of Kansas, 2003), 3.

28 Ibid., 4.

29 Giovanna Di Chiro, "Steps to an Ecology of Justice: Women's Environmental Networks across the Santa Cruz River Watershed," in Scharff, *Seeing Nature through Gender*, 284, quoting Scharff, "Man and Nature!"

30 Ibid., 288.

31 McNeill, "Observations on the Nature and Culture of Environmental History," 35.

32 Susan Schrepfer, *Nature's Altars: Mountains, Gender, and American Environmentalism* (Lawrence: University Press of Kansas, 2005), 6.

33 Kolodny, *Lay of the Land*, and *The Land before Her: Fantasy and Experience of the American Frontiers, 1630–1860* (Chapel Hill: University of North Carolina Press, 1984).

34 Schrepfer, *Nature's Altars*, 4.

35 Mabel Osgood Wright and Elliott Coues, *Citizen Bird: Scenes from Bird-Life in Plain English for Beginners* (New York: Macmillan, 1897).

36 Schrepfer, *Nature's Altars*, 6.

37 Di Chiro, "Steps to an Ecology of Justice," 285.

38 Judith A. Carney, *Black Rice: The African Origins of Rice Cultivation in the Americas* (Cambridge, MA: Harvard University Press, 2001); Dianne D. Glave, "'A Garden So Brilliant with Colors, So Original in Its Design': Rural African American Women, Progressive Reform, and the Foundation of an African American Environmental Perspective," *Environmental History* 8 (2003): 395–429, and "The African American Cooperative Service: A Folk Tradition in Conservation and Preservation in the Early Twentieth Century," *International Journal of*

Africana Studies 6 (November/December 2000): 85–100; Mart A. Stewart, *What Nature Suffers to Groe: Life, Labor, and Landscape on the Georgia Coast, 1680–1920* (Athens: University of Georgia Press, 1996), and "Rice, Water, and Power: Landscapes of Domination and Resistance in the Lowcountry, 1790–1880," *Environmental History Review* 15 (Fall 1991): 47–64; and Carolyn Merchant, *The Columbia Guide to American Environmental History* (New York: Columbia University Press, 2002), 39–58.

39 Kimberly Ruffin, *Black on Earth: African American Ecoliterary Traditions* (Athens: University of Georgia Press, 2010).

40 Mae M. Ngai, *Impossible Subjects: Illegal Aliens and the Making of Modern America* (Princeton, NJ: Princeton University Press, 2004).

41 Robert D. Bullard, "Anatomy of Environmental Racism and the Environmental Justice Movement," in *Confronting Environmental Racism: Voices from the Grassroots*, ed. Robert D. Bullard (Boston: South End Press, 1993), 15–16.

42 Agarwal, "The Gender and Environment Debate," 150.

43 Carolyn Merchant, "Shades of Darkness: Race and Environmental History," *Environmental History* 8, no. 3 (2003): 381. Exceptions to this trend include Mary E. Mendoza, "Unnatural Border: Race and Environment at the U.S.-Mexico Divide" (PhD diss., University of California, Davis, 2015); Connie Chiang, "Imprisoned Nature: Toward an Environmental History of the World War II Japanese American Incarceration," *Environmental History* 15, no. 2 (April 2010): 236–267; and Mario Sifuentes, *Of Forests and Fields: Mexican Labor in the Pacific Northwest* (New Brunswick, NJ: Rutgers University Press, 2016). Yet more work is needed in the realm of comparative racial and environmental histories, along the lines, perhaps, of Neil Foley's 1997 book, *The White Scourge: Mexicans, Blacks, and Poor Whites in Texas Cotton Culture* (Berkeley: University of California Press, 1997).

44 As the philosopher Theodore Adorno argues, "Nature is historical, not just because nature evolves and constantly changes, but because it has been profoundly—often negatively—affected by human history." Quoted in Deborah Cook, *Adorno on Nature* (New York: Routledge, 2014), 1. See also Aldo Leopold, *A Sand County Almanac: With Essays on Conservation* (1949; reprint, New York: Oxford University Press, 2001).

45 Joan Wallach Scott, *Gender and the Politics of History* (New York: Columbia University Press, 1999), 9.

46 Ibid.

47 Cook, *Adorno on Nature*, 3.

48 Emphasis mine. This Lockean formula went on to serve as the basis of homesteading and mining laws in the United States, which privatized huge swaths of the "public" land that had been recently dispossessed of Native nations. The Homestead Act, for example, required settlers to make improvements to the land they claimed. It was through these "improvements," or labor, that the land became privatized from the public domain. The General Mining Act likewise required that a mining claim be worked in order for it to be removed from the

public domain. See John Locke, "Chapter V: Of Property," *Second Treatise of Civil Government* (London: Awnsham Churchill, 1690).

49 Plumwood, *Feminism and the Mastery of Nature*, 19.

50 Ibid., 20.

51 Cuomo, *Feminism and Ecological Communities*, 3.

52 At least, it does in its most productive iterations. See note 6 above.

53 Simone DeBeauvoir, *The Second Sex* (1949; reprint, New York: Knopf, 2010), 157.

54 Cuomo, *Feminism and Ecological Communities*, 13–14, quoting Robert Utley.

55 Merchant, "Shades of Darkness," 382–383. This grouping of nonwhites and nonhumans reflects, more largely, the spectrum or field of what Mel Chen terms "animacies," or the "affective territory of mediation between life and death" that organizes how we understand and value everything from people to animals to ideas. See Mel Chen, *Animacies: Biopolitics, Racial Mattering, and Queer Affect* (Durham, NC: Duke University Press, 2012), 4. Animality, for Chen, has been used to mark the "analog or limit" of humanness, to the exclusion of many humans themselves.

56 Quoted by Hixson, *American Settler Colonialism*, 102.

57 Ibid., 101.

58 Plumwood, *Feminism and the Mastery of Nature*, 19. Gaard provides an excellent overview of these traps in "Ecofeminism Revisited." Chen, *Animacies*, offers a welcome exception to this gap in the literature, proposing complex new theoretical models for thinking about the field of differentiation organized around animacy (see note 53 above).

59 Marjorie Spiegel, *The Dreaded Comparison: Human and Animal Slavery* (London: Heretic Books, 1988). This comparison between speciesism and racism is not without its detractors, many of whom worry, with good reason, that further association between people of color and animals is too fraught a project in a social context in which the animalization of people of color remains a key part of how white supremacy is maintained.

60 Cuomo, *Feminism and Ecological Communities*, 15.

61 Ibid.

62 Ibid., 3.

63 Ibid.

64 This is evidenced in particular by scathing letters written by the Gulf Coast Tenant Leadership Development Project and the Southwest Organizing Project in 1990 to the "Group of Ten" (an environmental organization allied against the Reagan administration's assault on environmental regulation), as well as critiques offered by the 1991 First National People of Color Environmental Leadership Summit. The mainstream environmental movement as a whole was seen by these environmental justice activists as perpetuating "ignorance, ambivalence, and complicity" with environmental racism. See Phaedra C. Pezzullo and Ronald Sandler, "Introduction: Revisiting the Environmental Justice Challenge to Environmentalism," in *Environmental Justice and Environmentalism: The Social Justice*

Challenge to the Environmental Movement, ed. Ronald Sandler and Phaedra C. Pezzullo (Cambridge, MA: MIT Press, 2007), 3–4.

65 Ruth Wilson Gilmore, quoted by Lindsey Dillon and Julie Sze, "Police Power and Particulate Matters: Environmental Justice and the Spatialities of In/securities in U.S. Cities," *English Language Notes* 54, no. 2 (Fall/Winter 2016): 13–23.

66 Dana Alston, representing the Panos Institute at the First National People of Color Environmental Leadership Summit in Washington, DC, quoted by Pezzullo and Sandler, "Introduction," 7. This might be a productive inversion of Pellow's "racial discourse of animality" outlined in David N. Pellow, "Toward a Critical Environmental Justice Studies: Black Lives Matter as an Environmental Justice Challenge," *Du Bois Review* 13, no. 2 (2016): 6.

67 Mies and Shiva, *Ecofeminism*, xvi.

68 Referenced by Pezzullo and Sandler, "Introduction," 8.

69 Haraway, "Situated Knowledges," 581.

70 The Center for Health, Environment, and Justice was originally formed in 1980 as the Citizens' Clearinghouse for Hazardous Waste.

71 Joni Adamson and Rachel Stein, "Environmental Justice: A Roundtable Discussion," *ISLE: Interdisciplinary Studies in Literature and Environment* 7, no. 2 (2000): 158.

72 Hazel Johnson went on to found the People for Community Recovery.

73 Di Chiro, "Steps to an Ecology of Justice," 306.

74 Geraldine Terry, "No Climate Justice without Gender Justice: An Overview of the Issues," *Gender and Development* 17, no. 1 (2009): 5–18. Among climate refugees, for example, women experience alarming rates of sexual assault.

75 Mies and Shiva, *Ecofeminism*, xv.

76 Melissa W. Wright, "Necropolitics, Narcopolitics, and Femicide: Gendered Violence on the Mexico-US border," *Signs* 36, no. 3 (2011): 707–731, and "A Manifesto against Femicide," *Antipode* 33, no. 3 (2001): 550–566.

77 Mary Pardo, "Mexican American Women Grassroots Community Activists: 'Mothers of East Los Angeles,'" *Frontiers: A Journal of Women Studies* 11, no. 1 (1990):1–7.

78 "Mothers' Group Fights Back in Los Angeles," *New York Times*, December 5, 1989.

79 See Mies and Shiva, *Ecofeminism*; David Pellow, *Resisting Global Toxics: Transnational Movements for Environmental Justice* (Cambridge, MA: MIT Press, 2007);and Stein, *New Perspectives on Environmental Justice*.

9

I Tano' i Chamorro/Chamorro Land

Situating Sustainabilities through Spatial Justice and Cultural Perpetuation

MICHAEL LUJAN BEVACQUA AND
ISA UA CEALLAIGH BOWMAN

In January 2010, at the University of Guam Field House (a cavernous sports arena), military personnel began setting up posters with maps, showing locations on the island of Guam/Guahan that the U.S. military planned to use to accommodate an influx of new marines to the island's existing bases. The maps, with informational videos and text, sought to assure community members that the proposed firing ranges and other impacts on the environment in Guam would be negligible or offset.

Yet the U.S. military is one of the largest polluters on a global scale. While it presumes to protect and defend the interests of the United States at home and abroad, its wars abroad and its bases at home have had a serious detrimental impact on efforts to promote environmental sustainability and ecological consciousness. Petroleum-based fuel consumption, air pollution, the inhalation of toxins and resulting respiratory disorders, water contamination, and the degradation of natural resources are results of the war-related environmental impact of the United States' continuing foreign conflict zones in Iraq, Afghanistan, and Pakistan.[1] At home, the military has contributed to pollution, such as the infamous Camp Lejeune in North Carolina. The Pentagon acknowledges responsibility for 39,000 contaminated sites and 141 Superfund sites that qualify for special federal cleanup grants: The military accounts for 10 percent of all of the United States' Superfund sites, far more than any other polluter.[2]

This notion of the military buildup as being "sustainable" was tied to Guahan's history of militarization and the way that the United States has been elevated to the stature of liberator and social/economic savior. We survey the scholarly literature on the effects of U.S. military Draft Environmental Impact Statements on indigenous populations and discuss the effects on indigenous Chamorro people, specifically. We argue that the idea of the U.S. military promoting "sustainability" is an offshoot of unquestioning patriotism deliberately fostered in a colonized people, and, therefore, local Chamorro activists have sought to focus on intellectual and cultural demilitarization first, as a foundation for arguments to protect the environment. The ways in which demilitarization activists from groups such as Nasion Chamoru and We Are Guahan disrupted the fantasy of the buildup's sustainability helped the local community develop a more critical position in relation to the military's own stated environmental impacts, which may have broader impacts for locals fighting U.S. military pollution.

Tinituhun/Introduction

That 2010 evening in Guahan was just one in a series of public comment periods sponsored by the U.S. military and the local government. The Field House filled with more than 500 community members and residents of Guahan, the southernmost of the Mariana Islands, the home of the indigenous Chamorro people. Since World War II, following the intensive bombing campaign with which the U.S. military took back the island from the occupying Japanese, the unincorporated U.S. territory has sent its sons and daughters in droves to the military. Liberation Day every July commemorates the reoccupation of the island by the United States, and the Chamorro people, as well as the large Filipino community, have turned out by the thousands to celebrate the United States as a benevolent liberator.

Yet the notion of Guahan as superpatriotic would be challenged at this public hearing because the military's plans were viewed as repeating the island's painful history of land taking. Members of the Taotaomo'na Native Rights Group and We Are Guahan walked into the arena in force behind Nasion Chamoru leaders Danny "Pågat" Jackson and Josephine "Ofing" Jackson, as their grandson Cason Jackson sang the famous hymn "Fanoghe Chamoru" ("Rise, Chamorros"). One of the most affected areas under the military proposal was Pågat by the cliffs, a site registered with the Department of Historic Preservation as an archaeological site with the ruins of an ancient Chamorro village and historical artifacts. The cliffside area would be taken away from the Chamorro Land Trust so the military could use it as a firing range. These groups represented a vast groundswell of opposition to the U.S. military's environmentally catastrophic plans for its "buildup," which would include moving up to 75,000 more residents from the military and support industries to the small island.

The military originally issued a Draft Environmental Impact Statement (DEIS) that was more than 11,000 pages long and gave only ninety days to read, discuss, and offer comments on it. Because of Guahan's history of purported patriotism and widespread complacency in the face of U.S. military discourse, the military perhaps was not expecting the response it got:[3] 10,000, mostly critical, written comments, representing the voices of perhaps 20 percent of the population. In person, speakers came forward to register complaints about the plans that the U.S. military had for their island. Melvin Won Pat Borja, the twenty-eight-year-old scion of a powerful Guahan political family, reflected the concerns of many when he spoke that evening at the University of Guam Field House: "You are not alone. We must be united. We must never be silent! I think in the past the larger community has been misrepresented as being in full support of this build-up. I think a lot of our people have been misled into believing the general population is in full support of this move."[4] Similarly, the elder statesman Senator Vicente "Ben" Pangelinan said, "Ladies and gentlemen, they tell us that this process tonight is to listen to the people. Well, let me just say, that before the people have even started talking, they have stopped listening. . . . They're going to move forward, in which, no matter what decision we have here . . . nothing we say matters. They can move the Navy and will be given the authorization to not listen, to not honor the thoughts, the sentiments, and the feelings of the people which this process is designed to influence."[5]

Scholarly literature on U.S. military activities and training on indigenous communities shows very troubling trends. The Chamorro social scientist LisaLinda Natividad points out that the U.S. military's 2009 DEIS for its proposed military buildup on Guahan received the lowest possible rating from the U.S. Environmental Protection Agency (EPA)—"environmentally unsatisfactory"—and, further, the military's subsequent modifications of the plan were insufficient and continued to draw serious protest from the indigenous Chamorro people.[6] The Chamorro feminist scholar Christine Taitano DeLisle, in discussing the 2009 DEIS for Guahan, points out the absence of any references to, or respect for, indigenous feminist critiques in the U.S. military and EPA's documents; for her, "the US military's interest in Chamorro culture, coupled with the [tourist] industry's willingness to work with the military, reveals a more insidious form of hypermilitarization of an already heavily militarized island."[7] She contends that control over environmental impact should be in the hands of indigenous groups themselves, rather than entirely controlled by the U.S. federal government and the military.

Guahan's indigenous people do not enjoy certain levels of sovereignty that are allotted to Native American/First Nations peoples in North America, which enables a process, however flawed, of environmental planning. The political scientist and anthropologist Linda Moon Stumpff explains that "many, but not all, of the 556 federally recognized tribal governments have assumed responsibility for NEPA [National Environmental Policy Act] planning processes. . . . The future of Indian trust lands as natural and cultural homelands may depend in large part on the ability of tribes to implement planning strategies that assure continuous restoration."[8] However, too often the U.S. federal government and military earn criticism from indigenous groups regarding environmental impact statements. The Native American archaeologist Anna Cordova has analyzed Native Hawai'ian activism around U.S. military and federal land use, and she assesses U.S. federal and military statements as "paternalistic and colonial," "infantilizing the original caretakers of the land" with "hugely negative implications towards the Hawaiian community."[9] Similarly, Lindsay Eriksson and Melinda Taylor describe the Department of Homeland Security's DEIS for a Texas-Mexico border wall as "inadequate," as is its draft environmental assessment."[10] The sociologist Keri E. Iyall Smith describes the struggle of the indigenous Makah people to continue with sustainable, religiously and culturally important whale hunts against the U.S. government's refusal to complete even a DEIS.[11] June L. Lorenzo, Laguna Pueblo and Diné, describes the long and often unsuccessful struggle of indigenous tribes in New Mexico—Acoma, Laguna, Navajo Nation, Zuni, and Hopi—to prevent uranium mining companies from decimating their land, with the U.S. government's DEIS itself stating approval of the mining and conversations "ongoing" as of publication in 2017.[12]

The experiences of indigenous Chamorro activists in seeking to resist environmental degradation on their ancestral island by the U.S. colonial government and occupying military present a microcosm of the global struggles of indigenous peoples affected by the U.S. and European colonial powers, including their militaries and industries.

Hinangai-ña i Tinige'/Rationale

When the military buildup to Guahan was announced in 2005, it was first welcomed and lauded as an economic boon for the island. It was invoked in terms of sustainability and prosperity by island political and economic leaders, even prior to any details being released on what the buildup would actually entail. Although initial assessments indicated that the buildup could cause severe damage to the island in environmental, social, and economic terms, island leaders and media reports focused primarily on this increase as being the key to future "sustainability" for the island.

Guahan has long been of value to military empires in the Pacific Ocean. Three different colonizers have occupied Guahan, and its sister islands to the north. First came the Spanish (1668–1898), then the United States (1898–1941), the Japanese (1941–1944), and finally the return of the United States (1944–present). Guahan's status is as an organized unincorporated territory of the United States. Guahan is one of seventeen non-self-governing territories left in the world ("non-self-governing territory" being the United Nations's term for a colony). Each year, representatives of Guahan travel to United Nations conferences to draw attention to their continuing colonial status. The United States has stated that it considers Guahan to be a domestic issue only, with no international dimensions, and has insisted that Guahan is not a colony.

Discussing colonial status can be difficult, as Guahan is a "comfortable colony" because of the complicated status of its peoples.[13] In 1950, the U.S. Congress passed an Organic Act for Guahan, allowing residents the privilege of limited local self-government. People born in Guahan are birthright U.S. citizens. Although all laws passed by the U.S. Congress are assumed to apply to Guahan, Guahan does not have the right to participate in approving or rejecting those laws. Residents of Guahan do not have the right to vote for president and have no Electoral

College votes. Furthermore, although Guahan does have the privilege of sending a single representative to the U.S. Congress, that representative, as with those from the Commonwealth of the Northern Marianas Islands, American Samoa, Puerto Rico, the U.S. Virgin Islands, and Washington, DC, is non-voting.[14]

The Tip of the Spear

In 2006, the magazine *Foreign Affairs* published a short article that listed the six most important U.S. military bases in the world. Given the fact that the United States has close to 1,000 different types of facilities around the world today, being chosen as one of the six most important would reflect a great deal of strategic value.[15]

Guahan stands out among the others, which represent vital points through which the United States currently projects force in the Middle East and Asia, or black sites, where their strategic value is precisely the way they exist out of sight and out of mind of most Americans. When asked about the strategic importance of Guahan, William Fallon, a retired four-star admiral and a former commander of the Pacific Command, minced no words, remarking, "Look at a map":[16]

> U.S. officers often talk about the "tyranny of distance" in the Pacific Command's area of operations, which runs from the west coast of North America to the east coast of Africa. Guam . . . will provide a base for land, naval and air forces closer to targets than for forces on the U.S. mainland or Hawaii.[17]

The strategic flexibility that Guahan offers is critical to maintaining U.S. interests. Located right on the edge of Asia, Guahan, like Okinawa, helps to provide the United States the ability to contend with potential future threats from China, Russia, North Korea, or others. Yet both Guahan and Okinawa, these crucial bases, have also been environmentally disposable for the U.S. military:

> In the late 1980s, the United States military discovered levels of toxic polychlorinated biphenyls (PCBs) at land on Kadena Air Base that exceeded safe standards by many orders of magnitude. . . . Despite the possible risks

to service members and local Okinawans, it appears the U.S Air Force failed to alert Japanese authorities and has been concealing information about the contamination—which potentially remains dangerous today—for more than 25 years.[18]

Admiral Fallon alluded to a second strategic value of Guahan (one that it shares with places such as Diego Garcia and Guantanamo Bay): its political ambiguity. Guahan is a political entity that is both foreign and domestic at the same time, for it can be considered part of the United States in one instance or a mere possession of the United States in the next. Fallon notes that as an "American territory . . . the island does not have political restrictions, such as those in South Korea, that could impede U.S. military moves in an emergency."[19] The blurring of political lines in Guahan creates new strategic possibilities, as it is not a foreign nation that might seek to limit the activities of the U.S. military within its borders. But as a territory and not a full member of the United States, it also lacks political power within the U.S. system. The U.S. military can do things on Guahan it might not be able to do elsewhere, for those who call it home have no say in what the military may or may not do.[20]

Since 9/11, Guahan has been referred to by U.S. military commanders and personnel as "the tip of the spear," meaning that the island's strategic location on the edge of Asia operates as a real weapon in terms of projecting American power into Asia.[21] This name for the island is just one among a long legacy of diminutive and dismissive labels that Guahan has been given by the United States and its military. Others include the "trailer park of the Pacific," "Sleepy Hollow," "USS *Guam*," "Fortress Guam," and "unsinkable aircraft carrier."[22] All these labels deemphasize and, in many ways, completely strip away any semblance of the island as anything but an object, a piece of real estate through which the United States brandishes its military prowess. Yet this idea of Guahan as the tip of the spear is something that people on the island have taken up, not as a marker of disrespect, but rather as one of usefulness, of recognition—of something that nonetheless connects the island to the United States, thereby conferring value upon it. The reason such a clear and brutal objectification of Guahan can be endorsed is because this weaponization is, at its core, an *American* weaponization, a form of recognition and a chance for Guam to assert itself clearly as a part of America.

Land Trauma

With the U.S. return to the island in July 1944, the occupation was over, but the Chamorro struggles for sustainability and freedom did not end. Chamorros were elated at the United States' return because of its expulsion of the Japanese. However, even when the fighting had stopped in 1945, the United States kept taking land from the native inhabitants of the island. Thousands of Chamorros were displaced with the U.S. return. Guam, which had once been a sleepy navy base, thought of as a quiet coaling station, was now the largest harbor in the Western Pacific, with flat expanses in the south, center, and north, ideal for runways. Guahan was transformed into a military hub, for defending U.S. interests in the Pacific and Asia. At the height of this transformation, 85,000 acres had been taken by the United States, amounting to 63 percent of the entire land mass of Guahan, while the majority of the Chamorro people still had to live in refugee tents or Quonset huts, unable to return to their homes. Chamorros, although grateful for America's return, could not understand why the land taking continued and why, by 1948 and 1949, families were still being displaced, sometimes to create recreational areas for troops to relax.

Although the taking of Chamorro lands was supposedly authorized through the "eminent domain" clause of the U.S. Constitution, it was so extreme that it eventually attracted national attention. Newspapers began to publish articles shaming the U.S. military for its treatment of Chamorros. In a U.S. Senate hearing in 1946, Colonel Wilson, a marine corps commander, was asked if the land taking had been conducted legally. Wilson's response was, "I wouldn't say legally, but everything is legal in a time of war."[23] However, eminent domain applies only to U.S. citizens, while, at that time, Chamorros were recognized only as U.S. nationals. In response to local protests and international pressures, the U.S. Congress passed an Organic Act for Guahan in 1950. This act gave the island the privilege of having limited local government and also granted U.S. citizenship to Chamorros on Guam. Although the passage of the Organic Act is often attributed to American benevolence, it may have had more to do with legitimizing the postwar land theft. The day prior to the Organic Act going into effect, Carlton Skinner, who was appointed by President Harry Truman to be the first civilian governor of Guahan, signed a quitclaim deed that "authorized" the control of 36 percent of the island to the U.S. Department of Defense, used to retroactively legalize the lands that had been taken illegally from Chamorros.

The trauma of the land taking is something that still haunts Chamorros and their relationship to the United States today. According to the Chamorro scholar Robert Underwood, the issue of land, its theft, and its demanded return was the one issue that could turn any Chamorro—a nurse, a teacher, a serviceman, anyone—into an activist, and perhaps a radical one.[24] But for others, radicalization happened not through land, but bodies. Anghet Santos, the founder of the protest group Nasion Chamoru, was politicized not only by the taking of his land but by the illness and death of his daughter, which was thought to be connected to military pollution. Santos was credited for revealing the improper disposal of toxic waste on private property by the U.S. military, a practice that had been kept secret by the U.S. military itself. The bases not only represented a theft of native lands but also their polluting, and by extension the polluting of the people of the land or, as the Chamorro refer to themselves, *i taotao tåno'*.

The land takings displaced thousands of Chamorros who were not only unable to return to their lands but also unable to live as farmers and fishermen. Hence the systems of reciprocity, bartering, and subsistence farming began to slowly disappear. Changes in Guahan's governance after the war provided more options for employment.[25] Among Chamorros, these changes to the island economy mixed with new desires to Americanize and created a very different attachment to the United States, which was accompanied with a very aggressive set of militaristic policies for the island.

The Military Buildup to Guahan

Although the U.S. Department of Defense first announced its intentions to move thousands of marines from Okinawa to Guahan in 2005, it did not reveal its specific plans until late 2009. The lack of specifics, however, did not keep Guahan's politicians and economic leaders from ruminating on the important "golden ticket" opportunity this military increase could represent for Guahan. Media coverage stressed the economic boon and the increase in jobs the buildup would represent and emphasized financial sustainability through the military industry.

Lee Webber, chairman of the Armed Forces Committee of the Guam Chamber of Commerce, and the president and publisher of the *Pacific Daily News*, stated:

> This is not only great news for our economy but also for Guam and our nation, as it places the best fighting forces in the world on U.S. soil while simultaneously keeping them at the tip of the spear. . . . Marines cleared the way on Guam some 60 years ago and that has enabled our island to grow into its current position. . . . They will most certainly assist us in maintaining that growth position well into the future.[26]

The *Pacific Daily News* is the largest media outlet in the Western Pacific, and its pro-military personal opinion is evident in its coverage.[27] It focused on the great economic potential the buildup represented. When caution was urged, it was not directed toward the buildup, indicating that it might be something bad or unsustainable for Guahan, but rather that Guahan itself might not be ready, in terms of infrastructure, to take advantage of the opportunities the buildup would offer.

Gerry Perez, the general manager of the Guam Visitors Bureau, which is in charge of managing Guahan's tourist economy, said:

> This situation has made it difficult . . . to pay for necessary upgrades in our tourism plant and island infrastructure, while attending to critical health, education, and public safety issues. The military build-up will stimulate new markets, attract higher spending business travelers, and generate more income to pay for improvements in public service.[28]

The buildup became a sort of panacea that could quickly and easily solve so many economic woes, tied to possibilities for new sustainability and the use of alternative energy, as evidenced in an October 29, 2009, press release, "Guam Military Build-up to Usher in Era of Energy Efficiency."[29] The title of the article made it appear that the use of energy efficiency would extend to the island as a whole when it applied only to facilities on military bases and would not affect the civilian infrastructure.

Representatives of the Joint Guam Program Office, who were tasked with guiding the buildup process, were careful to note that anything and everything discussed was merely "notional" or "pre-decisional." By the middle of 2009, no concrete or detailed proposals about the U.S. military's intentions for this increase had been offered, yet the chorus of supporters continued unabated. The buildup was still seen as the path to economic improvement and sustainability.

Given the numbers invoked, it was clear that the buildup would be big and would come with significant costs or risks. Estimates by the Joint Guam Program Office indicated that the buildup might increase Guahan's population by 40,000, a 30 percent increase in just four years. Housing and training 8,000 Marines would require a substantial investment. Would the U.S. military stay within its existing footprint? Or would it seek new lands and expand its already significant holdings? How would an increase in population affect socioeconomic life on Guahan? How might such a large population increase cause problems?

The buildup was being touted as a chance for economic development and advancement for Guahan, a "golden ticket" that could lead to economic sustainability. But that mythical sustainability wasn't so much about the buildup itself but, rather, the way the buildup helped people on Guahan build a less colonial relationship to the United States.

Buildup Fantasy

Our conceptualization of fantasy is informed by Julie Sze's concept of eco-desire as articulated in her book *Fantasy Islands: Chinese Dreams and Ecological Fears in an Age of Climate Crisis*, especially in relation to Slavoj Žižek's definition of fantasy. In Sze's text, she discusses a variety of environmental discourses, each of which relies upon similar, necessarily excluded content in order for there to be the appearance of consistency or harmony.[30] Žižek in *Looking Awry* represents another insightful example of how social theory can be used to analyze and unpack different social challenges.[31] His theories assist us in portraying the acceptance and later rejection of the buildup by the Chamorro people in a complex fashion, allowing us to understand both how it was formed and later how it came to be disrupted. The buildup was a fantasy in the sense that it was not simply a wishful dream but, rather, a fiction upon which an economy of desire was based. The efficiency of this fantasy depended on certain content, some essential fact, being excluded. In this sense, an ideal fantasy space is empty, as one can project sustainability upon it. Fantasies can be unraveled or disrupted when the content that is supposed to be left excluded may somehow then be brought back into articulation and recognition.

The positive interpretations of the buildup and the optimistic assumptions about its sustainability in an economic and political sense were very much tied to negative feelings of colonial dependency in the people of Guahan. Without any actual details as to what the military was planning and how Guahan might benefit, the increase was nonetheless lauded like manna from heaven, a glorious panacea that Guahan required in order to sustain and improve itself.

Chamorro support for the buildup was high so long as the world of discourse that gave it meaning and shape was dominated by ideas that had nothing to do with the proposed actions. The buildup could fulfill nearly every colonial desire. It reinforced the concept of the benevolent United States. It confirmed the idea of the U.S. military being Guahan's most consistent and valuable connection to the United States, a way to cut through the colonial difference and complete the circle of political belonging. The embedded colonial ideas of the United States as the top of the binary for nearly everything became fodder for filling that fantasy.

Fantasies require an emptiness so people can put their desires into them, so they can use that emptiness to create something that will feel consistent and powerful. That something will protect what they perceive to be their enjoyment or primary source of their identity. In this instance, the military buildup was a fantasy void that allowed Chamorros, and others seeking to overcome the colonial difference, a chance to give life to their ideas of the United States being a bastion of freedom and democracy and being the richest and most generous nation in the world, a chance, through their patriotic support for the buildup, to forge a connection to the United States that would surpass that colonial difference and establish them within the circle of American belonging.

Lost in these initial discussions was the general environmentally destructive nature of U.S. military facilities, to the land both within their fences and without. For example, internationally, the U.S. military generates some 500,000 tons of toxic waste annually, more than the five largest U.S. chemical companies combined, according to the nonprofit watchdog group Project Censored.[32] Guahan's residents and veterans have most likely been affected by the storing of dangerous chemicals such as Agent Orange on Guahan during Vietnam or the fallout from nuclear testing in the nearby Marshall Islands in the 1950s and 1960s. Little attention was paid, however, to these historical instances of environmental damage, and as a result even less was mentioned about possible future contamination.

When the question of whether the buildup was sustainable first emerged, the fantasy fell apart. The plans for Guahan were too destructive.

The National Environmental Protection Act

On November 20, 2009, the Department of Defense at last released its Draft Environmental Impact Statement for the Guahan military buildup. As per the National Environmental Protection Act (NEPA), the DEIS was submitted to the Guahan community for review and comments, prior to the project being able to move forward:

> The NEPA process is part of a national policy that was developed to help protect the environment and mitigate related concerns. The process, which relies on the analysis and review of information, including public input, will help guide and evaluate the impacts of the military build-up on the island community.[33]

A DEIS has to be conducted by the federal government whenever it plans some public action or construction that may affect the people or the environment in the area. An average DEIS is only 100–200 pages long. The DEIS for the Guahan buildup was 11,000 pages long, the longest ever recorded. Owing to the unusual length of the DEIS, the comment period for the community was eventually extended, but only to ninety days. This would have required any interested or concerned individuals to read 122 pages each day of a document filled with sometimes confusing scientific jargon.

Privately, the U.S. military assumed that the public interest in the DEIS would be minimal, owing in part to its sheer size but also owing to the fact that the Department of Defense believed Guahan to be a very pro-military community that would not challenge or question an increase in the U.S. military presence. One employee of the Joint Guam Program Office stated that his office estimated that they would receive around 500 comments and that the public informational comment meetings that were planned would be filled with an outpouring of patriotic support. These assumptions proved to be far off.

What the Department of Defense's DEIS proposed would require the military to lease more than 1,000 acres of new lands to build firing ranges and would result in the destruction of dozens of acres of coral reef to build a berth for aircraft carriers. If its plans were carried out, the Department of Defense estimated that Guahan's population could increase by 75,000 in just four years. Guahan's population was already around 170,000.

The military buildup would include construction of facilities to house and support the transferred marines, their dependents, and tens of thousands of imported workers; the establishment of an Air and Missile Defense Task Force; the placement of a firing range complex on sacred lands; and the creation of a deep-draft wharf in Apra Harbor for nuclear-powered aircraft carriers. The buildup would create an unsustainable explosion of population, overrun public utility systems, an increase in the production of toxic waste, the appropriation of public land for weapons testing and training, the destruction of coral reefs, a rise in crime and sexual assault, and much more endangerment of marine and terrestrial life.

Prior to the DEIS comment period, the discourse was dominated by pro-military jobs, money, and patriotism. People who knew little about the buildup supported it because of those empty positives, in the same way in which people who know nothing about children or our future will say that children are it. Issues concerning traffic, land loss, disrespect, Pågat, and colonization had all been part of the conversation, but more and more people began to form their ideological cocoon using those ideas. As a result, empty negatives started to brim with life, and people soured on the buildup.

Even the United States's own Environmental Protection Agency strongly criticized the proposal by the U.S. military, declaring that it was "environmentally unsatisfactory" and that it "should not proceed as proposed." Nancy Woo of the EPA said, "The government of Guam and the Guam Waterworks cannot by themselves accommodate the military expansion. . . . It is not possible and it is not fair that the island bear the cost."[34] At the time, Guahan government officials put the total costs of the proposed buildup at about $3 billion, including $1.7 billion for infrastructure and $100 million for the already severely overburdened public hospital. On Guahan—where a third of the population at the time received food stamps, where a massive influx of impoverished immigrants from the surrounding islands was promoted by the United States, and where about 25 percent of the population lived below the U.S. poverty level—that price tag could never have been paid with local tax revenue.

Breaking the Fantasy

The sheer size of the DEIS and the challenges interpreting it presented ended up leading to the formation of a new community group critical of the military buildup. Named "We Are Guahan," it was originally started primarily by a group of young professionals, educators, and graduate students, some of whom had previous activist backgrounds in Guahan and the United States. They met to divide the DEIS into sections, read the sections in small groups, and then meet again to summarize the contents. Fueled by the statements they found in the thousands of pages of that document, the group evolved to become a public protest group, which would become the face and the voice of buildup resistance for several years.

One of the most powerful strategies employed by We Are Guahan in its anti-buildup advocacy was its members' choice to use the military's own words and own studies against it. The most powerful condemnations of the military buildup were quotes and statistics that came from the DEIS itself. At public hearings on the buildup, members of We Are Guahan produced protest signs, not with anti-military slogans per se, but rather with quotes from the DEIS with citations. In a more systematic sense, in an effort to counter the unrealistically positive portrayals of the military buildup in the media, We Are Guahan produced an informational series titled *The Grey Papers*.[35] In all, six handouts were released, each of which addressed a different aspect of life on Guahan that would be severely and negatively affected should the Department of Defense continue with its buildup as planned. We Are Guahan used information supplied by the DEIS itself, as well as other government agencies. Tiara R. Na'puti notes in her dissertation, where she provides an analysis of the rhetoric used in *The Grey Papers*, that,

> written in the very language and grounded in the content of the DEIS, the *Papers* rhetorically constructed opposition to the military build-up as well researched and factually accurate. By naming their series "grey," WAG [We Are Guahan] discursively communicates that the build-up was an extremely complex issue that could not easily be considered black or white, nor cut and dry. Instead, there were many objectives of the U.S. relocation that remained unclear, and generally grey.[36]

We Are Guahan sought to wrest the buildup from the fantasy in which it had been cloaked for years prior to its official announcement. During that time, people had projected onto the buildup their wildest dreams for economic wealth for the island, as well as for proving a patriotic relationship to the United States. It had been supported and celebrated as something that would solve Guahan's economic problems and also, perhaps, solve its colonial problems, as the buildup was, in the words of Congresswoman Madeleine Bordallo, a strong recognition of Guahan's importance and value to the United States.[37]

This strategy was built on showing the innards of the buildup, the stuff that it was made from. Its floating positivistic form was always buoyed by huge sums of money and vague notions of economic advancement. What the DEIS provided was more clarity over those very things. We Are Guahan's approach was to make those connections for people, even if the military or local buildup supporters did not want them to.

The more one delved into the thousands of pages of the DEIS, the less economically viable the buildup seemed to be. Economic benefits of the buildup seemed to not stretch as far as people might have hoped, and in fact the DEIS seemed to predict that, for middle- and low-income families on Guahan, the military buildup would increase the economic strain on them and offer them few benefits. Through the studies conducted by the Department of Defense to contribute to their DEIS, the buildup slowly filtered into more and more aspects of life, not only in positive senses, but in negative terms as well.

We Are Guahan honed in on those aspects of the DEIS, exposing to the island the fact that the Department of Defense was admitting to a whole host of negative impacts, which ranged from irritating to severe. If the buildup were carried out as planned, the DEIS predicted that there would be longer lines for residents at hospitals, increased crowding in schools, higher costs of living with no increases in wages, and dramatically increased traffic on major roads. Thus, as the buildup became more tangible, it became more and more attached to tangible things and to places, such as Pågat, a culturally significant site for Chamorros. Finally, it became possible to dissolve the buildup fantasy, which represented another strategy of We Are Guahan.

Hiking through the Fantasy

In understanding the power of Chamorro activism springing from an indigenous ethos of sustainability during this period, there is one aspect in particular that we would like to highlight as "hiking through the fantasy." Chamorro writers and activists sought to disrupt the militarized U.S. fantasy: The key lies not necessarily in disproving a fantasy, but, as Žižek argues, in forcing it to account for what it must erase or exclude in order for its fantasy to be constituted. It means to bring into the center of the fantasy that which was excluded for the fantasy to achieve consistency and formation of identity. Thus, the activists sought to re-center Chamorro lifeways and belief systems surrounding land use and sustainability in the service of social justice.

The fantasy of sustainability for the military buildup was built around the valorization of Guahan as being "Where America's Day Begins" and the concurrent exclusion of its ancestral being as *I Tano' i Chamorro*, the land of the Chamorro people. The buildup represented another way in which Guahan could reinforce the American identity proposed in that scene, a place where benevolence is demonstrated and where the greatness of America is illustrated. But the Chamorro connection, the ancient Chamorro claim to the land, must be erased for that fantasy to be coherent.

The Pågat location for the five proposed firing ranges was initially chosen by the military because of its isolation and also because much of the land that would be taken was owned by the Government of Guam, from which the military thought it would be easier to lease land than from individual landowners. Although an ancient village at Pågat still existed close to the cliffs, with the remnants of housing and living areas from Ancient Chamorros, the area near the road, at the start of the trailhead, was routinely used as a dumping ground for old furniture, appliances, and general bags of trash. From the military's point of view, the state of the trail didn't seem to indicate much community concern for its environment.

On January 2, 2010, the first of many hikes organized by We Are Guahan and other community groups took place to Pågat. More than 100 people made the three-hour trek into the Pågat area, visiting the freshwater cave, the ancient Chamorro village, and the natural arch along the coast. On February 6, 2010, We Are Guahan organized a four-hour snorkeling trip to visit outer Apra Harbor, the site of the seventy-one acres of coral that the Department of Defense was proposing to dredge to create a berth for nuclear-powered aircraft carriers.

Even after the DEIS public comment period had ended, We Are Guahan continued using the buildup as a fierce topic of public debate by organizing what they referred to as "Heritage Hikes." They held this series of twelve hikes total from November 2010 to December 2011 and focused primarily on guiding people to locations that have been historically affected by militarization in Guahan or that might be affected in the future.[38]

Pågat, given its centrality to the planned military buildup, was visited multiple times, but so were other locations that were also mentioned in the DEIS but that had not received as much attention. Each hike included lectures about the historical or cultural significance of the location, especially how each location connected to Guahan's historical relationship with the United States military. The hikes were grouped by threes, with each trio being arranged around a different theme. One series was called "I Kantan i Latte Siha," or "The Song of the Latte Stones," and introduced hikers to the ancient homes and villages of the Chamorro people, the latte stone dwellings with ancestral burial grounds, including Hila'an, an area recently returned to the Government of Guam; Haputo; and Pågat itself, where the U.S. military planned to build a firing range complex. Another series was called "Nå'i Tåtte, Chule' Tåtte" ("Give Back, Take Back") and was focused explicitly around places that had once been taken by the U.S. military and then returned to either the original landowners or the government of Guahan but that the Department of Defense was, in the conversation over the specifics for the military buildup, mulling over possibly taking again.

A third sequence of hikes was named "Un Nuebu na Inatan," or "A New Look," because of the way it centered around visiting two places that even residents of Guahan didn't associate with militarization of the past or present. One hike traveled to Tumon Bay, the tourist center of Guahan, which is a beautiful stretch of beach, with dozens of hotels and condo high-rises crowded around it. Prior to World War II this was an area where several families lived comfortably, enjoying the abundance that both the land and the sea provided. In 1948, the United States military condemned almost all the privately held property in Tumon, forcing hundreds of Chamorros out.

Another hike visited Sella Bay, the site of an ancient village, which is no longer inhabited. The area still possesses remnants of habitation, most notably an old Spanish bridge. To visit Sella Bay today, it might seem like nothing more than jungle, river, and beach. But in the 1970s this was a site of successful protest against a previous proposed military buildup in Guahan. During the Vietnam War, the U.S. Navy sought to take Sella Bay and transform it into an ammunition wharf. Local landowners resisted this, as did Chamorro activists, educators, and even certain members of the Guam Legislature. The protests were enough to stall the process for years, until the Navy eventually decided to scrap their plans.

Tiara Na'puti described the impact of these hikes:

> The hikes also provided a meaningful educational contribution by literally bringing people out to the land and teaching them the history of these places. In this way, WAG [We Are Guahan] created strong connections between the people, the land, and the cultural significance of these sites. These hikes provided a powerful visual opportunity, allowing hikers to experience the locations that would be affected by the military relocation. The hike series also instilled renewed interest in the surrounding environment. By bringing in speakers and experts to tell the stories of the locales, the hikes also conveyed the information about these sites while indicating the potential material damage and loss that would result from the build-up.[39]

"Un Nuebu na Inatan" is telling in terms of both the intent and the impact of We Are Guahan's activism against the military buildup. By taking hikers to these locations—some of which are targets for militarization, others former victims of it, and some examples of community protecting sites from militarization—the purpose is not simply to educate about the facts of the place but also to perhaps transform the very way they see the land and, most important, to whom it belongs.

As the buildup fantasy was built around the privileging of Guam as a site of *American* power, identity, and possibility, the new vision that these hikes were meant to inform was one rooted in the *Chamorro* connection to the land. Just as *The Grey Papers* were meant to fill up the buildup with critical facts and details, these hikes were intended to fill in the blanks of the buildup with images, artifacts, and histories of the places that might be destroyed or closed off. These hikes lead people on a trail to find the Chamorro signs, the Chamorro markers to these lands, contesting the claim that these places are for the United States to do with as it pleases. The visits to the sites of ancient villages, such as Pågat, helped to enliven that alternative way of seeing the land. As hikers walked among toppled stones that once served as the pillars for the homes of Ancient Chamorros, it was easier to perceive those claims, and once those concerns became more prominent in terms of the use of Pågat for firing ranges, the conversation shifted dramatically.

But during the DEIS period, activists began to work to fill the "buildup" as an idea with other things, which called into question the sustainability of the buildup and whether it would be good for the island. The buildup as a concept became filled with images of the ruins of ancient villages, the bones of Chamorro ancestors, with millions of rounds of ammunition being fired above. It became filled with the images of acres of coral reef destroyed to make way for massive aircraft carriers. It became filled with the stench of extended waiting time in traffic, the stress of longer waits at the hospital, and the shock of increased rent for low-income families.

As these hikes re-centered Chamorro history, they also led to an invoking of Chamorro *values* in opposition to the buildup. The disruption of the fantasy made it possible for people on Guahan to reevaluate their relationship to the buildup and to the parts of Guahan it would affect.

In the case of Pågat, resistance to its use became driven by the concept of *inafa'maolek*, an older Chamorro conception of inter-connectedness.

Inafa'maolek/Doing Good for One Another

On Guahan, after the buildup fantasy was disrupted, people began to question the idea of selling off land, historic and cultural sites, and the environment, to be taken over or destroyed by the U.S. military. A "Save Pågat" movement was born from different levels of activism to assert that Pågat wasn't simply jungle or stones but "I Sengsong Pågat," or "Pågat Village," a location for life, for history, and for culture, and not just empty jungle that can only achieve value if it is sold off or bulldozed over. This was a critical moment, as, during the height of debate over the military buildup and its impact on Guahan, suddenly people began to assert that we should have a very different relationship to this piece of land, that we should protect it and defend it and not just let it be closed off behind fences or let it be destroyed in construction to add more military facilities to an island already covered in U.S. military facilities.

The land was not an empty commodity but something still brimming with life. With the notion of sustainability through military buildup no longer effective for Guahan, or no longer as powerful and consistent, another discourse emerged to fill the space formed by the critiques and critical action. That discourse was formed from a variety of ideological sources. It came from those who had become resistant to the buildup because they didn't want to see their home change. It came from those who were riddled with discourses on environmental protection. It also came from those tied to indigenous rights, and, in some ways different, but other ways connected to this, it came from those who were hesitant about the buildup owing to Guahan's lack of consent to, or participation in, the process.

To address these concerns, many come together under the banner of *inafa'maolek,* a term used to refer to Chamorro epistemology and the appropriate relationship between humans, their ancestors, and the natural world. It breaks down to "the act of making things good for each other," but it is often translated in English to "interdependence," or it could be translated in modern terms as "sustainability"—protecting the people and the environment rather than harming or degrading them.

NOTES

1 Robert Miller and Mac Skelton, "Environmental Costs," Costs of War project, Watson Institute for International and Public Affairs, Brown University, April 2015, www.brown.edu.

2 Alexander Nazaryan, "The U.S. Department of Defense Is One of the World's Biggest Polluters," *Newsweek*, July 17, 2014, www.newsweek.com.

3 This expectation of complacency was despite the testimony of U.S. veterans that Agent Orange and other toxic defoliants were dumped on Guahan during the Vietnam War period, despite the existence of almost twenty Superfund toxic sites on the small island, and despite a significant history of public outrage at often uncompensated and coercive military land taking, which now amounted to nearly one-third of the entire land mass of the island. Jerick Sablan and Kyla P. Mora, "Congressman Introduces Guam-Inspired Agent Orange Bill," *Pacific Daily News*, February 3, 2017, www.guampdn.com.

4 Zita Taitano, "Military Buildup Rouses Guam Youth Activism," *Marianas Variety*, January 11, 2010, www.mvariety.com.

5 friendsofbenp, "Senator Ben Pangelinan Speaks at DSEIS Hearing," May 20, 2014, Santa Rita, Guahan, *YouTube*, https://www.youtube.com/watch?v=Sh-Psm5GeSo.

6 LisaLinda Natividad, "CHamoru Values Guiding Nonviolence," in *Conflict Transformation: Essays on Methods of Nonviolence*, ed. Rhea A. DuMont, Tom H. Hastings, and Emiko Noma (Jefferson, NC: McFarland, 2013).

7 Christine Taitano DeLisle, "Destination Chamorro Culture: Notes on Realignment, Rebranding, and Post-9/11 Militourism in Guam," *American Quarterly* 68, no. 3 (September 2016): 563–572.

8 Linda Moon Stumpff, "Reweaving Earth: An Indigenous Perspective on Restoration Planning and the National Environmental Policy Act," *Environmental Practice* 8, no. 2 (June 2006): 93–103.

9 Anna Cordova, "Scientific Colonialism in Indigenous Spaces: A Case Study in Hawai'i" (Master's thesis, University of Colorado at Colorado Springs, 2016), 42.

10 Lindsay Eriksson and Melinda Taylor, "The Environmental Impacts of the Border Wall between Texas and Mexico," *TexasLaw: The Texas-Mexico Border Wall*, n.d., www.utexas.edu, p. 3. Also see Denise Gilman, "Obstructing Human Rights: The Texas-Mexico Border Wall: The Working Group on Human Rights and the Border Wall," *TexasLaw: The Texas-Mexico Border Wall*, June 2008, www.utexas.edu.

11 Keri E. Iyall Smith, "Notes from the Field: 'Breathing Life' into the Declaration on the Rights of Indigenous Peoples," *Societies without Borders* 6, no. 1 (2011): 102–115; point noted at 110–111.

12 June L. Lorenzo, "Spatial Justice and Indigenous Peoples' Protection of Sacred Places: Adding Indigenous Dimensions to the Conversation," *justice spatiale / spatial justice*, no. 11, March 2017, 9–10, www.jssj.org.

13 Robert Underwood, "The Status of Having No Status," speech given at the Annual Research Conference of the College of Liberal Arts and Social Sciences, University of Guam, Mangilao, Guam, March 1999.

14 However, as the Obama Administration argued in 2014, the rights of people living in Guam, even if they are U.S. citizens, are not secure because of Guam's colonial status. They are instead privileges, as the U.S. Congress has the ultimate say over what aspects of the U.S. Constitution apply to Guam.

15 Daniel Widome, "The List: The Six Most Important U.S. Military Bases," *Foreign Policy*, May 2006, www.foreignpolicy.com.

16 Richard Halloran, "Guam Seen as Pivotal U.S. Base," *Washington Times*, March 11, 2006.

17 Ibid.

18 Jon Mitchell, "U.S. Military Report Suggests Cover-up over Toxic Pollution in Okinawa," *Japan Times*, March 17, 2014, www.japantimes.co.jp.

19 Halloran, "Guam Seen as Pivotal U.S. Base."

20 According to one member of Nasion Chamoru, a Chamorro grassroots activist group, "*Ya un tungo' sa' håfa* [and do you know why] we are important to them? It is because they can do things here that they can't at home and they can't do in other countries. We don't really have a say in what happens, if they want to do something" (David Herrera, interview with author Bevacqua, Seventh Day Adventist Clinic, Tamuning, Guam, May 21, 2004).

21 Christian Caryl, "America's Unsinkable Fleet: Why the US Military Is Pouring Forces into a Remote West Pacific Island," *Newsweek International*, February 26, 2007, www.msn.com.

22 See Todd Crowell, "Fortress Guam Gets More Crowded," *Asia Sentinel*, June 16, 2008, www.asiasentinel.com; Richard Marquand, "U.S. More Cautious than Wary as China's Reach Grows," *Christian Science Monitor*, November 18, 2005, www.csmonitor.com; James Brooke, "Looking for Friendly Overseas Base, Pentagon Finds It Already Has One," *New York Times*, April 7, 2004; Kristen Scharnberg, "Bracing for the Next Wave," *Chicago Tribune*, June 18, 2007; and Robert Rogers, *Destiny's Landfall: A History of Guam* (Honolulu: University of Hawaii Press, 1995), 126.

23 Michael Phillips, "Land Ownership on Guam," *Kinalamten Pulitikåt: Siñenten i Chamorro* (Issues in Guam's Political Development: The Chamorro Perspective) (Hagåtña, Guam: Political Status Education Coordinating Commission, 1996), 17.

24 Robert Underwood, "Afterword," in *Campaign for Political Rights on the Island of Guam, 1898–1950*, by Penelope Bordallo Hofschneider (Saipan: Commonwealth of the Northern Marianas Islands, Division of Historic Preservation, 2001), 211.

25 Anthony Leon Guerrero, "The Economic Development of Guam," *Kinalamten Pulitikåt: Siñenten i Chamorro* (Issues in Guam's Political Development: The Chamorro Perspective) (Hagåtña, Guam: Political Status Education Coordinating Commission, 1996), 86.

26 Gene Park, "7,000 Marines: Pentagon Announces Shift to Guam," *Pacific Sunday News*, October 30, 2005.

27 "Relocation of Marines to Guam Could Be a Good Thing," *Pacific Daily News*, November 7, 2005; "Let's Follow Okinawa's Example and Flourish with Marine Build-up," *Pacific Daily News*, August 15, 2006; and "Military Build-up, Relocations Will Change Island, Hopefully for Better," *Pacific Daily News*, December 4, 2006.

28 Amritha Alladi, " 'I'm Not Against the Buildup': Supporters Prepare in Anticipation of Economic Growth," *Pacific Daily News*, January 18, 2010.

29 Quoted in Jeff Marchesseault, "From Guam, Joint Region Marianas Leads Energy Conservation across the Pacific," *Peace and Justice for Guam and the Pacific* (blog), October 21, 2009, www.decolonizeguam.blogspot.com.

30 Julie Sze, *Fantasy Islands: Chinese Dreams and Ecological Fears in an Age of Climate Crisis* (Oakland: University of California Press, 2015).

31 Slavoj Žižek, *Looking Awry: An Introduction to Jacques Lacan through Popular Culture* (Cambridge, MA: MIT Press, 1991).

32 "Military Toxic Waste Sites: More Dangerous and Not EPA Regulated," Project Censored, July 16, 2015, http://projectcensored.org.

33 "Environmental Workshops on Buildup Start Today," *Marianas Variety*, October 27, 2009.

34 See Blaine Harden, "On Guam, Planned Marine Base Raises Anger, Infrastructure Concerns," *Washington Post*, March 22, 2010.

35 We Are Guahan, *The Grey Papers*, series, 2010, www.weareguahan.com.

36 Tiara R. Na'puti, "Charting Contemporary Chamoru Activism: Anti-militarization and Social Movements in Guåhan" (Dissertation, University of Texas at Austin, 2013), 146.

37 Sabrina Salas Matanane, "Bordallo on Obama's Refueling Stop," KUAM News, November 20, 2011, www.kuam.com.

38 I (Michael Lujan Bevacqua) worked as the main organizer for these hikes, and, given the controversy over the military build-up and lands, I decided to focus the hikes to cover the following types of lands of Guam: (1) land (sort of) returned by the federal government; (2) land currently held by the federal government, and (3) land that is being sought after by the federal government.

39 Na'puti, "Charting Contemporary Chamoru Activism," 184–185.

10

Equality in the Air We Breathe

Police Violence, Pollution, and the Politics of Sustainability

LINDSEY DILLON AND JULIE SZE

Donna Murch's history of the Black Panther Party, *Living for the City*, takes its title from a Stevie Wonder song: "living just enough / just enough for the city."[1] Wonder sings a familiar story of the Great Migration. As a young boy, the song's protagonist moves from rural Mississippi to the city—with its promises of opportunity—but economic conditions, police violence, the prison system, a toxic environment, and other forms of racism beat him down. The song was released in 1973, a few years after cities like New York adopted the policy of "planned shrinkage," or the removal of essential city services from poor neighborhoods, usually where black people lived.[2] In the song, the boy is arrested for a small street crime and sentenced to ten years in prison. In the city, then, he finds the "new Jim Crow."[3] In one of the song's final verses, Wonder tells us, "He spends his life walking the streets of New York City / He's almost dead from breathing air pollution / He tried to vote but to him there's no solution."[4] These images depict what the scholar Rob Nixon calls slow violence, "a violence that is neither spectacular nor instantaneous, but rather incremental and accretive, its calamitous repercussions playing out across a range of temporal scale."[5] They also speak to the geographer Ruth Wilson Gilmore's definition of racism as "the state-sanctioned and extralegal exposure of group-differentiated vulnerability to premature death."[6] And yet the song does not end in despair. Instead, Wonder hopes that "you hear inside my voice of sorrow" and that it "motivates you to make a better tomorrow." "Living for the City" thus opens up into life and the possibility of enacting other, more just worlds.

The Black Panther Party for Self-Defense—among other groups—sought to enact a more just world in the 1960s and 1970s. Their health clinics, free breakfast programs, "survival conferences," and other projects aimed to reverse social forces that tore at black lives in the United States while making connections with colonized people across the globe.[7] They inspired other decolonial movements in the United States at the time, like the Puerto Rican Young Lords in New York City. Today's Black Lives Matter movement is, at least in part, a legacy of the Black Panther Party. Both engage in a form of decolonial thinking and alternative world-making practices in the context of the state-sanctioned violences of our time. "Black Lives Matter is an ideological and political intervention in a world where Black Lives are systematically and intentionally targeted for demise," write the movement's organizers on its website.[8] The physical gesture of "Hands Up!" during anti–police violence protests and signs that read, "I can't breathe," attest to the ways race and racism manifest—as they did for the protagonist in Wonder's song—as everyday, embodied vulnerabilities. Yet Black Lives Matter is more than simply a protest against racialized violence. To quote its website, "It is an *affirmation* of Black folks' contributions to this society, our humanity, and our resilience in the face of deadly oppression."[9] The movement is about, as Alicia Garza, one of its founders, puts it, "broadening the conversation to include Black life."[10]

This chapter brings an interdisciplinary and social justice perspective to the concept and practices of "sustainability" by foregrounding the work of anti-racist struggles in U.S. cities, like Black Lives Matter. We assert that anti-racist struggles have always been struggles about life-sustaining environments, at least as "the environment" is defined by the environmental justice movement as the place where we "live, work, and play." Black and brown activists, scholars, and cultural figures like Stevie Wonder have not separated police violence from pollution in their political critiques—the social and the ecological are inseparably connected in the work of building a better world. As such, anti-racist movements offer a serious challenge to conventional notions of sustainability—asking sustainability practitioners to rethink their ideologies and practices through a politics of difference. *Whose* lives are to be sustained? *Which* environments are at stake? And how might social movements like Black Lives Matter offer powerful socioecological arguments about how to build sustainable futures? This chapter focuses on U.S. cities and specifically on resistance to the racialized geographies of pollution and police violence, two toxic vectors through which black and brown lives are rendered vulnerable in the United States today. We develop this argument through examples of social movements from our own research in San Francisco and New York and alongside other scholars and activists who emphasize the relationship among place, embodiment, and politics.

We are indebted to, and inspired by, scholars and activists who insist that any notion of sustainability should be inseparable from issues of equity and justice.[11] However, we hope our argument moves beyond the notion of bringing together anti-racist praxis with an already-existing sustainability movement, particularly as this movement has been defined by mainstream environmentalism of the Global North. Rather, we turn to anti-racist social movements as a distinct standpoint and sociospatial positionality from which to understand and articulate an alternative vision of "sustainability." This alternative vision of sustainability is emphatically *not* about sustaining the status quo but refers to life-sustaining practices and more livable worlds. In solidarity with Black Lives Matter and in reference to Eric Garner's last words, "I can't breathe,"[12] in the second half of the chapter we focus on breathing and the breath—that essential act of life that is often constrained or denied to people of color. We consider the breath as a geographical site of political struggle and resistance to unsustainable socioenvironmental conditions.

Black Geographies and the Unsustainable City

Drawing on Gilmore's writing on racism as a state-sanctioned, group-differentiated vulnerability, in this article we consider racism as embodiment.[13] This definition connects with the environmental justice movement, which has highlighted and challenged the health inequalities that have resulted from racialized exposures to industrial pollution. Environmental justice scholars have developed theoretical approaches to the entanglements of race and the environment. The geographer Laura Pulido demonstrates how race and racism *work through* the uneven production of place—specifically, through residential segregation and industrial pollution patterns in Los Angeles. Pulido draws on critical race scholarship and the analysis of race as a historically situated social formation, and she has extended these insights to urban geography. As

Pulido explains, racism is "a sociospatial relation, both constitutive of the city and produced by it."[14] The sociologist Valerie Kuletz and the ethnic studies scholar Traci Brynne Voyles explore a different relationship between race and space, demonstrating how the disposability of indigenous lands in the United States and the disposability of indigenous peoples have been historically linked—specifically how desert landscapes have become a sacrifice zone for uranium extraction and U.S. nuclear weapons production, testing, and disposal.[15]

In both urban and rural landscapes, the uneven, unequitable production of environmental conditions has resulted in "group-differentiated vulnerabilities to premature death."[16] Examples include the "slow violence" of chemical exposure in racially segregated cities and workplaces. It also includes forms of cultural death, as with the loss of indigenous practices and ways of being through settler colonialism and environmental degradation. Importantly, these toxic spatialities also led to environmental and health justice social movements, which have critiqued existing power relations and articulated other—often more life-sustaining—world-making practices. The Standing Rock Sioux Tribe's protest against the Dakota Access Pipeline, for example, involves long-standing claims to territorial sovereignty and the right to uncontaminated water, and it also advances notions of climate justice and the need to transition to a fossil-free economy.[17]

While environmental justice scholarship has traditionally focused on the relationship between race and industrial pollution, other scholars have shown how anti-racist social movements emerge in response to other life-diminishing and unsustainable conditions—toxic environments in a broad sense. Such social movements have drawn powerful connections between race and place or between social and spatial exclusions. The geographer Matthew Gandy and the communications scholar Darrel Wanzer-Serrano both explore how the impoverished and dirty streets of New York City's East Harlem in the late 1960s were contested by the Puerto Rican Young Lords, whose first direct action in 1969 was a "garbage offensive" to clean up uncollected trash. The accumulation of waste on the streets had become a physical symbol of Puerto Rican political marginality.[18] The Young Lords also organized free breakfast programs and medical clinics, modeled after the work of the Black Panthers. These programs offered life-sustaining interventions in a landscape—both social and physical—produced through racialized municipal neglect. The historians Robert Self and Donna Murch have also shown how the Black Panthers in Oakland organized in response to the racialized production of urban space, including segregation in housing and employment, a neighborhood worn down by capital divestment and the decline of its tax base, and physically torn apart by the postwar construction of freeways and the BART rail line through an African American residential community in West Oakland.[19]

Many Oakland activists, including the Black Panthers, found spatial metaphors—in part from the anti-colonial lexicon of the time—useful in describing their urban experience.[20] For example, in 1968 the community organizer Paul Cobb called West Oakland an "urban plantation," while Don McCullum, chairman of the West Coast Region NAACP, testified to the U.S. Commission on Civil Rights that "here in Oakland . . . we are ringed by a white noose of suburbia."[21] According to Robert Self, in Oakland "the Panthers defined as actual and metaphorical space the defense of which had become their mission."[22] Many Black Power activists drew from the anti-colonial writer and activist Frantz Fanon, who, in *The Wretched of the Earth*, describes the Manichean segregation of colonial space. Fanon writes, "The colonist's sector is a sector built to last, all stone and steel."[23] The colonized sector, in contrast, is "a world with no space, people are piled up on top of each other, the shacks squeezed tightly together."[24] Fanon's passage speaks to the mutual constitution of urban environments, social difference, and embodiment—including forms of violence and premature death.

The salience of these spatial metaphors can also be understood through the geographer Katherine McKittrick's concept of "black geographies."[25] As an analytical framework and historical method, "black geographies" refers to the ways black subjects and black lives have been marginalized and displaced, in both material and imaginative space. Black lives are marginalized through physical and social displacement (such as incarceration or gentrification), through the naturalization of black bodies in some spaces and not others (as in the idea that some people are "out of place" while others belong), and through the erasure of black knowledge and experience from scholarly disciplines.[26] McKittrick notes that black writers and activists have historically used spatial categories as a way of challenging dominant narratives and asserting the agency and specific geographies of black subjects. To the "urban planta-tion" in Oakland, add "the Middle Passage," "the underground railroad," bell hook's "margin" and "homeplace," Paul Gilroy's "the Black Atlantic," and Sylvia Wynter's "plots."[27] As the Young Lords recognized, political marginality is a spatial and environmental condition. Importantly for McKittrick's concept of black geographies, these spaces of marginality and displacement are not simply sites of domination; they also point us to other ways of knowing, to sites of potentiality and other world-making practices. The concept of black geographies is thus an affirma-tion of meaningful sites through which to imagine and realize more just and sustainable worlds.

McKittrick develops the concept of black geographies, in part, through Frantz Fanon. Fanon's writings also help us explore the breath as a black geography—a contested, geographical space through which to critique contemporary relations of power and to imagine other, more life-sustaining environments. We can imagine, for example, the "world with no space" Fanon describes in *The Wretched of the Earth* as a place where it is difficult to breathe. Indeed, in the concluding essay of *Black Skin, White Masks*, Fanon uses the breath and the inability to breathe as a metaphor for colonialism. In explaining the material conditions of the rebellion in Vietnam in the 1950s, he writes, "It is not because the Indo-Chinese has discovered a culture of his own that he is in revolt. It is because 'quite simply' it was, in more than one way, becoming *impos-sible for him to breathe*."[28] Fanon's words circulate today (in abbreviated fashion and without the reference to Vietnam) on signs used in Black Lives Matter protests, demonstrating that the breath is again a political space—a metaphor for police violence in the United States. As the so-ciologist Ruha Benjamin writes, "I can't breathe" "is the clarion call of a renewed movement for social justice."[29]

In the following section, we present a brief survey of existing ideas and practices of sustainability and conclude that conventional notions of sustainability are implicated within histories of race and racism. Our in-tention here is not to do away with the concept of sustainability entirely but to suggest that other frameworks and social movements offer an alternative basis from which to develop a more inclusive sustainability praxis. We illustrate this idea through two examples of the breath as a black geography, from our research in San Francisco and New York City.

Critiques of Existing Sustainabilities

As this volume demonstrates, "sustainability" is a conceptually ambiguous term that has been used in widely divergent political projects. Many sustainability projects and policies in fact exacerbate existing social and environmental inequalities and make it difficult for some people to breathe. Miriam Greenberg describes how corporations and urban growth coalitions have embraced sustainability as a market strategy, what she calls a "sustainability edge."[30] Greenberg describes the contours of market-oriented sustainability in New York City and New Orleans as a form of "green city branding" and shows how sustainability in this context works to reproduce many of the same economic activities that cause environmental problems in the first place. These environmental problems include the ways sustainability in urban planning has been more likely to lead to gentrification and displacement than to affordable housing. In a similar vein, Julie Sze's study of "eco-desire" in Chinese urban development plans demonstrates the political resonance of sustainability discourses with top-down state and corporate interests.[31] This point is developed by scholars who conceptualize "green gentrification" and the contradictions of urban growth coalitions that seek to both "green" and "grow" cities.[32]

Erik Swyngedouw explores how the fusion of a harmonious "Nature" (with a capital "N") and a technocratic optimism is characteristic of the mainstream discourse of sustainability today.[33] He argues that sustainability, insofar as it gets defined by a small group of experts as a technical and managerial problem, is "postpolitical" in that it evacuates any real political discussion and therefore the possibility of radical socioenvironmental change. As he puts it, "The fantasy of 'sustainability' imagines the possibility of an original, fundamentally harmonious Nature, one that is now out-of-sync but, which, if 'properly' managed, we can and have to return to by means of a series of technological, managerial, and organizational fixes."[34] Importantly, the idea of needing to return to and sustain a singular, abstract "Nature" also excludes the multiplicity of actually lived and other-possible natures, as well as the question of who, exactly, gets to define what "nature" is worth sustaining.[35]

As Raymond Williams argued, ideas of nature "contain an extraordinary amount of human history,"[36] and this is the case of the "Nature," or natures, at stake in sustainability discourses as well. In the United States, ideas of nature historically developed through distinct racial projects. Native American displacement and genocide emerged alongside, and in relation to, the desire by U.S. settlers to protect land from urban and industrial development. The idea of Yosemite as a pristine wilderness, requiring state protection as a national park, was only possible after the militarized removal of indigenous Americans. That which John Muir and the Sierra Club—along with today's visitors to Yosemite and other national parks—experienced as untouched "nature" was once an inhabited, managed landscape.[37] The life-and-death struggle over which "nature" is worth sustaining is also part of the reproduction of colonial social relations in Africa and U.S. militarization in Hawai'i and the Philippines.[38]

Race and racism have also worked *through* ideas of nature.[39] For example, social groups have been reduced and essentialized through presumably "natural" characteristics (such as laziness or irrationality) or seen as somehow "closer to nature" (as in the myth of the "ecological Indian") and thus farther from modernity. The ways race has worked through ideas of nature has had profound consequences for democratic inclusion—for who is imagined as a rational political actor, deserving of rights and state recognition. To the extent that popular discourses of sustainability rely on unexamined ideas of a harmonious and universal nature, they risk inheriting and reproducing these concepts and histories.[40]

Other social practices have always existed alongside these dominant ideas of nature. The Afro-American studies scholar Britt Rusert finds a precursor of today's concept of sustainability within the socioecological relations of plantation agriculture in colonial Caribbean islands.[41] Colonial planters of the time worried about threats to the stability of the plantation's ecology (and its profits) through invasive crops, diseases, inclement weather, and slave rebellions. And yet plantation ecologies—oriented as they were to production for global commodity markets—often did not produce enough food to sustain the slaves who lived on them (a dynamic that resembles farmworker food insecurity in industrial agriculture today).[42] As a remedy to unsustainable life on the plantation, slaves were often allowed to keep small garden plots, or provision grounds.[43] "Another history of sustainability," Rusert writes, "might be glimpsed in the everyday acts of enslaved and dispossessed peoples." More specifically, "despite the production of the slaves' provision rounds *through* colonial rule and power, such spaces also produced an alternative ecological vision."[44]

In making this claim, Rusert draws on the philosopher Sylvia Wynter's writings of slave plots as containing "secretive histories."[45] Slave plots were simultaneously produced by the plantation system *and* were sites of a flourishing folk culture, outside the plantation's racist logic. Katherine McKittrick also works with Wynter's notion of slave plots as enacting other possible worlds in her concept of "plantation futures."[46] She asks: How might we understand the legacies of the plantation in contemporary cities, which include "sites of toxicity, environmental decay, pollution and militarized action that are inhabited by impoverished communities," in ways that do not reduce and represent them as spaces of "unending black death?"[47] McKittrick turns to Wynter's concept of the "plot" as prefiguring a different, more humane way of living, to insist on a recognition of plot-*life* and, by extension, black-*life* as "anticipatory."[48]

In the 1970s, as Black Power activists and the Puerto Rican Young Lords struggled for more livable urban environments, black scholars theorized alternative ecologies that might also provide the basis for rethinking the definition of "sustainability." Nathan Hare, the first coordinator of the Black Studies Department at San Francisco State University (which was famously established after a five-month student strike, and which is now called Africana Studies), developed the concept of "black ecology" in a 1970 article in the *Black Scholar*, a journal he co-founded.[49] Hare suggests that "the concept of ecology in American life is potentially of momentous relevance to the ultimate liberation of black people."[50] He draws connections between the built environment and black health outcomes and argues that the problems of the urban "ghetto" constitute an ecological crisis: Spatial concentration and overcrowding, industrial pollution—all affect black psychological and physical health. According to Hare, from a black perspective, the ecological crisis requires a fundamental change in economics as well as a spatial analysis of metropolitan segregation and its environmental and health effects, including air pollution produced by white suburban commuters. Hare concludes that black ecology challenges "the very foundations of American society," and that "the real solution to the environmental crisis is the decolonization of the black race."[51]

Together, these insights from scholars and activists offer a critique of the idea of nature in the dominant sustainability movement. They sketch out an alternative notion of sustainability, as it has been long theorized by, and lived through, brown and black lives. Here we focus on the breath and on breathing—that essential act of life that is often constrained or denied to people of color in U.S. cities today. If "breathing spaces" in the United States today are racialized geographies, we believe they are also key sites through which to explore alternative, more just and livable worlds.[52]

Sustainable Urbanism and Air Quality in San Francisco

On December 2, 2015, San Francisco police officers shot and killed twenty-six-year-old Mario Woods in the city's Bayview Hunters Point neighborhood. Woods was African American, and he was carrying a kitchen knife. His body was ultimately riddled by twenty bullets. The following day, dozens of residents attended a candlelight vigil at the site of Woods's killing, gathering around a photograph of him and sign reading "Black Lives Matter." A year before, in 2014, San Francisco police killed Alex Nieto while he was eating dinner on a park bench. Born in San Francisco to Mexican immigrants, Nieto was killed in the once-working-class neighborhood of Bernal Heights, just north of Bayview Hunters Point, where he had grown up. The essayist Rebecca Solnit writes about Nieto in her article, "Death by Gentrification," in which she details how a white couple, walking in the Bernal Heights park that evening, had called 911 to report Nieto as a suspicious person. Both men in the couple worked in the tech business—an industry that bears much responsibility for San Francisco's unsustainable housing market, including the wave of evictions currently displacing longtime residents from the city. Today, Nieto's image joins those of Eric Garner and Michael Brown on a mural in the city's Mission District, painted to insist that "brown and black lives matter."[53]

In the context of these gentrification-related police killings and economic displacements, it may seem paradoxical that many of the gentrifying development projects in San Francisco take place through a discourse of sustainable urbanism. A short walk from the site of Woods's killing is the Hunters Point Naval Shipyard, an abandoned military base and an Environmental Protection Agency Superfund site, currently undergoing redevelopment by the real estate company Lennar. Lennar's seven hundred-acre project (which includes the site of the former Candlestick Stadium, adjacent to the shipyard) seeks to transform the area into a landscape of expensive townhomes, office buildings, and waterfront parks. The project is advertised through pictures of eco-friendly buildings and green spaces replacing older industrial areas. Design plans for the development have included solar panels, energy-efficient streetlights, native plant landscaping, and a project for monitoring nesting birds. In 2012, it was certified as a Leadership in Energy and Environmental Design (LEED) "Neighborhood Development" by the U.S. Green Building Council. On its website, Lennar advertises its development project as "sustainable living in the twenty-first century," relying on pictures of bicycles and the phrase, "Explorers welcome."[54] The image of new home buyers in Bayview Hunters Point as "explorers" recalls the geographer Neil Smith's foundational writing on gentrification, specifically the centrality of a frontier discourse. As Smith shows, one of the effects of imagining a place as a frontier—as empty and available for settlement—is to erase the histories of a landscape and contemporary opposition to gentrifying development.[55]

The Bayview Hunters Point neighborhood, which surrounds Lennar's redevelopment project, is a mixed industrial and residential place. Historically one of San Francisco's black neighborhoods—a legacy of postwar racial segregation—it is also a site of civil rights and environmental justice activism. Today Bayview Hunters Point is racially diverse, a population that is (according to U.S. census categories) predominantly one of African Americans, Asian Pacific Islanders, and Latinos. It is one of the poorest neighborhoods in San Francisco: 18 percent of the population lives at or below the poverty line, while the unemployment rate in Bayview Hunters Point is 14 percent, which is twice the average for San Francisco as a whole.[56] In addition to the naval shipyard, Bayview Hunters Point has housed San Francisco's heavy and noxious industries since the late nineteenth century and currently contains one-third of the toxic brownfield sites in the city, including underground leaking fuel tanks and the remains of chemical and metals manufacturers. The neighborhood also houses many current hazardous waste producers, the city's main sewage treatment plant, and a large waste transfer station.[57] Until

2008, an oil-fired power plant operated near the shipyard, sending emissions of nitrogen dioxide, carbon monoxide, sulfur dioxide, and volatile organic compounds into the breathing space of several public housing developments nearby. As one woman testified in a letter to the city attorney in 1995, as part of an environmental justice campaign,

> The air pollution in Hunter's Point is so bad I can't hang my laundry outside. I've tried and it gets so filthy that I have to wash it again. . . . I have breast cancer. . . . How many girls who go to school across the street . . . from me will grow up and become victims of breast cancer because of the filthy air they breathe? If filth sticks to my sheets as they dry in the "fresh" air, think about the filth that adheres to the lungs. I can wash my sheets but I can't wash my lungs.[58]

Her words speak to a feeling of environmental vulnerability, how the involuntary but necessary act of breathing—of life—rendered her vulnerable to premature death. The anthropologist Tim Choy writes about the "many means, practices, experiences, weather events, and economic relations that co-implicate us at different points as 'breathers.'"[59] Today, Bayview Hunters Point residents also breathe in diesel particulates from nearby freeways, trains, idling trucks, and emissions from the sewage treatment plant and industrial manufacturers. In the 2000s, the asthma hospitalization rate for Bayview Hunters Point residents was four times that of the San Francisco average, which local medical researchers called an "asthma epidemic."[60] In Bayview Hunters Point, the act of breathing has, historically, been inseparable from histories of racism, urban planning, and industrial and military waste.

In August 2000, an underground fire at the toxic Hunters Point Naval Shipyard added a new complexity to the local atmosphere. The fire, which burned for nearly a month, emanated from the site of the shipyard's landfills, which contain asbestos, industrial chemicals, and radioactive waste.[61] Residents of the public housing developments reported respiratory problems—the military's waste constricted their breathing—as they watched the fire's occasional but eerie, yellowy-green smoke climb into the air near their homes. Based on air-sampling data collected two weeks after the fire, the California Agency for Toxic Substances and Disease Registry (ATSDR) concluded that the Bayview

Hunters Point residents would only have experienced (what it calls) "short-term" health effects, such as "burning, itchy or watery eyes and sinuses, headache, nausea, breathing difficulty and asthma-like symptoms."[62] Against the ATSDR's conclusion that the fire was an inconsequential event, many Bayview Hunters Point residents connected this experience of physical vulnerability to a long history of environmental racism in the city. The fire and its aftermath rendered the often-invisible relations of breathing visible, as it became an event through which Bayview Hunters Point residents challenged the U.S. Navy's neglect of the shipyard's environmental hazards and the ways residents have been left vulnerable to its toxic effects.

The anthropologist Ali Kenner writes that breathing is "typically unnoticed, unconsidered, unseen—an *invisible other*"—that becomes visible in particular moments or for particular groups of people. Asthmatics, for example, have a sensitivity to air and breathing that is different from those who do not struggle to breathe.[63] Bayview Hunters Point residents have also politicized the local breathing space through protests against the dust and particulate matter produced through Lennar's work of demolishing old buildings and its new construction activities.[64]

These protests call attention to the exclusions and inequalities constitutive of market-based versions of "sustainability" and raise questions that include: Who is the urban redevelopment project sustainable for? Whose bodies bear the burden of this sustainable development project? Who is imaginatively and physically displaced in the process? Inclusive sustainability practices would begin from an understanding of political economy and histories of racism, and these considerations would be part of the design and development of sustainable projects and policies. Inclusive sustainability would also build from local knowledge and histories of activism in places like Bayview Hunters Point, where generations of activists have fought to make the neighborhood a healthier place for people to live.

"I Can't Breathe": From Metaphor to Materiality and Back Again

When Eric Garner was murdered by New York City police officers on a "quality-of-life" offense—selling loose cigarettes—by being put in an illegal chokehold, he pleaded thus with the officers: "I can't breathe."

Garner, who suffered from asthma, repeated "I can't breathe" eleven times. The violent encounter represented one of the worst instances of the abuse of police power, the only new element being that it was caught on cellphone video and widely disseminated. The mantra "I can't breathe" became—and remains—a common chant in the Black Lives Matter and anti–police brutality movements. It became a meme, worn on T-shirts by high-profile black athletes (LeBron James and Kobe Bryant), supported by entertainers like Jay-Z and even President Barack Obama. The phrase "I can't breathe" encapsulates a broader critique of police violence, and it also resonates with an environmental justice and public health standpoint.

Communities of color throughout the United States face elevated exposure to pollution, especially air pollution.[65] This is, in part, an outcome of the history of urban renewal in the United States, through which federal highway policies and the active destruction and forced removal of working-class and black communities (often by highway building, which leads to air pollution) produced a racially structured metropolitan space. According to recent federal health data, African Americans were 20 percent more likely to have asthma than non-Hispanic whites in 2012; African American children had asthma death rates seven times that of non-Hispanic white children.[66] Asthma is a complicated disease and has become a signature environmental health issue for urban communities of color. The disease is shaped by many factors—political, racial, and technological—that are both external and internal to bodies and that can exacerbate existing health and environmental inequalities. Asthma contributes to overall levels of poor health, high stress, and premature death.

Asthma remains a central concern of contemporary urban environmental justice activism and has been a focal point of activism since the 1960s. In New York City, racial disparities saturate occurrences of asthma. Child asthma rates reach 25 percent in some communities of color, four times the citywide average. Low-income women of color in particular are often blamed for these rates, owing to individual prenatal exposures or what is deemed poor housekeeping, which some say leads to asthma. In response, environmental justice activists in New York have pushed back at public rallies and in campaign documents by emphasizing the environmental factors at play in the disease.[67] Drawing on their critiques, we think about asthma as a specific embodiment of racial and gender inequalities in the United States.[68]

Breath and the racialized difficulties of breathing are therefore both real in the sense of Eric Garner's asthma and an effective symbol of neglect. News accounts reported that Garner's asthma, as he lay on the ground, was ignored by the medical first responders, who thought he was "faking it." At the same time, prosecutors in the grand jury trial that followed settled on his asthma as one of the main factors in his death.[69] In addition to asthma, Garner suffered from hypertension and diabetes, other environmentally related illnesses common in low-income communities of color.

Although the city medical examiner ruled Garner's death a homicide, the officer who put Garner in the chokehold was not prosecuted. Garner's asthma, hypertension, diabetes, and obesity were all listed as factors that contributed to his death. We pause here to note that Garner's body was already vulnerable to police violence, in part, because of these preexisting health and environmental conditions. And yet, although these chronic illnesses were recognized as contributing to his premature death, they were understood as an *individual* issue rather than a *social* problem—rather than as an embodiment of race and racial residential segregation in the United States.

Moreover, the physical chokehold on Garner—the direct, overt violence by the police—was *not* recognized as a factor in his premature death. In a sense, then, the state criminalized Garner's own body: his chronic illnesses and his socially produced difficulties in breathing became the causes of his death. We find this criminalization of embodiment similar to the ways Michael Brown's body, in Ferguson, Missouri, was described as a "demon" and like "Hulk Hogan" by the police officer who killed him—racist stereotypes that deprived Brown of his humanity.[70] Whereas Brown's body was too dangerous, Garner's body was too sick (although the officer also feared him as large and menacing).[71]

In the renewed attention to police violence in the context of Black Lives Matter, mainstream accounts of air pollution and its differential exposures have refocused attention to this classic environmental justice concern. For example, an article by Max Ehrenfreund in the *Washington Post* was titled, "The Racial Divide in America Is This Elemental: Blacks and Whites Actually Breathe Different Air."[72] He writes at the end of this piece: "Of all the measures of equality we deserve, the right to feel assured and safe when you draw a breath should be paramount."[73] In this vein, we interpret the phrase "I can't breathe" as condensing the histories of persistent patterns of pollution and police violence, both of which have denied breath and healthy breathing spaces to low-income communities of color. In this sense, the inability to breathe can be understood as both a metaphor and material reality of racism, which constrains not just life choices and opportunities but also the environmental conditions of life itself.

In "Death by Gentrification," Rebecca Solnit explicitly ties police killings with gentrification and the increased policing of "quality-of-life crimes" (defined as "disorderly conduct" or "loitering") and, thus, the fates of Alex Nieto and Eric Garner.[74] Gentrification can be fatal. Solnit writes, "Displacement has contributed to deaths, particularly of the elderly. In the two years since Nieto's death, there have been multiple stories of seniors who died during or immediately after their eviction. . . . It also brings newcomers to neighborhoods with nonwhite populations, sometimes with atrocious consequences. . . . White people sometimes regard 'people of color who are walking, driving, hanging out, or living in the neighborhood' as 'criminal suspects.'"[75] "Quality-of-life" policing in a context of economic and spatial inequalities in cities can lead to direct physical violence. Criminalizing minor nuisance crimes (for example, selling "loose" cigarettes) directly leads to the deaths of people of color deemed "dangerous" or "out of place."

Green gentrification in New York, as in San Francisco, contributes to spatial displacement and growing economic inequalities. In Sunset Park, Brooklyn, real-estate developers took over what was historically known as the Bush Terminal, a group of seven massive buildings on the waterfront that was the iconic site of a Brooklyn industrial development. The developers called it Jamestown and partnered with other investors to buy a controlling interest in the site from the previous owners who had defaulted in the wake of the massive damage from Superstorm Sandy.[76] The real estate developers are best known for Chelsea Market, a development in what used to be a dilapidated meat market district of Manhattan but is now an extremely high end residential area. The developers renamed the site "Industry City" and sought to brand the area through artisanal food, "innovation economy" companies, and through events like large D.J. dance parties.[77] The community group UPROSE, which is fighting Industry City, objects to the developers' plans on gentrification grounds. UPROSE developed a climate resiliency plan based on local, situated knowledge, grounded in relationships. Social and environmental justice is at the center of their resiliency plan.[78] Their approach to climate adaptation takes capitalism and racial justice seriously and together.

Conclusion

Since the killing of Eric Garner, most news has focused only on the conditions of his death. The poet Ross Gay responds in a different vein in "A Small Needful Fact":

> A SMALL NEEDFUL FACT
> Is that Eric Garner worked
> for some time for the Parks and Rec.
> Horticultural Department, which means,
> perhaps, that with his very large hands,
> perhaps, in all likelihood,
> he put gently into the earth
> some plants which, most likely,
> some of them, in all likelihood,
> continue to grow, continue
> to do what such plants do, like house
> and feed small and necessary creatures,
> like being pleasant to touch and smell,
> like converting sunlight
> into food, like making it easier
> for us to breathe.[79]

As Gay told the *PBS Newshour*, "What that poem, I think, is trying to do is to say, there's this beautiful life, which is both the sorrow and the thing that needs to be loved."[80] The poem can also be thought of as an assertion of black life in the context of an overwhelming focus on black death. Gay's poem centers on the freeing of breath (". . . making it easier / for us to breathe") by planting trees, rather than breath's constriction.

It centers on life rather than death. Garner's work in horticulture—as a gardener, tending a small plot of the earth—is a small but needful fact because it asks that we understand him not as a criminal or victim (the two roles he is allowed in the current media discourse) but as a complex being who played a role in making the city a more livable place. Writes McKittrick, "This black urban presence—black life—uncovers a mode of being human that, while often cast out from official history, is not victimized and dispossessed and wholly alien to the land; rather it redefines the terms of who and what we are vis-a-vis a cosmogony that, while painful . . . honors our mutually constitutive and relational versions of humanness."[81]

We have suggested that black and brown activists and scholars who have theorized and struggled for more livable urban environments can help uncover alternative genealogies and practices of "sustainability." These alternative genealogies and practices are sorely needed to contest the conventional, market-based notions of sustainability—so amenable to corporate interests, to state surveillance and policing—that have exacerbated social and spatial inequalities, constricting the breathing spaces of already marginalized social groups.

Rather, we have argued that the question of which natures to sustain, and who gets to answer this question, can be asked within the context of the racially segregated U.S. city and the anti-racist social movements and political critiques that have emerged from it. The social movements and critiques we explored in this chapter challenge conventional sustainability by foregrounding race, class, and other relations of power in the task of building better, more livable worlds. They offer a basis for articulating alternative notions of sustainability, oriented not to markets but to valuing and sustaining multiple natures and "versions of humanness."

Acknowledgments

Ideas in this essay were first developed in an article commissioned by Janice Ho and Nadine Attewell for *English Language Notes*: Lindsey Dillon and Julie Sze, "Police Power and Particulate Matters: Environmental Justice and the Spatialities of In/securities in U.S. Cities, *English Language Notes* 54 (Fall/ Winter 2016): 13–23. We thank Managing Editor

Jenny Cookson and *English Language Notes* for their allowing us to reprint portions of this article. We also thank Ross Gay for permission to use his poem.

NOTES

1 Donna Jean Murch, *Living for the City: Migration, Education, and the Rise of the Black Panther Party in Oakland, California* (Durham: University of North Carolina Press, 2010).

2 Deborah Wallace and Rodrick Wallace, *A Plague on Your Houses: How New York Was Burned Down and National Public Health Crumbled* (New York: Verso, 1998); and Mindy Fullilove, *Root Shock: How Tearing Up City Neighborhoods Hurts America, and What We Can Do about It* (New York: One World/Ballantine, 2009).

3 Michelle Alexander, *The New Jim Crow: Mass Incarceration in the Age of Colorblindness* (New York: New Press, 2012).

4 Stevie Wonder, "Living for the City," *Innervisions* (Detroit: Tamla Records, 1973).

5 Rob Nixon, *Slow Violence and the Environmentalism of the Poor* (Cambridge, MA: Harvard University Press, 2011), 2.

6 Ruth Wilson Gilmore, *Golden Gulag: Prisons, Surplus, Crisis, and Opposition in Globalizing California* (Berkeley: University of California Press, 2007), p. 28.

7 Murch, *Living for the City*; Robert O. Self, *American Babylon: Race and the Struggle for Postwar Oakland* (Princeton, NJ: Princeton University Press, 2005); Alondra Nelson, *Body and Soul: The Black Panther Party and the Fight against Medical Discrimination* (Minneapolis: University of Minnesota Press, 2011); and Nik Heynen, "Bending the Bars of Empire from Every Ghetto for Survival: The Black Panther Party's Radical Antihunger Politics of Social Reproduction and Scale," *Annals of the Association of American Geographers* 99, no. 2 (2009): 406–422.

8 See the *Movement for Black Lives*, https://policy.m4bl.org. This platform is similar to the First National People of Color Environmental Leadership Summit, held October 24–27, 1991, Washington, DC, *EJnet.org: Web Resources for Environmental Justice Activists*, www.ejnet.org.

9 Our italics; see Black Lives Matter, https://blacklivesmatter.com.

10 Alicia Garza, "A Herstory of the #BlackLivesMatter Movement," *Feminist Wire*, October 7, 2014, www.thefeministwire.com.

11 Julian Agyeman, Robert D. Bullard, and Bob Evans, eds., *Just Sustainabilities: Development in an Unequal World* (Cambridge, MA: MIT Press, 2003).

12 "'I Can't Breathe': Eric Garner Put in Chokehold by NYPD Officer—Video," *Guardian*, December 4, 2014, www.theguardian.com.

13 "Embodiment" is a term the public health scientist Nancy Krieger uses to talk about the ways "our bodies tell stories about—and cannot be studied divorced from—the conditions of our existence." See Nancy Krieger, "Embodiment: A

Conceptual Glossary for Epidemiology," *Journal of Epidemiology and Community Health* 59, no. 5 (2005): 350–355, quote at 350.

14 Laura Pulido, "Rethinking Environmental Racism: White Privilege and Urban Development in Southern California," *Annals of the Association of American Geographers* 90, no. 1 (2000): 13. More recently, Pulido has argued that environmental racism is an example of the everyday functioning of racial capitalism, and she developed this point through the case of the state-sanctioned poisoning of drinking water in Flint, Michigan. See Laura Pulido, "Geographies of Race and Ethnicity II: Environmental Racism, Racial Capitalism and State-Sanctioned Violence," *Progress in Human Geography* 41, no. 4 (2017): 524–533, and "Flint, Environmental Racism, and Racial Capitalism," *Capitalism Nature Socialism* 27, no. 3 (2016): 1–16. Not all environmental justice scholars have used this language; we specifically point to environmental justice scholarship in conversation with critical race theory.

15 Traci Brynne Voyles, *Wastelanding* (Minneapolis: University of Minnesota Press, 2015); and Valerie Kuletz, "The Tainted Desert," *Environmental and Social Ruin in the American West* (New York: Routledge, 1998). Nixon's *Slow Violence* also elaborates on what he calls "displacement in place" by focusing on the effects of extractive industries on local communities, but this can also describe the wasting of indigenous lands.

16 Gilmore, *Golden Gulag,* 28.

17 For example, see Kyle Powys Whyte, "Why the Native American Pipeline Resistance in North Dakota Is about Climate Justice," *The Conversation*, September 16, 2016, www.theconversation.com.

18 Darrel Wanzer-Serrano, *The New York Young Lords and the Struggle for Liberation* (Philadelphia: Temple University Press, 2015); and Matthew Gandy, *Concrete and Clay: Reworking Nature in New York City* (Cambridge, MA: MIT Press, 2003).

19 Self, *American Babylon*; Murch, *Living for the City*; and Nelson, *Body and Soul.*

20 Robert Self makes this argument in *American Babylon.*

21 Quoted in ibid., 211.

22 Ibid., 226.

23 Frantz Fanon, *The Wretched of the Earth* (New York: Grove Press, 2004), 4.

24 Ibid.

25 Katherine McKittrick, *Demonic Grounds: Black Women and the Cartographies of Struggle* (Minneapolis: University of Minnesota Press, 2006).

26 Carolyn Finney, *Black Faces, White Spaces: Reimagining the Relationship of African Americans to the Great Outdoors* (Durham: University of North Carolina Press, 2014); Donald S. Moore, Jake Kosek, and Anand Pandian, eds., *Race, Nature, and the Politics of Difference* (Durham, NC: Duke University Press, 2003); Patricia Hill Collins, *Black Feminist Thought: Knowledge, Consciousness, and the Politics of Empowerment* (New York: Routledge, 2002); Charles Mills, cited in David Pellow, *Resisting Global Toxics: Transnational Movements for Environmental Justice* (Cambridge, MA: MIT Press, 2007); and Charles W. Mills, "Black Trash," in *Faces*

of Environmental Racism: Confronting Issues of Global Justice, 2nd ed., ed. Laura Westra and Bill E. Lawson (Oxford: Rowman & Littlefield, 2001), 73–92.

27 bell hooks, "Choosing the Margin as Space of Radical Openness," *Framework: The Journal of Cinema and Media* 36 (1989): 15–23; Paul Gilroy, *The Black Atlantic: Modernity and Double Consciousness* (Cambridge, MA: Harvard University Press, 1993); and Sylvia Wynter, "Novel and History, Plot and Plantation," *Savacou* 5 (1971): 95–102.

28 Italics added. See Frantz Fanon, *Black Skin, White Masks* (New York: Grove Press, 2008), 226.

29 Ruha Benjamin, "Catching Our Breath: Critical Race STS and the Carceral Imagination," *Engaging Science, Technology, and Society* 2 (2016): 146.

30 Miriam Greenberg, "'The Sustainability Edge': Competition, Crisis, and the Rise of Green Urban Branding," in *Sustainability in the Global City: Myth and Practice*, ed. Cindy Isenhour, Gary McDonogh, and Melissa Checker (New York: Cambridge University Press, 2015), 105–130.

31 Julie Sze, *Fantasy Islands: Chinese Dreams and Ecological Fears in an Age of Climate Crisis* (Berkeley: University of California Press, 2015).

32 Kenneth A. Gould and Tammy L. Lewis, *Green Gentrification: Urban Sustainability and the Struggle for Environmental Justice* (London: Routledge, 2016); Melissa Checker, "Wiped Out by the 'Greenwave': Environmental Gentrification and the Paradoxical Politics of Urban Sustainability," *City and Society* 23, no. 2 (2011): 210–229; Lindsey Dillon and Miriam Greenberg, "Geographies of Sustainability in the San Francisco Bay Area," *Association of American Geographers Newsletter*, August 31, 2015, www.news.aag.org.

33 Erik Swyngedouw, "Impossible 'Sustainability' and the Post-political Condition," in *The Sustainable Development Paradox: Urban Political Economy in the United States and Europe*, ed. Rob Krueger and David Gibbs, 13–40 (London: Guilford Press, 2007).

34 Ibid., 23.

35 On this point, see Miriam Greenberg, "What on Earth Is Sustainable?" *Boom: A Journal of California* 3, no. 4 (2013): 54–66.

36 Raymond Williams, *Problems in Materialism and Culture: Selected Essays* (London: Verso, 1980), p. 68.

37 See William Cronon, *Uncommon Ground: Toward Reinventing Nature* (New York: Norton, 1995); Rebecca Solnit, *Savage Dreams: A Journey into the Landscape Wars of the American West* (Berkeley: University of California Press, 1994); Mark Spence, "Dispossessing the Wilderness: Yosemite Indians and the National Park Ideal, 1864–1930," *Pacific Historical Review* 65, no. 1 (1996): 27–59; and Kat Anderson, *Tending the Wild: Native American Knowledge and the Management of California's Natural Resources* (Berkeley: University of California Press, 2005). Richard Drayton also writes about the origins of environmentalism in tropical colonies in *Nature's Government: Science, Imperial Britain, and the "Improvement" of the World* (New Haven, CT: Yale University Press, 2000).

38 Roderick P. Neumann, *Imposing Wilderness: Struggles over Livelihood and Nature Preservation in Africa* (Berkeley: University of California Press, 1998); and Vernadette Vicuña Gonzalez, *Securing Paradise: Tourism and Militarism in Hawai'i and the Philippines* (Durham, NC: Duke University Press, 2013). There is a vast and important literature on the entanglements of race, colonialism, and nature.

39 Moore, Kosek, and Pandian, *Race, Nature*; Donna Haraway, *Primate Visions: Gender, Race, and Nature in the World of Modern Science* (New York: Routledge, 1989); and Jake Kosek, *Understories: The Political Life of Forests in Northern New Mexico* (Durham, NC: Duke University Press, 2006).

40 As another example, Julie Guthman has shown how many alternative food practices are "coded as white"—including those that are associated with a "sustainable" lifestyle. In her study of farmer's markets and community supported agriculture programs in a university setting, Guthman details the cultural politics that work as barriers to non-white students' sense of inclusion or identification with these alternative food practices. As she puts it, this sociospatial coding "not only works as an exclusionary practice, it also colors the character of food politics more broadly and may thus work against a more transformative politics." See Julie Guthman, "'If They Only Knew': The Unbearable Whiteness of Alternative Food," in *Cultivating Food Justice: Race, Class, and Sustainability*, ed. Alison Hope Alkon and Julian Agyeman (Cambridge, MA: MIT Press, 2011), 263–282, quote at 264.

41 Britt Rusert, "Plantation Ecologies: The Experimental Plantation in and against James Grainger's *The Sugar-Cane*," *Early American Studies: An Interdisciplinary Journal* 13, no. 2 (2015): 341–373.

42 Sandy Brown and Christy Getz, "Farmworker Food Insecurity and the Production of Hunger in California," in Alkon and Agyeman, *Cultivating Food Justice*, 121–146.

43 Also see Judith Ann Carney and Richard Nicholas Rosomoff, *In the Shadow of Slavery: Africa's Botanical Legacy in the Atlantic World* (Berkeley: University of California Press, 2011).

44 Rusert, "Plantation Ecologies," 372–373.

45 Ibid., 373.

46 Katherine McKittrick, "Plantation Futures," *Small Axe* 17, no. 3 (2013): 1–15.

47 Ibid., 10.

48 Ibid., 11.

49 Nathan Hare, "Black Ecology," *Black Scholar* 1, no. 6 (1970): 2–8.

50 Ibid., 2.

51 Ibid., 8.

52 For other scholars on breathing spaces, see Gregg Mitman and Stephen Bocking, *Breathing Space: How Allergies Shape our Lives and Landscapes* (New Haven, CT: Yale University Press, 2007); *The Asthma Files*, http://theasthmafiles.org; Timothy K. Choy, *Ecologies of Comparison: An Ethnography of Endangerment in Hong Kong* (Durham, NC: Duke University Press, 2011); and Ali Kenner, "Invisibilities:

Provocation," Field Notes: Invisibilities series, edited by William Girard, *Cultural Anthropology* (journal website), June 15, 2013, https://culanth.org.

53 Oliver Laughland, "Chronicle of a Death Untold," *Guardian*, June 2, 2015, www .theguardian.com; "The Counted: People Killed by Police in the U.S." *Guardian*, 2015–, www.theguardian.com; Rebecca Solnit, "Death by Gentrification," *Guardian*, March 21, 2016, www.theguardian.com. For a connection between Mario Woods, pollution from the Hunters Point power plant, and gentrification, see Jamillah King, "How Gentrification Shadows Protests over San Francisco's Latest Police Killing," *Mic*, December 10, 2015, https://mic.com.

54 Lennar, www.lennar.com. On the connections between bicycle activism, the notion of a livable city, and gentrification, see John Stehlin, "Cycles of Investment: Bicycle Infrastructure, Gentrification, and the Restructuring of the San Francisco Bay Area," *Environment and Planning A* 47, no. 1 (2015): 121–137.

55 Neil Smith, *The New Urban Frontier: Gentrification and the Revanchist City* (London: Psychology Press, 1996).

56 San Francisco Department of Public Health, "Your Neighborhood at a Glance: Bayview Hunters Point and Visitacion Valley" (San Francisco: San Francisco Department of Public Health, 2012), www.sfdph.org.

57 Lindsey Dillon, "Race, Waste, and Space: Brownfield Redevelopment and Environmental Justice at the Hunters Point Shipyard," *Antipode* 46, no. 5 (2014): 1205–1221; U.S. Environmental Protection Agency, "Targeted Brownfields Assessments, Bayview Hunters Point" (Washington, DC: U.S. Environmental Protection Agency, 2012), posted at San Francisco Mayor's Office of Housing and Community Development, http://sfmohcd.org; Greenaction for Health and Environmental Justice, "A Toxic Inventory of Bayview Hunters Point" (San Francisco: Greenaction for Health and Environmental Justice, 2004), www.greenaction.org.

58 Quoted in Clifford Rechtschaffen, "Fighting Back against a Power Plant: Some Lessons from the Legal and Organizing Efforts of the Bayview-Hunters Point Community," *Hastings West-Northwest Journal of Environmental Law and Policy* 3 (1995): 407. Also see Alan Ramo, "Hunters Point: Energy Development Meets Environmental Justice," *Environmental Law News* 5, no. 1 (Spring 1996): 28–32.

59 Choy, *Ecologies of Comparison*, 128. Also see T. Choy and J. Zee, "Condition—Suspension," *Cultural Anthropology* 30, no. 2 (2015): 210–223.

60 Ken Kloc, "Air Pollution and Environmental Inequity in the San Francisco Bay Area" (San Francisco: Golden Gate University of Law, Center on Urban Environmental Law, 2011); "Community Health Status Assessment," San Francisco Healthy Homes Project, n.d., posted at City and County of San Francisco, SF Environment, https://sfenvironment.org; and Shannon M. Thyne, Joshua P. Rising, Vicki Legion, and Mary Beth Love, "The Yes We Can Urban Asthma Partnership: A Medical/Social Model for Childhood Asthma Management," *Journal of Asthma* 43, no. 9 (2006): 667–673.

61 Agency for Toxic Substances and Disease Registry, "Health Consultation: Parcel E Landfill Fire at Hunters Point Shipyard" (Washington, DC: Agency for Toxic

Substances and Disease Registry, 2009). This file used to be retrievable at the Agency for Toxic Substances and Disease Registry website, www.atsdr.cdc.gov, but in 2017, the agency took the report offline. To access the report, send an email request to the ATSDR. Also see "EPA Faults Navy for Handling of 4-Week Landfill Fire," *Los Angeles Times*, September 12, 2000, www.latimes.com.

62 Agency for Toxic Substances and Disease Registry, "Health Consultation: Parcel E Landfill Fire at Hunters Point Shipyard."

63 Kenner, "Invisibilities: Provocation." Also see Mitman and Bocking, *Breathing Space*; and *The Asthma Files*.

64 "Developer Sued over Hunters Point Toxics," *San Francisco Chronicle*, March 18, 2007, www.sfgate.com; "Resident Voiced His Concerns over Dust," *San Francisco Chronicle*, March 10, 2007, www.sfgate.com; and "Hunters Point Groups Say Lennar, Government, Hid Asbestos Risks," *San Francisco Examiner*, March 22, 2011, www.sfexaminer.com.

65 Julie Sze, *Noxious New York: The Racial Politics of Urban Health and Environmental Justice* (Cambridge, MA: MIT Press, 2007).

66 U.S. Department of Health and Human Services, "Asthma and African Americans" (Washington, DC: U.S. Department of Health and Human Services, Office of Minority Health, n.d.), www.hhs.gov.

67 There is a large medical and public health literature on health disparities and asthma. Much less work is from the sociological perspective on asthma, but for a general overview, see Cara Chiaraluce, "The Politics of Asthma: Disease Frameworks and Direct Action," in *Issues and Controversies in Science and Politics*, ed. B. Steele (Thousand Oaks, CA: Sage Publications, 2014); Julie Sze, "Gender, Asthma Politics, and Urban Environmental Justice Activism," in *New Perspectives on Environmental Justice: Gender, Sexuality, and Activism*, ed. Rachel Stein (New Brunswick, NJ: Rutgers University Press, 2004), 177–190; and Gregg Mitman, *Breathing Space: How Allergies Shape Our Lives and Landscapes* (New Haven, CT: Yale University Press, 2008).

68 Krieger, "Embodiment."

69 Al Baker, J. David Goodman, and Benjamin Mueller, "Beyond the Chokehold: The Path to Eric Garner's Death," *New York Times*, June 13, 2015, www.nytimes.com.

70 Jessica Glenza, "'I Felt like a Five-Year-Old Holding on to Hulk Hogan': Darren Wilson in His Own Words," *Guardian*, 25 Nov 2014, www.guardian.com.

71 Calvin John Smiley and David Fakunle, "From 'Brute' to 'Thug': The Demonization and Criminalization of Unarmed Black Male Victims in America," *Journal of Human Behavior in the Social Environment* 26, nos. 3–4 (2016): 350–366.

72 Max Ehrenfreund, "The Racial Divide in America Is This Elemental: Blacks and Whites Actually Breathe Different Air," *Washington Post*, December 4, 2014, www.washingtonpost.com.

73 Ibid.

74 On efforts to increase policing of "quality of life crimes," see Vivan Ho, "Prop. R, SF Anticrime Measure, Faces Stiff Criticism," *San Francisco Chronicle*, September 16, 2016, www.sfchronicle.com.

75 Solnit, "Death by Gentrification."

76 Neil de Mause, "As Industry City Promises a New Sunset Park, Some Residents Fight to Maintain the Old One," *City Limits Magazine*, October 27, 2015, https://citylimits.org.

77 Erica Berger, "Gentrification Inc," *Fast Company*, August 7, 2014, www.fastcompany.com.

78 See "Climate Justice Resilience Center," UPROSE, www.uprose.org.

79 Ross Gay is a poet and professor at Indiana University. See "A Detail You May Not Have Known about Eric Garner Blossoms in Poem," *PBS Newshour*, July 20, 2015, www.pbs.org.

80 Ibid.

81 McKittrick, "Plantation Futures," 12.

AFTERWORD

From More than Just Sustainability to a More Just Resilience

DAVID N. PELLOW

SUSTAINABILITY AND ENVIRONMENTAL JUSTICE

Julie Sze's *Sustainability: Approaches to Environmental Justice and Social Power* is a welcome and much needed collection that advances our thinking and material possibilities around sustainability in the twenty-first century. Ideas concerning sustainability gained great prominence in the 1980s and 1990s among scholars, activists, policy makers, and media around the globe as the socioecological crises facing the planet and its denizens came into focus with the publication of the World Commission on Environment and Development's (1987) report *Our Common Future* and the UN Conference on Environment and Development in Rio de Janeiro in 1992. Critics have rightly noted the myriad and gaping limitations of the sustainability discourse, including Julian Agyeman (2005), who pointed to what he called the "equity deficit" that persists in the language, theory, and practices associated with sustainability. In response, he and his colleagues coined the term "just sustainability" to address the urgency of social needs, social welfare, and economic opportunity for people within any "ecological" sustainability framework. Specifically, "just sustainability" is defined as "the need to ensure a better quality of life for all, now and into the future, in a just and equitable manner, whilst living within the limits of supporting ecosystems" (Agyeman, Bullard, and Evans 2003, 5). While I agree fully with Agyeman and his colleagues and the contributors to this volume that we have much work to do with respect to deepening, grounding, and situating our understanding of sustainability and its possibilities, I am reminded that we can learn from important moments when some of this work was undertaken in the recent past.

In the fall of 1991, activist delegates to the historic First National People of Color Environmental Leadership Summit in Washington, DC, adopted the Principles of Environmental Justice—a sort of founding document of the U.S. environmental justice movement. The Preamble reads,

> WE, THE PEOPLE OF COLOR, gathered together at this multinational People of Color Environmental Leadership Summit, to begin to build a national and international movement of all peoples of color to fight the destruction and taking of our lands and communities, do hereby reestablish our spiritual interdependence to the sacredness of our Mother Earth; to respect and celebrate each of our cultures, languages and beliefs about the natural world and our roles in healing ourselves; to ensure environmental justice; to promote economic alternatives which would contribute to the development of environmentally safe livelihoods; and, to secure our political, economic and cultural liberation that has been denied for over 500 years of colonization and oppression, resulting in the poisoning of our communities and land and the genocide of our peoples, do affirm and adopt these Principles of Environmental Justice.

There are seventeen of these principles in all, and here I would like to briefly highlight five of them since they are most relevant to this discussion. Principle no. 1 "affirms the sacredness of Mother Earth, ecological unity and the interdependence of all species, and the right to be free from ecological destruction." Principle no. 2 "demands that public policy be based on mutual respect and justice for all peoples, free from any form of discrimination or bias." Principle no. 3 "mandates the right to ethical, balanced and responsible uses of land and renewable resources in the interest of a sustainable planet for humans and other living things." Principle no. 5 supports "the fundamental right to political, economic, cultural and environmental self-determination of all peoples." And Principle no. 7 "demands the right to participate as equal partners at every level of decision-making, including needs assessment, planning, implementation, enforcement and evaluation."

At a gathering of environmental justice activists and scholars in 2013, a well-regarded environmental justice leader gave a presentation during which he stated that it was high time to reevaluate and revisit the Principles of Environmental Justice because they were apparently outdated and not entirely well suited to the twenty-first-century social and environmental landscape. I was scheduled to speak at that same gathering the next day and stayed up much of the night revising my remarks because I was struck by how much that speaker's charge to us resonated with me, but in an unexpected fashion. Specifically, my view was not that we needed to reevaluate the Principles; rather, we might be better served by reevaluating our commitment to those Principles and the degree to which our scholarship and advocacy have measured up to them, rather than the other way around. The delegates to the meeting in 1991—commonly referred to as the first Environmental Justice Summit—set forth, in the Principles of Environmental Justice, their clear opposition to racism, patriarchy, the excesses of the state and market forces, speciesism, imperialism, and ecological harm. They also recognized the inherent worth of non-human natures, acknowledged the inseparability of humans and the more-than-human world, and articulated a vision of environmental justice that easily matches and exceeds any definition of sustainability or just sustainability I have encountered. In my presentation the next day, I concluded by declaring that the Principles of Environmental Justice were and remain far more transformative, radical, far-reaching, and visionary than most of the environmental justice scholarship and activism that have followed, so we actually need to do a much better job of "catching up" and living up to those Principles than we have thus far.

This volume poses three key questions: (1) What does sustainability mean, and how does it work? (2) What are the key contexts for how sustainability is conceptualized, enacted, and contested? And (3) What is sustainable, for whom, why, and how? Throughout this volume, contributors present powerful and compelling answers to each of these questions. The authors rightly contend that no single definition or approach to sustainability will address our multi-dimensional socioecological crises—multiple approaches are needed. The contributors organize much of the volume around one such approach: the concept of "situated sustainability," which begins with an acknowledgment of the many ways in which sustainability is envisioned and enacted across place, space, and culture and embraces the core values of environmental justice scholarship, including a focus on praxis, social/racial justice, and multi-disciplinarity. Thus the authors make clear that sustainability must be situated within contexts, histories, actions, and conversations that are both interdisciplinary and rooted in social justice, otherwise efforts aimed at practicing sustainability are not only limited, they are actually unsustainable. Thus democracy, social justice, and inclusivity of diverse knowledges and ways of knowing are what make sustainability possible. Unfortunately, there are far too many instances when these connections are not forged, and the results have been disastrous. Consider the historic and ongoing dispossession and displacement of indigenous peoples in the pursuit of conservation through the creation of national parks in the United States, Latin America, and elsewhere. Or witness the discourse and rhetoric that name human population growth as the greatest threat to our ecosystems and blame low-income, working-class immigrants as the source of that problem, while ignoring the primary threats to our life support systems in military, state, and corporate practices. In contrast, we also see many instances where connections that embrace situated sustainability *do* occur. For example, we can witness this in the solidarity work between mainstream environmentalists and environmental and social justice activists (as we saw when the Sierra Club endorsed the Black Lives Matter movement) and through the telling of stories that allow us to think, visualize, represent, and act in ways that produce critical linkages that may not have been articulated previously. The Campaign to Fight Toxic Prisons (FTP) is a coalition of social justice, racial justice, environmental justice, and prison abolition groups and activists who have come together to document the ways in which the prison industrial complex produces and exacerbates environmental and social justice risks to inmates, corrections officers, and surrounding communities and ecosystems. The Campaign to Fight Toxic Prisons is building on the earlier work of groups like the California Prison Moratorium Project, Critical Resistance, and Mothers of East LA (MELA), which brought a similarly uncommon alliance together at the beginning of this century. Drawing on art, humanities, scientific and social scientific methods, and the experiences of prisoners and their families, these formations imagine and work to bring into existence a world in which both prisons and environmental injustice are abolished.

Situated sustainabilities are often made possible by "situated solidarities"—actions that produce knowledge in the interests of challenging privilege and inequalities and benefiting the disadvantaged. In one way or another, each chapter in this book offers up clear and persuasive examples of this and presents new questions and insights that build the foundation for such practices (for example, the Humanities for the Environment initiative, campus-community partnerships in Philadelphia, and the Baltimore Ecosystem Study), thus demonstrating ways of "joining up" various fields of study, research and practice, and academia and grassroots communities.

RESILIENCE AND JUSTICE

Recent scholarship has taken up the call for exploring the idea and practice of resilience, and I applaud this development. For example, Caniglia, Vallee, and Frank (2016) contend that environmental justice scholars have done an admirable job of documenting the unequal and unjust exposure of various marginalized populations to environmental harms, but they note that we have also struggled to offer alternative frameworks that pinpoint key social vulnerabilities in these communities that, if addressed, could be helpful for supporting mechanisms for mitigation before threats emerge. They argue that, in confronting those vulnerabilities—or "injustices-in-waiting"—communities could build capacities that could reduce the impacts of environmental injustices and improve a population's capacity to rebound afterward. In other words, resilience.

I have urged scholars and activists to go beyond the boundaries of the state and capital to explore the ways that humans and more-than-humans can and do resist the current social order to bring new imaginings, visions, practices, relationships, and communities into being that are anti-authoritarian and sustainable and that embody what I call "just resilience"—a resilience marked by social and environmental justice. "Just resilience" is an important concept for environmental studies scholars because, among many reasons, there are forms of resilience that are *unjust*, and we should distinguish between them. For example, as scholars of political economy have noted for decades, one of the defining features of states, capital markets, and dominant social institutions is that these systems and structures are often forced to display resilience, as they frequently deflect, displace, absorb, incorporate, and assimilate myriad challenges from various corners of society, whether it be the entry of new ethnic groups, the emergence of revolutionary social movements, or the growth of political ideologies that might challenge their hegemony. States, corporations, markets, and their constituent institutions seek to maintain their dominance through various forms of *unjust resilience* on a regular basis. When community leaders urge corporations to build social and environmental responsibility into their investment practices, they are sometimes (though not often) met with acceptance and, later, the realization that, while some activities have changed, the overall profile and direction of the company is largely unaltered. When climate activist groups like 350.org urge colleges and universities to divest funds from fossil fuel markets, too often those institutions that have agreed to such demands have done so only after careful analyses reveal that such a change will have a minimal effect on their finances. Moreover, those institutions communicate this message to their investors and assure them that this is an exception being made to the (generally ecologically unsustainable and unjust) overall investment orientation to which they remain firmly committed. These are examples of how dominant institutions retain their hegemony through *unjust resilience*. That resilience is unjust because it generally maintains socially and ecologically unequal, discriminatory, and unsustainable practices and relationships. *Just resilience* would be a set of practices and relationships characterized by deeper and broader commitments to equity, social, and environmental justice. While just sustainability is a major step forward in the integration of the concepts of environmental justice and sustainability, it may not directly address the need for a community's capacity to rebound and rebuild (that is, *resilience*) in the wake of myriad threats and harms and to do so with a focus on justice. Just resilience seeks to offer such a framework. An instance where just resilience may have taken root was in the Gulf Coast region during the aftermath of Hurricane Katrina. Thousands of people came together to support and strengthen already existing local grassroots community groups and networks and to form new ones (like the Common Ground Collective) in order to improve the community's capacity to rebuild after that disaster and to articulate a vision of a future that was more democratic and socially and environmentally just than the structures and practices under which they had lived prior to that.

The editors of and contributors to *Sustainability: Approaches to Environmental Justice and Social Power* offer insightful analyses and explorations of how just sustainability, situated sustainabilities, situated solidarities, and just resilience are enacted and engaged across a range of fields and social contexts, and I look forward to the conversations and actions this powerful collection inspires in the years ahead.

WORKS CITED

Agyeman, Julian. 2005. *Sustainable Communities and the Challenge of Environmental Justice*. New York: New York University Press.

Agyeman, Julian, Robert Doyle Bullard, and Bob Evans. 2003. "Introduction: Joined-Up Thinking: Bringing Together Sustainability, Environmental Justice and Equity." In *Just Sustainabilities: Development in an Unequal World*, ed. Julian Agyeman, Robert Doyle Bullard, and Bob Evans, 1–18. Cambridge, MA: MIT Press.

Caniglia, Beth Schaefer, Manuel Vallee, and Beatrice F. Frank, eds. 2016. *Resilience, Environmental Justice, and the City*. New York: Routledge.

"Principles of Environmental Justice." 1991. *EJnet.org: Web Resources for Environmental Justice Activists*. www.ejnet.org.

World Commission on Environment and Development. 1987. *Our Common Future*. Brundtland Report. Oxford: Oxford University Press.

ACKNOWLEDGMENTS

This publication is supported by a grant from the NYU Abu Dhabi Institute, a major hub of intellectual and creative activity, and advanced research. The institute hosts academic conferences, workshops, cultural events, and other public programs and is a center of scholarly life in Abu Dhabi, bringing together faculty and researchers from institutions of higher education throughout the region and the world.

ABOUT THE EDITOR

Julie Sze is Professor and the Founding Chair of American Studies at the University of California, Davis. Sze's first book, *Noxious New York: The Racial Politics of Urban Health and Environmental Justice*, won the 2008 John Hope Franklin Publication Prize, awarded annually to the best published book in American Studies. Her second book is called *Fantasy Islands: Chinese Dreams and Ecological Fears in an Age of Climate Crisis* (2015). She has written or co-authored forty-five peer-reviewed articles and book chapters and has given talks in China, Abu Dhabi, Canada, Germany, France, and Italy.

Joni Adamson is Professor of Environmental Humanities and Director of the Environmental Humanities Initiative at Arizona State University. She is the author and co-editor of many books and special issues that have helped to establish and expand the environmental humanities and environmental studies, including *Humanities for the Environment* (2017), *Ecocriticism and Indigenous Studies—Conversations from Earth to Cosmos* (2016), and *Keywords for Environmental Studies* (New York University Press, 2016). She has lectured internationally and published over seventy articles, chapters, and reviews.

Lawrence Baker applies his hybrid education in ecology and environmental engineering toward his research on applied biogeochemistry. In recent years he has focused his research on urban ecosystems—cities and farms—with the intent of finding novel ways to reduce pollution, leading him to work at the science-policy interface. He has published more than 120 articles and has edited two books, most recently *The Water Environment of Cities*. He served as Associate Editor for the journal *Urban Ecosystems* for ten years, currently serves on the University of Minnesota's Water Council, and is completing a term on the Safe and Sustainable Waters Subcommittee for the U.S. Environmental Protection Agency's Board of Scientific Counselors.

Thomas (Tom) D. Beamish is Professor of Sociology at the University of California, Davis. Dr. Beamish's research and teaching have topically focused on issues of risk, environment, social organization, and economy. Reflecting these areas, he teaches courses on society and the environment, organizational sociology, and social movements. His books include *Silent Spill: The Organization of an Industrial Crisis* and *Community at Risk: Biodefense and the Collective Search for Security*. He has also published widely in leading peer-reviewed journals.

Michael Lujan Bevacqua (familian Kabesa/Bittot) is Assistant Professor in Chamorro Studies at the University of Guam and a longtime blogger, artist, writer, and poet. His academic work deals primarily with the effects of colonization on the Chamorros and their islands and theorizing the possibilities for their decolonization. His work has been published in the journals *American Quarterly*, *Micronesian Educator*, and *Marvels and Tales:* Journal of Fairy-Tale Studies. He is a member of Guam's Commission on Decolonization, co-chair for the Independence for Guam Task Force, and is frequently invited by the United Nations Committee of 24 to testify as an expert on the state of affairs in Guam at its annual regional seminars.

Isa Ua Ceallaigh Bowman is Assistant Professor of Comparative Literature and Director of the Women and Gender Studies Program at I Unibetsedåt Guahan (the University of Guam). Recent publications include an essay in *Interdisciplinary Literary Studies* on Mary Wortley Montagu's translation of a Turkish love poem and an essay in *Marvels and Tales: Journal of Fairy-Tale Studies* (co-authored with Michael Lujan Bevacqua) on CHamoru activist reclaiming of ancient legends. Current and planned projects include the Fino' CHamoru oral narrative collection at the Hongga Mo'na Project (www.HonggaMona.com) and essays on World War II human trafficking and sex slavery on Guam, female sexuality in "Stetit puella" from the *Carmina Burana*, and a performance of Canada Lee in whiteface.

M. L. Cadenasso is Professor of Landscape and Urban Ecology in the Department of Plant Sciences at the University of California, Davis. Her research links landscape pattern to ecosystem function and focuses on understanding how human activities alter that link. She spans systems and scales in her research, and she works in the metropolitan regions of Sacramento and Baltimore and the savannas of California and South Africa. She has co-authored four books and more than seventy-five peer-reviewed articles and thirty book chapters.

Chris Caldwell is an enrolled member of the Menominee Indian Tribe of Wisconsin. He has over twenty-five years of technical, administrative, and leadership experience working for various Menominee Tribal institutions and federal agencies dedicated to sustainable forestry and natural resources management. Since 2012 he has served as Director of the Sustainable Development Institute at the College of Menominee Nation, where he leads applied research, education, and outreach projects centered on indigenous sustainability.

Giovanna Di Chiro is Professor of Environmental Studies at Swarthmore College. She has published widely on the intersections of environmental science and policy, with a focus on racial, gender, and economic disparities and human rights. She is co-editor of the volume *Appropriating Technology: Vernacular Science and Social Power* and is completing a book titled *Embodied Ecologies: Science, Politics, and Environmental Justice*. Di Chiro's research, teaching, and activism focus on community-driven approaches to sustainability and the intersections of social justice and environmental change.

Lindsey Dillon is Assistant Professor of Sociology at the University of California, Santa Cruz. Her work looks at environmental justice social movements and the politics of toxic cleanup and redevelopment in U.S. cities. She has a Ph.D. in geography from University of California, Berkeley.

Liza Grandia is Associate Professor in the Department of Native American Studies at the University of California, Davis; Director of the Indigenous Research Center of the Americas (IRCA); and Associate Director of the Native American Language Center.

Miriam Greenberg is Professor of Sociology at University of California, Santa Cruz, where she directs the web project *Critical Sustainabilities: Competing Discourses of Urban Development in California*. Her research applies a range of theoretical and historical tools to the study of cities, social and cultural movements, and the environment. She is the author of *Branding New York: How a City in Crisis Was Sold to the World* (2008), co-author of *Crisis Cities: Disaster and Redevelopment in New York and New Orleans* (2014), and co-editor of the volume *The City Is the Factory: New Solidarities and Spatial Strategies in an Urban Age* (2017).

Jonathan London is an educator, researcher, and community-builder with experience in participatory research, rural community development, and community engaged planning. He is Associate Professor and Director of the Center for Regional Change at the University of California, Davis.

Beth Rose Middleton is Associate Professor in the Department of Native American Studies at the University of California, Davis. She focuses on creative, interdisciplinary approaches to support Indigenous-led land and water stewardship and climate change planning. Middleton is the author of *Trust in the Land: New Directions in Tribal Conservation* (2011), on Native applications of conservation easements, and *Upstream* (2018), on the history of Indian allotment lands at the headwaters of the California State Water Project.

David N. Pellow is the Dehlsen Chair and Professor of Environmental Studies and Director of the Global Environmental Justice Project at the University of California, Santa Barbara. His teaching and research focus on environmental and ecological justice in the United States and globally. He has served on the boards of directors for the Center for Urban Transformation, Greenpeace USA, and International Rivers.

Tracy Perkins is Assistant Professor in the Department of Sociology and Criminology at Howard University. She specializes in social movements, social inequality, and the environment through a focus on environmental justice activism. She has an M.S. in community development from the University of California, Davis, and a Ph.D. in sociology at the University of California, Santa Cruz. See more of her work at tracyperkins.org.

S. T. A. Pickett is a plant ecologist with the Cary Institute of Ecosystem Studies. Dr. Pickett's projects relate to the role of spatial heterogeneity in community and landscape structure and dynamics. Specific projects include research on urban ecosystems, the function of landscape boundaries, and plant community succession. The question motivating all these studies is, How does the spatial heterogeneity of a system or area control system function and change?

Anne Rademacher is Associate Professor of Anthropology and Environmental Studies at New York University. She is the author of *Building Green: Architects and the Struggle for Sustainability in Mumbai* and *Reigning the River: Urban Ecologies and Political Transformation in Kathmandu*. She is co-editor, with K. Sivaramakrishnan, of *Places of Nature in Ecologies of Urbanism* and *Ecologies of Urbanism in India: Metropolitan Civility and Sustainability*.

Laura Rigell hails from east Tennessee and has been an avid advocate for environmental and climate justice since 2010. From the halls of the United Nations to mountain hollers in Appalachia affected by mountaintop-removal coal mining, Laura's activism has spanned from the global to the local scale. Earning a bachelor's degree in environmental studies from Swarthmore College and a master's of city planning from the University of Pennsylvania, Laura uses her interdisciplinary background to bring together social justice concerns with sustainability initiatives in the city of Philadelphia. She is a community organizer and co-founder of Serenity Soular, a community organization that aims to develop solar enterprises in North Philadelphia. Laura also works as the solar manager at the Philadelphia Energy Authority, where she administers Solarize Philly, a citywide initiative to support residential solar for all Philadelphians.

Marie Schaefer is a Ph.D. student in community sustainability at Michigan State University and is a former research assistant at the College of Menominee Nation's Sustainable Development Institute. Her research focuses on how Indigenous knowledges and scientific knowledge can be braided together to contribute to sustainable communities. Currently, she is working on how Indigenous knowledges surrounding *manoomin* (wild rice) are being revitalized and how collaborations between Indigenous knowledge and scientific knowledge systems can contribute to the revitalization of *manoomin* in the Great Lakes.

Aaron Soto-Karlin is a design researcher, film producer, and innovation consultant with ten years of experience at the intersection of business, government and nonprofits in the United States and Central and South

America. He focuses on how to deliver human-centered solutions through design thinking and dramatic storytelling.

Traci Brynne Voyles is Associate Professor of Women's and Gender Studies at Loyola Marymount University. She is the author of *Wastelanding: Legacies of Uranium Mining in Navajo Country* (2015) and winner of the Border Regional Library Association's Southwest Book Award in 2015. Her research interests revolve around environmental justice, environmental history, feminist theory and gender studies, ecofeminism, and comparative ethnic studies.

Louis Warren is W. Turrentine Jackson Professor of Western U.S. History at the University of California, Davis. His research specialities are in environmental, U.S. West, California, and Native American History.

Kyle Whyte holds the Timnick Chair in the Humanities and is Associate Professor of Philosophy and Community Sustainability at Michigan State University. His research focuses on Indigenous climate justice and food sovereignty and the ethics of knowledge exchange between Indigenous peoples and climate scientists.

Mike Ziser is an Associate Professor of English at the University of California, Davis.

INDEX

Note: Page references followed by f indicate figures.

Acre, Brazil, 102, 104
Adamson, Joni, 17, 67
Afrofuturism, 84
agricultural activities, water pollution
  by, 46, 134
Agyeman, Julian, 3, 99n20, 271
air pollution, 107, 256–258, 259, 260–261.
  See also REDD
Akwesasne Mohawk Nation, 165–166, 213
Alaimo, Stacy, 201
American Society of Environmental
  History (ASEH), 56, 61
animalization, of women/people of color,
  207–210, 253
Anthropocene era, 11, 58–60, 63–64
"Anthropocene,' The" (Crutzen and
  Stoermer), 58–59
anthropocentric ecosystems, 124
anti-racist struggles, 20, 246–263; black
  geographies and unsustainable city,
  248–251; critiques of existing sustainabilities, 252–255; "I can't breathe"
  phrase, 258–262; spatial metaphors
  in, 250–251; sustainable urbanism
  and air quality in San Francisco,
  255–258
anti-toxics organizing, women as majority
  in, 212–213
Apra Harbor, Guahan, 235, 239
aquifers, 126, 127f, 133–134
Archive of Hope and Cautionary Tales,
  63–66

Arch Street United Methodist Church
  (North Philadelphia), 76, 82, 92
Arizona, 69–71, 124–125
Armstrong, Jeanette, 164
arts of futurity, 70
Asberg, Cecilia, 68–69
Association for the Study of Literature and
  Environment (ASLE), 57, 61
asthma, 257, 258, 259–260

Baker, Lawrence, 17–18
Baltimore, Maryland, 13, 47. *See also*
  Chesapeake Bay
Baltimore Ecosystem Study (BES-LTER),
  16–17, 124
Bayview Hunters Point neighborhood,
  San Francisco, California, 255,
  256–258
Beauvoir, Simone de, 209
Benjamin, Ruha, 251
Bevacqua, Michael Lujan, 20
binaries, in Western epistemology, 201,
  209–210
Biodiversity Group, 67, 68
biopiracy, 112
Black communities. *See* anti-racist
  struggles; North Philadelphia Black
  community; people of color
black ecology, 254
black geographies, 250–251
Black Lives Matter movement, 5, 20, 247,
  251, 255, 259, 274